PROPERTY OF:
DAVID O. McKAY LIBRARY
BYU-IDAHO
REXBURG ID 83440-0405 JUN 2 4 2024

DAVID O. McKAY LIBRARY
BYU-IDAHO

APR 1 8 2008

P9-CJS-662

Toward an Islamic Reformation

Contemporary Issues in the Middle East

Toward an Islamic Reformation

Civil Liberties, Human Rights, and International Law

ABDULLAHI AHMED AN-NA'IM

Foreword by
JOHN VOLL

SYRACUSE UNIVERSITY PRESS

Copyright © 1990 by SYRACUSE UNIVERSITY PRESS
Syracuse, New York 13244-5160

All Rights Reserved

First Paperback Edition 1996

05   6   5   4

This book was published with the financial assistance of the Publications Committee and
the Sallows Trust, University of Saskatchewan, Saskatoon, Canada.

Mohamad El-Hindi Books on Arab Culture and Islamic Civilization are published with
the assistance of a grant from Ahmad El-Hindi.

The paper used in this publication meets the minimum requirements of American National Standard
for Information Sciences—Permanence of Paper for Printed Library Materials, ANSI Z39.48-1984.∞™

Library of Congress Cataloging-in-Publication Data

Na'īm, 'Abd Allāh Ahmad, 1946–
    Toward an Islamic reformation.
    (Contemporary issues in the Middle East)
    Includes bibliographical references.
    1. Public Law (Islamic Law) 2. International Law
(Islamic Law) I. Title. II. Series.
LAW   340.5'9   89-21828
ISBN 0-8156-2484-0 (alk. paper) 0-8156-2706-8 (pbk.; alk. paper)

This publication was prepared in part under a grant from the Woodrow Wilson International Center
for Scholars, Washington, D.C. The statements and views expressed herein are those of the author and
are not necessarily those of the Wilson Center.

Manufactured in the United States of America

Proclaim (that) your Lord is Most Benevolent:
(Who) taught human being(s) through the pen
that which (they) did not (previously) know.

The Qur'an 96:3–5

No person is perfect enough to be entrusted
with the liberty and dignity of others.

Mahmoud Mohamed Taha

ABDULLAHI AHMED AN-NA'IM is a professor of Law at Emory University. He has taught at the University of Khartoum, UCLA, and the University of Saskatchewan, and was the Olaf Palme Visiting Professor at the Faculty of Law, Uppsala University. He has served as fellow of the Woodrow Wilson International Center of Scholars in Washington, D.C.; scholar-in-residence at the Cairo office of the Ford Foundation; and executive director of Human Rights Watch/Africa. He is the author of *Sudanese Criminal Law;* editor of *Human Rights in Cross-Cultural Perspectives: Quest for Consensus;* coeditor (with Francis Deng) of *Human Rights in Africa: Cross-Cultural Perspectives;* and translator of *The Second Message of Islam* (Syracuse University Press).

CONTENTS

FOREWORD

JOHN O. VOLL

CONTEMPORARY MUSLIMS are in the midst of an era of great debate and intellectual challenge. The issues are the major ones being debated in all societies in the contemporary world: what is the nature of the just society, how can people be free as individuals and what are their obligations to their communities, how can resources be used and distributed so that no one is deprived? This book presents the controversial ideas of a Sudanese Muslim jurist and provides a challenging statement of one way that the Islamic traditions can provide answers to the critical contemporary questions.

Abdullahi Ahmed An-Na'im, the author, is part of the contemporary generation of Muslim scholar-activists who have combined careers of scholarship with involvement in public affairs. In contrast to many of the more visible scholar-activists, An-Na'im is not in that broad grouping which some observers have identified as "fundamentalist." Instead, he is identified with a group which has been described as "unorthodox, reformist," the Republican Brotherhood in the Sudan.[1] In this position, he is often opposed by more conservative and more fundamentalist Muslim leaders.

This book provides the intellectual foundations for a total reinterpretation of the nature and meaning of Islamic public law. The argument is based on the teachings of Mahmoud Mohamed Taha, the founder of the Republican Brotherhood, but it develops Taha's general principles into a concrete analysis of their implications for Islamic public law.

An-Na'im argues that the Shari'a (Islamic law) as historically developed and understood by Muslims is based on the concrete experience of the Muslim community in Medina in the seventh century. Although such a foundation may have been appropriate for medieval times, An-Na'im believes that other foundations *within* Islam are available for a transformed Islamic law that will be appropriate for modern times. This alternative foundation is the revelation to the Prophet Muhammad in the first stage of his mission, while he was preaching in Mecca.

An-Na'im rejects the traditional formulations of Islamic law that developed during medieval times. He also does not accept modernist efforts to reform the medieval legal structure if they accept the medieval assumptions. In place of the old Shari'a, An-Na'im advocates a wholly new system of Islamic law which he believes provides a suitable foundation for Islamic life in the contemporary world. This is a comprehensive formulation dealing with political structure, the social order, criminal justice, international law, and basic human rights.

It is important to recognize that this book is not a dispassionate presentation. It is a book of advocacy, involving itself in the significant debates of the age, globally and within the world of Islam. It represents a radical departure from both the Islamic modernist and the Islamic fundamentalist positions which dominate contemporary thought in the Muslim world. It is neither an attempt to integrate Western and traditional Islamic thought (as is usually the case with modernist positions) nor a fundamentalist effort to return to pristine principles. An-Na'im is attempting to transform the understanding of the very foundations of traditional Islamic law, not to reform them. The significance of his thinking lies in providing the case of the radical extreme of the spectrum, offering a transformation of the very structure of the Islamic perspective. In the global debates, such a voice needs to be heard.

An-Na'im's ideas did not develop in a vacuum. His own experience as a student and lawyer involved in public affairs in the Sudan has shaped his thinking. The greatest influence was his involvement with the Republican Brotherhood in the Sudan.

The Republican Brotherhood gained international attention when its leader, Mahmoud Mohamed Taha, was executed in 1985 by the Sudanese regime of Ja'far Numayry, who was overthrown during that same year. The Republicans had, however, been an established if small group in the Sudan for many years. The organization was founded by Taha as the Republican party in the midst of the Sudanese nationalist struggle at the end of World War II. Taha worked to create an alternative to the larger nationalist political parties because he felt they were dominated by the leaders of the traditionalist Muslim groups in the Sudan. The party had little electoral success, but Taha began to emphasize the need for Islamic reform and liberation from domination by "sectarian" forces.

In the following two decades, Taha developed a comprehensive basis for reinterpreting Islam. The fullest presentation of his ideas appears in *The Second Message of Islam*, first published in 1967 and published in an English translation by Abdullahi An-Na'im in 1987.[2] This work, and the thinking of Taha in general, represents, in An-Na'im's words, "a modern and revolutionary interpretation of the Qur'an."[3]

An-Na'im became associated with the Republicans while he was a law student at the University of Khartoum in the late 1960s. He attended a number of lectures by Taha and soon began to join the informal discussions in "Ustaz Mahmoud's" house. This was at the time of the original publication of *The Second Message of Islam*, which had a profound influence on An-Na'im. By early 1968, An-Na'im had formally become a member of the Republican Brotherhood.

When he completed his law studies in Khartoum, An-Na'im went to Great Britain, where he received an LL.B. and a Diploma in Criminology at the University of Cambridge in 1973. He continued his advanced studies in law, receiving a Ph.D. from the University of Edinburgh in 1976. He then returned to the Sudan, where he became an attorney and a lecturer in law at the University of Khartoum. By 1979 he had become the head of the Department of Public Law in the Faculty of Law at the University of Khartoum.

While teaching law, An-Na'im became a prominent spokesman for the ideas of Mahmoud Mohamed Taha, writing articles for the local press and speaking with a variety of interested people.[4] This was an important function because Taha had been banned from participating in public activities since the early 1970s. Although the Republican Brotherhood did not actively oppose the government of Numayry at that time, Numayry at times restricted the activities of followers of Taha.

These limitations reached a peak in the early 1980s. At that time, Numayry initiated significant policies with regard to Islam. He had come to power as the leader of a group of younger soldiers in 1969 and had gone through an initial phase of relatively radical socialism. In the mid-1970s, Numayry's position was strengthened when he negotiated an end to a major civil war fought primarily between the Muslim northern Sudan and the non-Muslim southern Sudan. By 1978, however, Numayry had begun to identify himself more clearly with activist Islamic sentiments in the northern Sudan, reaching a climax with the forceful imposition of his interpretation of Islamic law in 1983. At that time, Taha and the Republican Brotherhood made their opposition to Numayry's Islamization program publicly clear.

For about a year and a half, Taha and about thirty Republican leaders, including An-Na'im, were interned without charge. They were released briefly late in 1984, but Taha was quickly rearrested, tried on charges of sedition and other offenses, and publicly executed in January 1985. Others were also arrested and tried, but only Taha was killed. In this process, An-Na'im took the lead in negotiating release of as many as four hundred members, but he was not able to secure the pardon of his teacher. The group agreed not to engage in political activities and formally to dismantle their organization.[5]

Since the killing of Mahmoud Mohamed Taha and the subsequent overthrow of Numayry, the group has not formally reorganized. It remains as a social community dedicated to the cause of Islamic reform in the tradition of Taha. Leaders emphasize that the group has always been interested in the reform of faith and practice rather than direct political action. An-Na'im himself stresses that the message represents an approach, not a political party.

This does not mean, however, that the era of activity is over. In recent years, An-Na'im has been lecturing and writing, primarily outside of the Sudan. He feels that it is his responsibility to take the basic teachings of Taha and develop them. He has been writing in his own field of specialization, public law, reinterpreting Islamic law from the perspective of the teachings of Mahmoud Mohamed Taha.[6]

This book represents the culmination of years of study and writing. An-Na'im feels that it provides the necessary next step in the mission of Islamic transformation begun by Mahmoud Mohamed Taha. An-Na'im believes that secular ideologies will have little appeal in the long run for most Muslims. "To seek secular answers is simply to abandon the field to the fundamentalists, who will succeed in carrying the vast majority of the population with them by citing religious authority for their policies and theories. Intelligent and enlightened Muslims are therefore best advised to remain within the religious framework and endeavour to achieve the reforms that would make Islam a viable modern ideology."[7]

It is to provide an alternative to both the secularists and the fundamentalists that An-Na'im has written this book. Many Muslims will disagree with An-Na'im's views, but the book is a contribution to the continuing debate in the Islamic world. It reflects the intellectual dynamism and diversity that characterize contemporary Muslim life.

PREFACE

The task set for this book is enormous and exceedingly delicate because of the nature of the relationship between Islam (as a religion) and the historical formulations of Islamic law, commonly known as Shari'a. As a Muslim, I am particularly sensitive to the religious implications of attributing inadequacy and injustice to Shari'a, which is perceived by many Muslims to be part of the Islamic faith. Nevertheless, I believe that the questions raised here must be confronted and resolved as a religious as well as a political and legal imperative if the public law of Islam is to be implemented today.

Various reliable estimates place the total Muslim population of the world at over 830 million people. Although there are Muslims on all continents of the world, their largest concentrations are to be found in a broad belt extending from North and West Africa, through the Middle East and Central Asia to South and Southeast Asia. Exact numbers of Muslims and their percentage of the total population in each country of this region are not easy to determine. Nevertheless, it can be safely assumed that Muslims constitute at least 70 percent of the total population in thirty-five countries. The term *Muslim country* will herein refer to one of those countries.

It is true, of course, that sociological or religious majority does not necessarily translate into political majority. In other words, it cannot always be assumed that the Muslim majority in any given country will act as such politically. Nevertheless, recent trends seem to indicate that Muslim majorities are becoming politically assertive. It is this phenomenon which raises the issues of the modern application of Shari'a in the public domain to be discussed in this book.

As a preliminary work introducing a revolutionary approach to Islamic legal reform, this book will be confined to a few fundamental issues in the constitutional, penal, and international law and human rights

xiii

fields. For the same reason, I shall present a theoretical and legalistic case for accepting the proposed approach to Islamic law reform. Although some reference to recent practical application of relevant aspects of Shari'a in Iran and the Sudan will be made to illustrate the arguments used, this book is not about the application of Islamic law in any particular country. To the extent that Islam and Islamic law are universal, the analysis and conclusions drawn here should be relevant and applicable to any Muslim country in the world.

It is true that the interpretation and practice of all religions, including Islam, are greatly affected by the sociological, economic, and political circumstances of a particular community. The same is true of a religious legal system, such as Shari'a. However, in relation to the particular religion, or the particular legal system, there is a limit to local variation and specificity, or else we would have to speak of a different religion or a different legal system.

An assumption of the thesis presented is that there are certain universal aspects of Islam, and of Shari'a, without denying that there is room for variation in terms of sociological or other circumstances. To the extent that there are universal aspects, this work would be useful as a framework for the reform of Islamic public law. But the study and analysis of the local or country-specific conditions and circumstances affecting the detailed application of the proposed reform methodology are not within the scope of this book.

I begin by considering the shifting basis of public law in the Muslim world and the sources and development of Shari'a in order to substantiate one of my basic arguments, namely, that Shari'a is not the whole of Islam but instead is an interpretation of its fundamental sources as understood in a particular historical context. Once it is appreciated that Shari'a was *constructed* by its founding jurists, it should become possible to think about reconstructing certain aspects of Shari'a, provided that such reconstruction is based on the same fundamental sources of Islam and is fully consistent with its essential moral and religious precepts. I also survey the objectives, methods, and achievements of modernist reform efforts since the nineteenth century, a necessary step toward understanding the limitations of reform within the framework of Shari'a and appreciating the need for a more revolutionary approach, such as the one I propose.

Given the reality of the nation-state in an increasingly interdependent and interactive world, I focus on the implications of the modern application of Shari'a to constitutionalism, criminal justice, international law, and human rights. In order to demonstrate the need for drastic reform of Shari'a in these fields, I explain what may be taken to be imperative principles in the particular field, contrasting them with the corresponding principles and rules of Shari'a, and highlighting the prospects of reconciliation, whether within or from outside Shari'a, but always in accordance with Islamic precepts. An underlying theme of this book is the need for balance between competing Muslim and non-Muslim rights to self-determination. Another fundamental concern is to maintain Islamic legitimacy for the proposed reforms. Toward that end, I seek to provide an Islamic rationale for the objectives of reform and ensure the Islamic validity of the reform methodology to be used in achieving those objectives. Islamic validity is thus seen as essential for the political viability of the proposed reforms.

I frequently refer to secondary sources written in English by well-recognized scholars of Islam because these are the sources which the readers can easily consult. I adopted this style because the relevant facts of Islamic history and principles of Shari'a are well known. The works referred to mention the primary Arabic sources for readers interested in consulting those sources. I have also cited authoritative primary Arabic sources when the asserted Shari'a principle may be disputed in argument.

Finally, a few technical points of style need to be clarified. First, translations of the Qur'anic and Sunna are my own, except where otherwise indicated. In preparing my own translations of Qur'anic texts, I have consulted Abdullah Yusuf Ali, *The Holy Qur'an, Texts, Translation and Commentary*, but sought to simplify the language while retaining the exact meaning of the text to the best of my ability. The Qur'an is cited, whether in the text or in a note, by chapter and verse; for example, the fifth verse of *Surat al-Tawba* is cited as 9:5.

Second, Arabic terms and phrases are kept to a minimum. Whenever an Arabic term or phrase is used, it is written in accordance with the American National Standard System for the Romanization of Arabic. However, diacritical marks of that style are omitted except (') and (') for medial *'ayn* and *hamza*, respectively. Arabic terms and phrases are italicized except for proper names and the most commonly used terms such as the Qur'an, Sunna and Shari'a.

I have developed some of the ideas expressed in this book while teaching Islamic law at the School of Law, University of California at Los Angeles, in 1985-87. I am grateful for that opportunity, and to students and colleagues who helped develop those ideas.

The first draft of the manuscript was prepared under a generous research and writing grant from the John D. and Catherine T. MacArthur Foundation. I did most of the research and writing of that draft while a Fellow of the History, Culture, and Society Program of the Woodrow Wilson International Center for Scholars, Washington, D.C. I am indebted to the MacArthur Foundation and the Wilson Center for their support.

I have undertaken revisions and final preparation of the manuscript while occupying the Ariel F. Sallows Chair in Human Rights at the College of Law, University of Saskatchewan, Canada, in 1988–89. I sincerely appreciate the help and support of Dean Peter MacKinnon and his colleagues and staff.

I am grateful to Professor Ann Mayer and Mr. Robert Bowman, attorney, for reading and commenting on some of my draft chapters. I also wish to acknowledge the research and editorial assistance of Ms. Laura Cooley and the editorial assistance of Ms. Charmaine Spencer.

Toward an Islamic Reformation

≻ 1 ≺

Public Law in the Muslim World

*T*HIS BOOK is based on the premise that the Muslim peoples of the world are entitled to exercise their legitimate collective right to self-determination in terms of an Islamic identity, including the application of Islamic law, if they wish to do so, provided that they do not violate the legitimate right of self-determination of individuals and groups both within and outside the Muslim communities.[1] As I will argue in the context of each of the four specialized areas discussed in this book, the universal principle of reciprocity requires a person to treat others as he or she would like to be treated by them, that is, to claim and exercise their own individual and collective rights to self-determination, Muslims must concede and guarantee that same right to others. According to this basic premise, the right to self-determination, whether claimed by an individual or a group of persons, is a relative concept. It is necessary to speak of the legitimate right of an individual or group to indicate its limitation by the legitimate right of other individuals and groups. The crucial questions, therefore, would be, What are these limitations, and how are they to be stated and enforced in practice?

These and related questions are discussed in this book from an Islamic legal point of view. In particular, this book is concerned with the likely consequences of applying historical Shari'a in the public domain, by which I mean the constitutional order, criminal justice, international relations, and human rights, that is, matters governed by what may be called public law. These may be distinguished from matters pertaining to religious practice and private or personal law. The distinction between public and private law is, of course, not absolute because these fields of the law overlap and interact. For example, some private law matters involving family and inheritance have clear constitutional and other public law implications.

I believe that the application of the public law aspects of histori-

1

cal Shari'a in public life would create severe problems and hardships. Nevertheless, I submit that it is possible to evolve an alternative and modern conception of Islamic public law that can resolve those problems and hardships. This alternative modern conception would be the modern version of Shari'a in that it would be derived from the same basic sources of Islam. To avoid confusion between the two conceptions or versions of Islamic law, the term *Shari'a* will be reserved in this book for historical Islamic law.

This chapter sets the scene for the discussion of the likely consequences of the application of the public law aspects of Shari'a. An explanation of these matters is also helpful in assessing the possibility of evolving alternative principles of Islamic public law. The recent historical background and current manifestations of what is commonly known as Islamic resurgence is the impetus behind the movement toward the application of Shari'a as the public law of the many Muslim countries today. Some understanding of the sociological and political nature of this phenomenon is important for appreciating the legal implications and assessing the prospects of reconciling the objectives of Islamic resurgence with the legitimate claims of those who may have good reason to fear the consequences of applying Shari'a as the public law of the land.

Although the writings of the early Muslim jurists did not distinguish between public and private law, this distinction is appropriate to the social and political circumstances prevailing throughout the Muslim world today. In the context of the organization of the nation-state and its internal and external relationships, the term *public law* is a convenient way of identifying those fields of the law which raise their own distinctive issues and problems. This book will assess the modern applicability of Islamic public law in terms of these issues and problems.

There are many competing imperatives for change in the public law of Muslim countries. The negative constitutional and human rights consequences of Shari'a appear to be entrenched by the assumed religious authority and inviolability of Shari'a. I believe that it is imperative to challenge and modify this assumption if we are to achieve significant improvements in the public policy and practice of Muslim countries. Yet, unless such challenges and modifications have religious legitimacy, they are unlikely to change Muslim attitudes and practice.

THE GENESIS OF ISLAMIC RESURGENCE

The phenomenon of Islamic resurgence has been the subject of numerous scholarly and popular discussions since the Iranian revolution of 1979.[2]

Some of the writers on Islamic resurgence use the term *fundamentalist* in reference to contemporary Muslim activists who demand complete conformity with the precepts of Islam, as they understand them, including the total and immediate application of the public law of Shari'a.[3] The term *fundamentalist* appears to have been first used with reference to a movement in American Protestantism in the early twentieth century.[4] Without drawing conclusions about the potential applicability of this term in the context of other religious traditions, I will not use it with reference to the above-mentioned Muslim activists.[5] My main objection to the use of this term is that, insofar as it implies a commitment to the fundamentals of Islam, it would apply to such a broad spectrum of Muslims that it would cease to be useful as a tool for identifying a specific group.

The crucial question, to my mind, is not whether a Muslim is committed to the fundamentals of Islam because this is a sentiment shared by the vast majority of Muslims but rather how to implement that commitment in concrete policy and legal terms today.[6] As suggested by Michael Hudson, "the question to be asked is not the crude, falsely dichotomous 'Is Islam compatible with political development?' but rather 'How much and what kinds of Islam are compatible with (or necessary for) political development in the Muslim world?.'"[7] In this light, I will classify Muslims according to their commitment to the implementation of the totality of Shari'a, including its public law, or their willingness to accept the need for significant revisions and reformulations of some aspects of that law.

As explained by Bernard Lewis, if we are to understand anything at all about what has happened in the past and is happening today in the Muslim world, we must appreciate the universality and centrality of religion as a factor in the lives of the Muslim peoples.[8] In contrast to other major world religions, "Islam from the lifetime of its founder *was* the state, and the identity of religion and government is indelibly stamped on the memories and awareness of the faithful from their own sacred writings, history, and experience."[9] Moreover, for Muslims, religion has traditionally "constituted the essential basis and focus of identity and loyalty."[10] It is not surprising, therefore, to find that most of the significant political and social movements in modern Muslim history have drawn heavily on Islam as a unifying and motivating force.[11]

Although it is important to understand the particular conditions under which each individual movement has evolved, and the broader Islamic historical context within which each movement operated, the current manifestations of Islamic resurgence should be seen as reflecting a long-standing and continuing dimension of Islamic history.[12] "Despite their individual differences and characteristics," noted one writer, "pre-modern revivalist movements provided a common legacy to modern Islam both in their ideology and methodology." The element common to the premodern and modern revivalist movements was their focus on the weakened and disorganized condition of the community, which they attributed to the Muslim departure from true Islamic belief and practice. Both premodern and modern movements prescribed the return to Islam as the cure. The premodern reformers also emphasized the need for reform, rejected blind acceptance of tradition, and stressed that the social and moral revival of Islamic society required political action and activism. These themes have been adopted and developed further by the proponents of modern resurgence.[13]

It has been suggested that the current Islamic resurgence is the natural response to a protracted crisis of political, economic, and military dimensions.[14] By offering a formula of religious legitimation in opposition to Western secularism[15] and the principle of social justice against economic injustice, as well as religious sanction for the militant pride and honor, "Islam does appear to provide a practical political alternative as well as a secure spiritual niche and psychological anchor in a turbulent world."[16] According to W. C. Smith, throughout the modern period almost every Islamic movement in almost every part of the Muslim world has been in some way a variation on the double theme of protest against internal deterioration and external encroachment.[17] A contemporary Muslim writer sees the phenomenon as the Muslim response to Western secularization and domination of the Muslim world and as a response to a crisis in leadership among Muslims. In this respect, the current cycle of resurgence reflects a continuing tradition in Islamic history. It is not inherently antagonistic to the West, but rather is hostile to whatever or whoever is perceived to be the cause of frustration and oppression, be it internal or external.[18]

It is therefore reasonable to conclude that Islamic resurgence, in its essential conception and purpose, is natural and healthy to the extent that it seeks to provide the Muslims with adequate answers from within their own tradition to the social, political, and economic problems facing Muslim societies.[19] It is not surprising that Muslims seek to reassert their cultural identity and to summon forces from within their faith and tradition to challenge the causes of social disorganization, political powerlessness, and economic frustration. The essential conception and purpose of current Islamic resurgence, then, is the right to self-determination. But an individual or collective right to self-determination is limited by the right to self-determination of other individuals and collectivities. This is particularly true in public life, where competing rights to self-determination are most likely to come into conflict, requiring mediation and accommodation.

THE CHANGING BASIS OF PUBLIC LAW IN THE MUSLIM WORLD

Classifications of law as public, private, commercial, and so on are relative to the nature and history of the particular legal system. Thus, whereas such classifications were used by Roman law and adopted by modern European legal systems, they were never used by the early Muslim jurists. The jurists of Shari'a knew no distinction between public and private law. As explained by Joseph Schacht, the distinction made by early Muslim jurists between the "rights of God" and the "rights of human beings" has nothing to do with the distinction between public and private law.[20]

In fact, public law has traditionally been the least developed aspect of Shari'a.[21] Although this lack of development may tell us much about those principles and rules which the founding jurists of Shari'a did formulate in this field, what is available in the nature of public law tends to be sketchy and fragmented.[22] One is therefore forced to search for whichever principles of Shari'a appear to be relevant and to discuss them in the context of the issues and concerns of public law as we know them today.

One should be careful in using the writings of early and "classic" premodern Muslim scholars on constitutional and political questions, sometimes described as Islamic political theory or thought. Although this literature was written by scholars who were experts in Shari'a and who were keenly aware of the need to conform to its dictates, it cannot be assumed that what they produced was necessarily identical to or even consistent with Shari'a. For the most part it would seem, those scholars were writing under circumstances that were not particularly conducive to strict application of Shari'a. Muslim scholars working at the time of the decline of the Abbasid dynasty in the eleventh and twelfth centuries were primarily concerned with maintaining the unity and security of the Muslims under extremely unstable political conditions.

It was under those conditions that al-Mawardi, for example, justified usurpation of power in the provinces by force, on grounds of necessity, though admitting that such usurpation was contrary to Shari'a. H. A. R. Gibb has commented: "But by justifying disregard of the law on the grounds of political necessity and expediency, al-Mawardi in effect admits that in certain cases might is to be given the semblance of right. Once this is allowed, the whole superstructure of the juristic system breaks down."[23] Consequently, some of those scholars had to make concessions to the realities of the Muslim situation by deemphasizing certain aspects of Shari'a in an effort to reconcile it with what they perceived to be in the best interest of the Muslim community at the time.

Other scholars simply disregarded reality and addressed themselves to an ideal situation in theorizing on what *ought* to be the case.

Ibn Taymiyya is the primary example of this group. In his work, he emphasized the duty to obey Shari'a, regardless of whether the ruler followed it himself. He also postulated close cooperation between the ruler and the jurists, whereby the ruler would consult with and abide by the opinions of the jurists on the requirements of Shari'a in any given situation.[24] This approach was of no help when rulers violated Shari'a in their official functions and failed to consult with jurists or ignored their advice.[25]

The lack of a clear conception of public law by early Muslim jurists would not necessarily preclude the classification of certain aspects of Shari'a as of public or private law nature.[26] In this book *the public law of Shari'a* will be used as a generic term for those aspects of Shari'a which applied, or were supposed to apply, in the public life of Muslim communities until they were replaced by secular public law during the nineteenth and early twentieth centuries. James Norman D. Anderson described the two types of legal "reforms" undertaken in the Muslim world during the last century: "First, that the Shari'a was more and more widely displaced in practice — in such matters as commercial law, criminal law, and much else — in favour of codes of largely alien origin, applied by a system of secular courts; and, secondly, that even in the sacred sphere of family law (administered as this still was, the most of the countries concerned, in specifically Shari'a courts) a number of most significant changes were made in the way in which it [Shari'a family law] was interpreted and applied."[27]

Herbert Liebesny explained the displacement of Shari'a by European laws as a paradigm of five concentric circles.[28] Using this paradigm, we find that commercial law falls in the outermost circle, which means that the earliest and most thorough displacement of Shari'a by European law occurred in the commercial field. Foreign influence and displacement of Shari'a followed in penal law, real estate, contract, and torts. Family law and inheritance, the innermost circle, remained the least affected; they continued to be governed by Shari'a throughout the Muslim world, subject to the changes indicated by Anderson.[29]

The psychological rationale behind the displacement of Shari'a seems to have been that Muslims preferred to keep Shari'a intact and inviolable in theory even if that was not possible in practice.[30] As Anderson explains, "To a Muslim, it has always been a far more heinous sin to deny or question the divine revelation than to fail to obey it. So it seemed preferable to continue to pay lip-service to an inviolate Shari'a, as the only law of fundamental authority, and to excuse departure from much of it in practice by appealing to the doctrine of necessity *(darura)*, rather than to make any attempt to adapt that law to the circumstances and needs of contemporary life."[31] Recent Islamic resurgence and its demands for the reinstatement of Shari'a to all the fields from which it has been excluded demonstrate that many Muslims are no longer satisfied with this logic of necessity. Instead, the proponents of Shari'a are now claiming that it is no longer necessary to make this concession to the pressures and demands of modern life.

The pretext of necessity is no doubt getting increasingly weaker in an age of self-determination and political and economic independence and confidence. Muslims can no longer maintain their sense of self-respect and pride while neglecting their religious duty to abide by the dictates of Islam. Nevertheless, the public law of Shari'a raises very serious moral and practical problems. This tension between a religious commitment to Islamic law and the manifest inadequacy of some aspects of that law in its Shari'a form is crucial to the thesis of this book. Islamic law has to adapt and adjust to the circumstances and needs of contemporary life within the context of Islam as a whole, even if this should involve discarding or modifying certain aspects of historical Shari'a.

One of the major factors requiring and conditioning the proposed process of adapting and adjusting to contemporary life has to do with the reality of the modern nation-state. Despite the supposed religious unity of all Muslims and the consequent theoretical universal application of Shari'a throughout the Muslim world, the Muslim peoples are now organized in nation-states and are likely to remain so for the foreseeable future. This form of political organization, effectively established in the Muslim world after the European colonial intrusion of the late nineteenth and early twentieth centuries, brought into the region its own structures of power and legal concepts.[32] In particular, if the nation-state is to conform to the standards of constitutionalism, as I believe it should, it must guarantee equal rights of citizenship for its entire population, such as equality before the law and equal participation in the government of their own country. Moreover, the nation-state must provide all the legal and other resources necessary for the continuous development and fulfillment of individual and collective identity.[33]

Since the concept of the nation-state did not evolve out of their own historical experience or from within their own cultural traditions, Muslim peoples find it difficult to assimilate and implement this concept. Like other peoples of Africa and Asia, the Muslim peoples will have to undergo a painful and protracted process of adjustment and reformulation of long-standing institutions and practices before they can implement the structures and institutions of the nation-state. This book is not concerned with the sociological, economic, and political issues associated with the processes of modernization in the context of the nation-state in the Muslim world. Without minimizing the importance of these issues, this study takes the existence and likely continuation of the nation-state in the

Muslim world for granted and proceeds to discuss its implications from the Islamic legal point of view.

Given the pervasive and persistent Islamic resurgence, the process of adjustment and reformulation can take place only when the nation-state is legitimized in Islamic terms and is reconciled with principles of Islamic law. In other words, although the establishment of the nation-state in the Muslim world was accompanied by secularization of aspects of the law, the comprehensive nature of Islam and its dramatically increasing role in the public life of many Muslim countries require the provision of an Islamic legal environment for the nation-state, or at least its reconciliation with Islamic law.[34]

Secular public law was introduced into the Muslim world with the establishment of the modern nation-state, and this branch of the law will have to be Islamized in recognition of the Muslim right to self-determination. Such Islamization must conform to the limits of the Muslim right to self-determination.

COMPETING IMPERATIVES FOR CHANGE

Two competing imperatives for change in the public law of Muslim countries emerge from the preceding discussion. There is growing demand for the restoration of Shari'a as the public law of Muslim countries. Yet both Muslim and non-Muslim citizens of these countries have come to take the benefits of the secularization of public life for granted. If historical Shari'a is applied today, the population of Muslim countries would lose the most significant benefits of secularization. Moreover, current international law, including the human rights standards established thereunder, cannot co-exist with corresponding principles of Shari'a.

The non-Muslim peoples in Muslim countries have enjoyed the status and rights of full citizenship under secular public law and will never accept the inferior status allocated to them by Shari'a. Shari'a does not afford non-Muslim subjects of an Islamic state constitutional and legal equality with its Muslim citizens. The strong objection of the non-Muslim population to being relegated to the status of second-class citizens will have the support of international public opinion, as well as that of a significant portion of the Muslim population of the Muslim countries.

Muslim women are in a similar situation. Under secular public law, Muslim women have enjoyed a significant improvement in their status and rights with increased access to public life and opportunities for higher education and employment. Although much remains to be done in this regard, the status and rights of Muslim women under secular public law are already clearly superior to their status and rights under Shari'a. The restoration of the public law of Shari'a would therefore have a negative effect on these women.

Even Muslim men, who are the only full citizens of an Islamic state under Shari'a, stand to lose some of their fundamental constitutional rights if Shari'a is restored as the public law of the land. As will be explained in Chapter 4, the freedoms of belief, expression, and association of Muslim men will be negatively affected by the law of apostasy and by the extensive powers of the ruler under Shari'a.

At the international level, Shari'a authorizes the aggressive use of force to propagate Islam and does not recognize the equal sovereignty of non-Muslim states. These aspects of Shari'a repudiate the basis of modern international law. Moreover, Shari'a violates some of the most fundamental international human rights standards. For example, slavery is lawful under Shari'a and can be reestablished if the conditions set by Shari'a for this institution are satisfied. This aspect of Shari'a is now universally condemned, even by the majority of Muslims, and constitutes a clear violation of international law and human rights.

Thus we have Muslim demands for self-determination by the application of Islamic law in public life. Yet such Islamic law cannot possibly be Shari'a as historically established. The only way to reconcile these competing imperatives for change in the public law of Muslim countries is to develop a version of Islamic public law which is compatible with modern standards of constitutionalism, criminal justice, international law, and human rights.

Although the early Muslim jurists did not use the term *public law*, they did deal with its subject matter — the conduct of the official organs of the state as it affects private persons, whether individually or collectively. Thus it is possible to take any of the main issues involving public law in the modern sense of the term and look for the corresponding principle or rule of Shari'a. We can then discover the relevant Shari'a principles and assess their applicability as modern public law. It is my hypothesis that when we do that, we will find that there are areas of serious conflict and tension between Shari'a and the essential purposes and necessary implications of public law in the context of the modern nation-state.

Having identified those areas, we can then proceed to resolve the conflict and tension within the framework of Islam as a whole, albeit not necessarily within the framework of historical Shari'a. The aim of this book is to argue for the adoption of the most viable methodology for achieving genuine and sufficient reform of the public law of Islam. The envisaged version of public law would be as Islamic as Shari'a has ever been because it will draw on the same basic sources of Islam from which the relevant principles of Shari'a were constructed by the early jurists.

However drastic this thesis may appear to many Muslims, it is presented here as an Islamic thesis to be evaluated as such. The aim of this book is to contribute to the process of changing Muslim perceptions, attitudes, and policies on *Islamic* and not secular grounds. Unless a religiously acceptable case for genuine modernist reform is established, present and future Muslims face only two alternatives: either to implement the public law of Shari'a, despite its inadequacies and problems, or to abandon it in favor of secular public law. I find neither alternative satisfactory, and I hope to reconcile Muslim commitment to Islamic law with the achievement of the benefits of secularism within a religious framework.

It may seem like a contradiction in terms to speak of achieving the benefits of secularism within a religious framework because secularism is, by definition, the relegation of religion to the domain of private faith. Yet if we can identify and resolve the problems that gave rise to secularism, it may become possible to have Islamic religious legitimacy for public law in Muslim countries without the problems historically associated with the close identification of religion with politics. The first step in this direction is to show that the public law of Shari'a, as developed by the founding Muslim jurists, is not really divine, thereby making it possible to replace aspects of Shari'a without violating the religious sensibilities of Muslims.

On the Sources and Development of Shari'a

𝒯o Muslims, Shari'a is the "Whole Duty of Mankind," moral and pastoral theology and ethics, high spiritual aspiration, and detailed ritualistic and formal observance; it encompasses all aspects of public and private law, hygiene, and even courtesy and good manners.[1] To attribute inadequacy to any part of Shari'a is regarded as heresy by the majority of Muslims, who believe that the whole of Shari'a is divine. This widespread view creates a formidable psychological barrier, which is reinforced by the threat of criminal prosecution for the capital offense of apostasy *(ridda)*, a real threat today in countries such as the Sudan.[2]

The first step in overcoming this obstacle is to show that the public law of Shari'a is not really divine law in the sense that all its specific principles and detailed rules were directly revealed by God to the Prophet Muhammad. If it can be shown that Shari'a was constructed by the early Muslim jurists out of the fundamental sources of Islam, namely the Qur'an and Sunna, contemporary Muslims may become more willing to accept the possibility of substantial reform.

Although this study is primarily concerned with the public law aspects of Shari'a, it is necessary to start with a general discussion of the sources and development of Shari'a because the subsequent analysis of the public law of Shari'a can be understood only in the context of the system as a whole. The sources and development of Shari'a will show that Shari'a, as known to Muslims today, is not divine in the sense of being direct revelation. Rather, it is the product of a process of interpretation of, and logical derivation from, the text of the Qur'an and Sunna and other traditions.

The literature on the sources and development of Shari'a is too extensive for comprehensive treatment here. Within that literature, however, it may be possible to highlight the most significant events and personalities relevant to arguing for an adequate methodology for establishing modern Islamic public law. In this examination of the formative stages of Shari'a and the development of Islamic jurisprudence, I am not concerned with Shari'a in an abstract sense or as it may exist under any conceivable interpretation of the Qur'an and Sunna but rather with Shari'a as it has actually evolved and has come to be determined in the concrete historical experience of the Muslims. This is the Shari'a which traditionalist and "fundamentalist" Muslims purport to apply today. We have to be clear on what Shari'a *is* today before we can embark on a quest of what it *ought* to be in the future.

HISTORICAL BACKGROUND

The Prophet Muhammad was born in Mecca, a commercial town in western Arabia, in 570 A.D. Following a short career as a trader, including a partnership with his first wife, Khadija, the Prophet is reported to have undertaken rigorous worship and meditation in and around Mecca. By 610 A.D., the Prophet is believed to have started receiving divine revelation, the Qur'an, whereupon he began propagating his message of religious and social reform. The general reaction of the Meccan community, constituted mainly of Quraysh, the Prophet's own tribe, was extremely negative and hostile, but the Prophet persisted and managed to win a few supporters over the thirteen years of the Mecca stage of his mission. As a result of mounting and increasingly violent persecution of himself and his followers, the Prophet sought a more receptive environment for his message, which he eventually found in Medina, a mainly agricultural community in western Arabia. In 622 A.D., the Prophet and his first followers, who became known as *al-muhajirun* (the migrants), left Mecca and settled in Medina, where they were welcomed by *al-ansar* (the supporters). This decisive move, known as *hijra* (migration) has been taken as the beginning of the Muslim calendar.[3]

The *hijra* marked not only a dramatic change in the growth of the number of Muslims and the establishment of the first Muslim polity or state in Medina but also a significant shift in the subject matter and content of the message. It is generally agreed that during the Mecca period the Qur'an and Sunna contained primarily religious and moral precepts and did not express specific political and legal norms until the Medina period. An obvious explanation for this shift is that in Medina the Qur'an and Sunna had to respond to the concrete social and political needs of an established community. With the freedom to develop their own institutions and apply the norms of their new religion, the Muslims needed more detailed instruction and guidance.

The significance of the shift in content, as distinguished from subject matter, of the message may not be so obvious and does not seem to have received adequate attention in the past. It is my thesis that it was not only a shift from the general to the specific, from the religious and moral to the political and legal, but also one in the meaning and implications of the Qur'an and Sunna. I believe that the specific political and legal norms of the Qur'an and Sunna of Medina did not always reflect the exact meaning and implications of the message as revealed in Mecca. An adjustment had to be made, and was successfully made, to provide for a specific political community in its concrete historical and geographical context.

For the ten remaining years of his life after *hijra*, the Prophet concentrated on consolidating the Muslim community in and around Medina. The hostility of the Quraysh tribe and its allies continued, leading to several major battles and raids until a truce was declared under what is known in Muslim history as *sulh* (peace treaty of) *al-hudybiya* in 628 A.D.[4] When that treaty was violated by Quraysh about two and a half years later, the Prophet and his followers were strong enough to march unopposed into Mecca. Thus, by the time of his death in 632, the Prophet had established Muslim rule throughout Arabia and converted most of its population to Islam.

The choice of a successor to the Prophet as the religious and political head of the community presented the Muslims with their first serious crisis. Some of the ramifications of that crisis persist up to the present day. Not only was the position of successor to the Prophet, caliph, contested by the two main segments of the community, *al-muhajirun* (those who migrated with the Prophet from Mecca in 622) and *al-ansar* (those who hosted and supported him in Medina), but it was also contested among the leading personalities of *al-muhajirun*, the segment that prevailed in the broader contest.[5] Abu Bakr (the Prophet's first adult male follower and long-standing friend) became the first caliph. Those Muslims who supported Ali (the Prophet's first cousin and son-in-law) in that first and subsequent contests over the position of caliph eventually developed into the separate sect of Islam known as the *Shi'a* (partisans of Ali).

Abu Bakr was succeeded by two leading *muhajirun*, Umar and Uthman, before Ali had his turn as caliph. Ali's reign, however, was short and turbulent, ending in his assassination and the establishment of the Umayyad dynasty in 661. Umayyad rule lasted until 750, when it was overthrown and replaced by the Abbasid dynasty, which continued for several centuries.[6] These are the main stages of early Muslim history which are significant for the sources and development of Shari'a.

THE FORMATIVE STAGES OF SHARI'A

It is reasonable to assume that the formulation of Shari'a, like any other legal system, followed the main stages of the development of the community it purported to regulate. The techniques through which Shari'a was derived from the divine sources and the ways in which its fundamental concepts and principles were formulated are clearly the product of the intellectual, social, and political processes of Muslim history. It is not possible to discuss in a comprehensive and exhaustive fashion all the relevant processes, but a brief outline may be helpful in understanding the way Shari'a was constructed.

The first three centuries of Islam (seventh to ninth centuries A.D.) were the formative period for Shari'a. During that time the main historical determinants in the formulation of Shari'a included the territorial and demographic nature of the Muslim communities and their political and sociological context.[7] The stages of Muslim expansion and the concomitant conversion of a wide variety of ethnic and cultural groups are also important. These territorial and demographic factors determined the political and sociological nature of the Muslim state and provided the raw material from which its institutions and policies developed during the crucial first three centuries of Islam. The combination of these factors had considerable impact on the formulation of Shari'a.

Historical sources are in agreement on the main features of the extraordinary Muslim expansion from the city-state of Medina into a vast empire extending from Spain in the west to northern India in the east within a few decades of the death of the Prophet in 632. This phenomenal expansion over such a short period brought into Islam a wide variety of ethnic and cultural groups, some of whom had their own ancient and sophisticated civilizations and systems of law and government. The late Umayyad and early Abbasid eras were periods of consolidation and assimilation, in which these diverse groups became a coherent and integrated Islamic whole. This process of Islamization involved the adoption and adaption of pre-Islamic norms and institutions of both Arab and non-Arab segments of the Muslim population.[8] The process of Islamization was slow and protracted because it was limited by the methods of transportation, communication, and other technological resources of the seventh and eighth centuries. Nevertheless, it was a thorough and effective process that set the scene for the development of Shari'a and the arts and sciences of the Islamic civilization over the next several centuries.

The following quotation from Fazlur Rahman reflects the common Muslim view of the nature of the state and its relationship to Shari'a until to the end of the Umayyad dynasty:

> During the period of the first four Caliphs (up to about 40/660),[9] the Muslim state and government was headed by the Caliph but was indistinguishable from the public body thanks to the large numbers of Companions [of the Prophet] in Medina, especially the senior members who advised on, controlled and participated in both legislative and executive functions. Indeed, at this stage, law can hardly be separated or even distinguished from administration. Legislation in this period can, therefore, mainly by courtesy be attributed to the contemporary Caliph, for it was the joint work of the Community or its senior members. With the Umayyad, however, the government became vested in the ruling autocracy which became distinguished from the public. The Umayyad rulers carried on their administration from Damascus, largely guided by the Qur'an and the Sunna, but these were interpreted by their advisers and officers on the principle of expediency and in the light of local practices in different provinces. . . . The first Umayyad Caliph to take the application of the Shari'a law seriously and systematically was 'Umar ibn 'Abd al-'Aziz around the close of the first/early eighth century.[10]

It is often said that genuine and thorough Islamization of the government and administration of justice were not high priorities with the Umayyads because of their preoccupation with the external expansion and internal cohesion of their domain.[11] Nevertheless, some degree of Islamization must have taken place during the Umayyad era, if only in the service of their overriding concern with internal cohesion and external expansion. The Abbasids, who mounted their successful challenge to Umayyad rule on the ground that the latter failed to pursue rigorous Islamization, are said to have applied Shari'a in a more comprehensive and strict fashion.[12] This may have been true in practice at the very beginning of Abbasid rule, but in due course political expediency caused Abbasid practice to depart from the theory of Shari'a.[13] Nevertheless, the importance of the initial practical (and continued theoretical) commitment of the Abbasids to Shari'a rule must not be underestimated. That commitment accounted for the establishment of the sources and techniques of Shari'a and the formulation of its fundamental concepts and general principles. The vast majority of

Muslims today are followers of the four surviving Sunni schools of Islamic jurisprudence, *madhahib* (singular *madhhab*), which were established during the early Abbasid era.[14]

To recognize the paramount importance of the early Abbasid period is not to deny the significance of the earlier periods. It would be better to see the early Abbasid period as the culmination of a long process and fusion of the various elements and factors contributing to the formulation of Shari'a. After all, Shari'a is fundamentally based on the Qur'an and Sunna as understood through the practice of the first few generations of Muslims. The clear and definite verses of the Qur'an and texts of Sunna must have been applied by the Prophet himself and his immediate Companions *(sahaba)*[15] and following generations.[16]

DEVELOPMENT OF ISLAMIC JURISPRUDENCE

The first stage in the development of Islamic jurisprudence is shrouded in controversy over the extent to which the opinions and rulings attributed to the Prophet and his Companions were genuine or merely fabrications projected back from the second century of Islam to enlist the support of earlier and stronger authority for subsequently developed propositions of Shari'a. This controversy is complicated by the lack of independent objective sources for verifying the alleged historical facts and developments. For the purposes of this study, it is sufficient only to note the following points.

First, the Muslim community existed as an independent political entity in need of daily regulation and provision for its government and administration of justice since 622 A.D. The fundamental sources for such regulation and provision were the Qur'an and the guidance and leadership of the Prophet during his lifetime. Upon his death, the Muslims were left with the text of the Qur'an and the Sunna of the Prophet, as reported and understood by his surviving Companions.[17] It is also clear that the opinions of the Companions were given strong weight even when they did not purport to be expressly based on a specific Sunna of the Prophet. But because such regard for the opinions of the Companions was based on the assumption that the particular Companion had benefited from his association with the Prophet, the weight given to the opinion of each Companion varied with his rank, which was based on perceptions of his character and degree of identification with the message of Islam. Another consideration was whether other leading Companions approved or acquiesced to the particular opinion. This second consideration was developed later into the concept of *ijma* (consensus) as a source of Shari'a. A similar process occurred in relation to the opinions of the scholarly members of the second generation, as assessed and accepted or rejected by the third generation of Muslims.

Second, although specific rulings and opinions by the Prophet and by the first and second generations of Muslims existed, the vast majority of them remained in the form of informal oral tradition for several decades before they were gradually collected and recorded for systematic study and development in the second century of Islam.[18]

Third, in the second century of Islam the systematic study of the traditions of the first and second generations of Muslims (as distinguished from the Sunna of the Prophet) sifted through the wealth of detail to categorize and rank the various views and judge them in the light of the Qur'an and Sunna. By this time, Sunna had acquired a specialized and more authoritative sense as a source of Shari'a. The traditions of the first and second generations of Muslims continue to carry weight with the vast majority of contemporary Muslims and are still available in primary and secondary sources. They are used, even now, to support propositions of Shari'a under the criteria established by *usul al-fiqh* (the science of the roots or foundations of Shari'a).

Finally, whatever specific opinions and rulings existed in the first century of Islam, they were not developed into general principles or integrated into the legal system which we know today as Shari'a until the second century of Islam.[19] This does not mean that there was a complete legal vacuum before the second century. Rather, it means that such specific legal norms which existed in the Qur'an, Sunna, traditions of the earliest Muslims, and customary practices (the raw material from which Shari'a was subsequently constructed) were not developed into a systematic and coherent legal system until the second century of Islam.

The construction of Shari'a in the second century of Islam built on the work of earlier individual jurists/judges working in several Muslim centers: Medina and Mecca in western Arabia, Basra and Kufa in southern Iraq, Damascus in Syria, and in Egypt.[20] Because of its independent and individualistic nature, the work of the early jurists/judges was characterized by a wide range of local variations, which were accepted as natural and legitimate.[21] The founders of the surviving Sunni schools of Islamic jurisprudence were individual jurists working in their respective local centers.

For a variety of political and sociological reasons, the early Abbasid era, from 750 A.D. onward, marked the beginning of a process of consolidation and systemization of the work of certain individual jurists and their students into separate schools of thought on Shari'a.[22] As noted by Noel Coulson, "Islamic jurisprudence thus began [as a result of the political and sociological factors associated with the downfall of the Umayyad dynasty] not as the scientific analysis of the existing practice of courts whose authority was accepted, but as the formulation of a scheme of law in opposition to that practice."[23]

That scheme of law was constructed by certain leading jurists, in some cases by students in the name of their master jurist.[24] In this way, Abu Hanifa (d. 150/767) and his two leading students, Abu Yusuf (d. 181/797) and Shaybani (d. 189/805), founded the Hanafi school in Iraq. Awaz'i (d. 157/774) founded a school in Syria, which was overcome by that of Malik (d. 179/795), originally founded in Medina. Shafi'i (d. 204/819) was a student of Malik who is credited with founding *usul al-fiqh* and the establishment of a separate school. Shafi'i's insistence on the use of the Sunna of the Prophet alone, rather than the tradition of the first and subsequent generations of Muslims, was carried to an extreme by Ibn Hanbal (d. 241/855), the founder of the fourth and last of the surviving Sunni school of Islamic jurisprudence.[25]

As the dates of the deaths of these founding jurists clearly show, the most active period in the construction of Shari'a was between the middle eighth and the end of the ninth centuries, the second and third centuries of Islam. Both the masters and their leading students who founded the schools lived and worked during that period. It is true that the founding jurists were working with source materials from the earlier period (the Qur'an, Sunna, and the traditions of the first and second generations of Muslims), but those founding jurists were removed from the Prophet's time by at least a century and a half.

The key to the maturation of Islamic jurisprudence and to the founding of the schools of thought in the early Abbasid era was the refinement of the definition of the sources of Shari'a and the development of the techniques by which general principles and specific rules were derived from those sources. The eighth and ninth centuries witnessed phenomenal activity in the interpretation of the Qur'an and the authentication and recording of the Sunna of the Prophet as distinguished from other traditions. The jurist most commonly credited with the founding of *usul al-fiqh* is Shafi'i.[26] With his work (and that of his immediate predecessors, contemporaries, and successors) the sources and techniques of Shari'a were molded and settled into their present form. Ever since that time, generations of Muslims and their jurists have been content with *taqlid* (the close and faithful following of their respective school).

A few exceptional jurists purported to challenge *taqlid* and maintained that scholars and jurists should be able to resort directly to the Qur'an, Sunna, and traditions of the earliest Muslims without the intermediacy of the established schools. But these so-called renewers were operating within the framework of the established jurisprudence and did not introduce significant changes in the sources, techniques, or general concepts and principles of Shari'a. Ibn Taymiyya, the prime example of this class of renewers, was operating within the framework of the Hanbali school and did not introduce any significant changes in the principles and rules of the public law of Shari'a developed by his predecessors.[27]

THE SOURCES AND TECHNIQUES OF SHARI'A

The four sources of Shari'a are the Qur'an, Sunna of the Prophet, *ijma*, and *qiyas*, the last two commonly translated as consensus and reasoning by analogy, respectively. *Ijtihad* (independent juristic reasoning), which is sometimes mentioned as a source of Shari'a in records of early traditions, will be considered further in the next section.

The logic of Shari'a as a religious legal system clearly indicates that it is to be derived first from direct divine revelation, the Qur'an; second from the traditions or Sunna of the Prophet, who received that revelation; and finally from the "reliable" and "guided" action of the individual persons and the community who have lived in accordance with that revelation and tradition. Although *ijma* and *qiyas* are not expressly mentioned in the Qur'an or Sunna as sources of Shari'a, the development of these concepts as sources of Shari'a was the product of an expressly sanctioned source, the *ijtihad* of the founding jurists of the second and third centuries of Islam.[28]

Qur'an

The full text of the Qur'an, which Muslims believe to be the literal and final word of God,[29] was collected very early in Muslim history. The text of the Qur'an is accepted as accurate and beyond dispute by all Muslims.[30] What needs to be reexamined, I suggest, is the use of the Qur'an as the basis of positive law.

The key to understanding the role of the Qur'an in the formulation of Shari'a is the appreciation that the Qur'an primarily sought to establish certain basic standards of behavior for the Muslim community rather than to express those standards as rights and obligations. As stated by Coulson, the role of the Prophet in establishing the standards of behavior "precedes, both in point of time and emphasis, his role as a political legislator" specifying the legal consequences of violating those standards.[31] The Qur'an contains the basic notions underlying civilized society, such as compassion, fairness, and good faith in commercial dealings and integrity and incorruptibility in the administration of justice, and expresses them as the Islamic religious ethic.[32] Except for a few specified offenses (*hudud* and *qisas*, to be explained in Chapter 5), the Qur'an does not set out the legal consequences of its "public law" injunctions. Rather, it "looks beyond this to the effect that [human] actions may have upon the conscience and eternal soul of the one who performs them. In short, the primary purpose of the Qur'an is to regulate not the relationship of man with his fellows but his relationship with his Creator."[33]

Thus "the Qur'an is not and does not profess to be a code of law or even a law book. . . . Rather, it is an eloquent appeal to mankind to obey the law of God which, it is (in the main) implied, has already been revealed or is capable of being discovered. Nevertheless, it would be a grave mistake to overlook the influence of the Qur'an in the creation of the Islamic legal system."[34] It is true, on one hand, that only about 500 (600 according to some scholars) out of a total of 6,219 verses of the Qur'an have a legal element, and the vast majority of these deal with worship rituals, leaving only about 80 verses of legal subject matter in the strict sense of the term.[35] On the other hand, not only have these 80 verses been constructed "so as to extract the utmost ounce of meaning from them," but the nonlegal verses have also been constructed to render legal content and guidance in various ways.[36] Most important, the Qur'an is the source of the Muslim conviction that Shari'a is the direct and comprehensive command of God. Consequently, all other sources and techniques, as well as any individual principle or rule of Shari'a, have to be either based on the Qur'an or at least shown to be consistent with its precepts.

Schacht has suggested that "apart from the most elementary rules, norms derived from the Koran [Qur'an] were introduced into Muhammadan law [Shari'a] almost invariably at a secondary stage." This statement cannot be taken to mean, I submit, that the Qur'anic rule was not applied from the very beginning whenever it was seen to be relevant and applicable. As indicated by Schacht and other scholars, there are examples of very early reference to the Qur'an as a source of legal rules.[37] The Qur'an's detailed rules of family law and inheritance, for example, have always been applied. Therefore, the lack of reference to the Qur'an in any given instance during the early period may be simply because the particular scholar or jurist did not see any verse of the Qur'an to be relevant to the issue at hand. Conversely, the more frequent reference to the Qur'an in the second and third centuries of Islam was the result of exceptional jurisprudential activity in the interpretation of the Qur'an and the development of

Shari'a during that period. In this way, the use of the Qur'an as a source of Shari'a was subject to differences in opinion over the relevance and interpretation of the verses in question. *Ijma* (consensus) was used to establish certain opinions and interpretations as the most authoritative statements of Shari'a on any particular subject.

Of particular interest in the present context, however, is the principle of *naskh* (the abrogation or repeal of the legal efficacy of certain verses of the Qur'an in favor of other verses). The principle of *naskh* is accepted by the vast majority of Sunni jurists and schools of thought and is clearly at the foundation of many principles and rules of Shari'a, especially in the public field. As a matter of Shari'a, an abrogated or repealed verse(s) of the Qur'an was to remain abrogated to maintain consistency. From that point of view, positive law developed on the basis of the subsequent revelation of the Medina period abrogating apparently inconsistent revelations of the earlier Mecca period.[38] Is it possible for contemporary Muslims to reconsider the process of abrogation? Is it permissible to take verses that have been previously abrogated as the new basis of Islamic law and to that end deem previously enacted verses to be abrogated from the legal point of view? I submit that it is not only possible to rethink the rationale and consequences of *naskh,* but that it is imperative to do so if we are to resolve the problems raised by the modern application of the public law of Shari'a.[39]

Sunna

The Arabic verb *sanna* means to fashion a thing and produce it as a model. The verb is also applied to model behavior.[40] Such exemplary conduct can either be initiated by setting an example or be drawn from the practice of the forefathers of, say, a tribe or community. As explained by Fazlur Rahman, the concept has two elements: an (alleged) historical fact of conduct and its normativeness for succeeding generations.[41] In the Muslim context, the concept is explained by another scholar as follows: "Among the pious successors of Muhammad and in the oldest Muslim community *sunna* came to mean anything that could be proven to have been the practice of the Prophet and his oldest disciples. Just as the pagan Arab adhered to the *sunna* of his ancestors, so was the Muslim community enjoined to uphold and follow the new *sunna.* Thus the Muslim concept of *sunna* is a variant of an ancient Arab concept."[42]

There is some disagreement among modern scholars of Islam as to the exact time of the emergence of the concept of Sunna of the Prophet, as distinguished from other early Muslim traditions. Some scholars, such as Joseph Schacht, maintain that this specialized concept of Sunna was a relatively late concept, while others, such as Fazlur Rahman, maintain that this concept existed from the beginning.[43] It is beyond dispute, however, that the precise sense of Sunna of the Prophet as the only Sunna constituting the authoritative second source of Shari'a was a product of the late second century of Islam.[44] Throughout the first century of Islam, the term *sunna* was used to refer to *both* the Sunna of the Prophet and the *sunna*, in the sense of traditions of an individual Muslim or that of the community in general.[45] The existence of the broader sense of *sunna* as the traditions of leading individuals or of the community of Muslims in early Islam is not inconsistent with the existence of *riwayat* (verbal transmissions) of Prophetic model behavior since the earliest times of Islam. As explained by Fazlur Rahman, the nature of the Companions' relationship with the Prophet (as disciples trying to live and embody the master's teaching and not merely students recording it) made it difficult for the formal traditionalists, the scholars who collected and recorded the Sunna of the Prophet, and for subsequent generations to disentangle the strictly prophetic element from the alleged dicta and facta of the Companions.[46]

As the Sunna of the Prophet acquired its paramount role as a source of Shari'a during the second century of Islam (late eighth and ninth centuries A.D.) its authenticity, exact wording, and the circumstances of its origin became extremely important.[47] S. G. Vesey-Fitzgerald is helpful in understanding the phenomenon of fabrication and the need for authentication of Sunna during that period:

> That there has been wholesale fabrication of traditions [Sunna] is universally admitted by Muslim and Western scholars alike. Indeed, the existence and danger of such fabrication was well known from almost the earliest period of Islam. At the first it may have been innocent enough. Many of the Companions were people who had known the Prophet intimately; and the psychological step from feeling confident of what the Prophet's view would probably have been to persuading oneself that he had in fact so decided is one which an honest mind might easily take without being conscious that it has crossed the border between opinion and fact. As time went on, many of the traditions were obviously attempts to read back the controversies, or the conditions of later ages, into that earlier period from which guidance was sought.[48]

The process of verification of authenticity and recording of Sunna was undertaken by a large number of Muslim scholars of the second century of Islam, but only the compilations of six scholars have come to be accepted by the majority of Muslims as containing sound or genuine

Sunna.[49] These and other scholars of Sunna developed very strict criteria or apparatus for verifying the authenticity of reports of Sunna and ranking them according to reliability or acceptability.[50] Vesey-Fitzgerald notes, "Unfortunately, this apparatus suffered from the cardinal defect which is inherent, even to this day, in the Islamic theory of evidence—the presumption that a respectable man who would not willingly tell a lie is therefore necessarily telling the truth. Of faulty memory, wishful thinking, reading back the present into the past, casting the color of one's opinion on the facts, and the effect of leading questions . . . they [Muslim scholars of Sunna] were in the main completely unconscious."[51]

The defects of the apparatus of authentication, when judged by modern standards, may logically support the proposition that some fabricated Sunna may have crept into even the six compilations currently accepted as authoritative by all Sunni Muslims. It is also possible that some genuine Sunna were rejected or ranked so low as to have no impact as a source of Shari'a. Nevertheless, I believe that any attempt to sift the genuine from the false, or to reinstate previously discredited reports of Sunna, is a hopeless task to undertake today.

Ijma

When Sunna was specified to be that of the Prophet alone, the "living tradition" of his Companions and succeeding generations was relegated to a lower status but survived as *ijma* (consensus), the third source of Shari'a.[52] Besides its logical rationale, Sunna was also enlisted by Muslim jurists in support of *ijma* as a source of Shari'a. It is reported that the Prophet said: "My people *(Ummati)* shall never be unanimous *(tujmi'u)* in error."[53] Verse 4:115 of the Qur'an is also cited in support of the authority of *ijma*.

Despite problems with defining its scope and operation, *ijma* was a powerful force in the development of Shari'a, not only as an independent source but also in determining the authoritative text and interpretation of the Qur'an and Sunna themselves. At one level, the early record of the Qur'an and subsequent selected compilations of Sunna have become authoritative and conclusive through *ijma*. Moreover, it was established that "only that interpretation and application of the Qur'an and *sunna* [Sunna] are correct which have been taken over by the consensus *[ijma]*. . . . Only those men and writings are regarded as authoritative whom the consensus *[ijma]* of the community has acknowledged as such, not in synods or councils, but through a nearly subconscious voice of the people which in its universality was regarded as not being subject to error."[54]

Although the principle of *ijma* as a source of Shari'a was accepted

early in the day, its meaning and scope were the subject of much controversy.[55] What constitutes *ijma?* Does it require complete unanimity or can
it be formed despite some disagreement or minority dissent? Whose *ijma*
is binding and upon whom? Is it the consensus of the Companions and
their community of Medina, that of Muslim scholars and jurists in general
(or in a given locality), or that of the totality of Muslims? Is it the *ijma*
of a single generation (of either scholars or the Muslim community) or
that of several generations? Is the *ijma* of an earlier generation (or generations) necessarily binding on all subsequent generations? All these and other
questions relating to the nature and scope of *imja* were, and continue to
be, controversial.

The controversy over these and other related questions was to some
extent the result of the inadequacy in methods that would provide the community (whether of scholars or of Muslims at large) with the means to
arrive at *ijma* over any given matter.[56] Given the modern means of organization, transport, communication, and the like, this procedural aspect
is no longer a problem. What is problematic are the policy aspects of the
nature and scope of *ijma*. For example, which population should be competent to establish binding *ijma*, and what should be the relationship of
their *ijma* to that of earlier, contemporary, and subsequent generations?
Can it be argued, for example, that *ijma* is the consensus of a particular
political community of Muslims, say that of a nation-state, and that it may
be determined by the elected representatives or through referendum of the
particular community? If so, can such "democratic" *ijma* of a given modern political community be allowed to repudiate a concept or principle of
Shari'a based on the *ijma* of an earlier Muslim community, especially the
earliest generations, which are assumed by the vast majority of Muslims
to enjoy particularly strong religious authority? At the heart of these questions and their possible answers is the fundamental question of the rationale
of *ijma:* is it based on the principle of popular sovereignty or on an assumption of religious authority, piety, and morality? These questions of
fundamental policy cannot be settled here. It is hoped, however, that the
present study will contribute to their resolution.

Qiyas

In applying *qiyas* (analogy) a jurist is "concluding from a given
principle embodied in a precedent that a new case falls under this principle or is similar to this precedent on the strength of a common essential
feature called the "reason" ('illa)."[57] Since the determination of the *illa* or
reason behind the original precedent or previous rule, and the presence

of the same in the new case is the opinion of the jurist, *qiyas* has been resisted as basing Shari'a on human reason rather than divine revelation. Such a charge can be avoided only if *qiyas* is limited to cases in which none of the other sources is applicable and the outcome is seen to be fully consistent with the totality of Shari'a as well as with any of its established principles and rules.

Although obviously related to *ijtihad* (independent juristic reasoning) and one of its techniques,[58] it may have been useful to recognize *qiyas* as an independent source of Shari'a, especially since the gates of *ijtihad* were supposed to have been closed after the ninth century A.D. It thus became possible to continue to deduce rulings for new cases out of the precedents of earlier established principles and rules of Shari'a without claiming to exercise *ijtihad* as such.

Minor or Subsidiary Techniques

These techniques include *istihsan, istislah* or *maslaha, istishab, darura,* and *urf.* It has been said that the best English translation for *istihsan* is "favorable construction" because the concept has been applied mainly to avoid having strict *qiyas* abolish an already existing and salutary or at least harmless practice or causing an unnecessarily harsh result.[59] Another possible translation is "juristic preference." Instead of following strict *qiyas,* a jurist may prefer or elect *(yastahsinu)* another solution. Originally contrasted with usual *qiyas* in the work of Malik and Abu Yusuf during the second half of the eighth century A.D., the term *istihsan* came to mean "a method of finding the law which for any reason is contradictory to the usual *kiyas [qiyas].*" Shafi'i and his disciples rejected *istihsan* as opening a loophole for arbitrary decision, while the supporters of the technique, mainly in the Hanafi school of Islamic jurisprudence, defended it as concealed or subtle *qiyas (qiyas khafi),* a divergence from an externally obvious *qiyas* to an inner and self-conditioned decision, preference based on a reason sanctioned by established authority.[60]

Istislah or *maslaha* (public good) is related to, and sometimes confused with, *istihsan* in that it is also conceived in contrast to the more obvious method of deducing legal decisions, although the latter may be traceable further back than the former. Al-Ghazzali is reported to have defined *maslaha* as consideration for what is aimed at for humankind in the law, namely, the maintenance of religion, life, reason or mind, descendants, and property. According to al-Ghazzali, such maintenance is generally guaranteed by the legal texts and therefore coincides with usual *qiyas.* If that were not the case, then *maslaha* is decisive only when there are cogent and unequivocally defined considerations affecting the whole community. Otherwise it is not allowed to use *istislah*.[61] In this sense, it has been said, the concept of *istislah* or *maslaha* seems to be very similar to the English idea of "public policy" or "the policy of the law."[62]

Being concerned with avoiding anything that opens the way to tampering with the law of God, Shafi'i preferred the stricter doctrine of *istishab*. By this he meant seeking a link, a principle of evidence whereby an existing state of affairs may be presumed to have had a lawful origin and to continue in existence until the contrary is shown.[63] In other words, this is no more than a presumption of legitimacy for ancient practices until the contrary is proved.

Contrasting the views of two Muslim jurists on the implications of *istislah* or *maslaha* is instructive on the potential of this concept for modern law reform. Ibn Taymiyya was skeptical about the concept because he thought that Shari'a had already provided for "legitimate" *maslaha*. If a human being thinks that there is *maslaha* in some principle, then such *maslaha* is either already provided for and needs only to be discovered or it is an imaginary and not real *maslaha*, that is, it is illegitimate or should not be pursued. Al-Tawfi, by contrast, maintained that *maslaha* is decisive over even the text of the law *(nass)* and *ijma* (consensus) if the latter cannot be reconciled with regard for the general welfare insofar as the legal aspects of everyday life are concerned.[64] In other words, except for matters relating to worship rituals and practices *(ibadat)*, al-Tawfi perceived of *maslaha* as paramount and capable of overruling the text of Shari'a.

Darura or necessity may be seen as derived from *qiyas* or analogy to a principle contained in verses of the Qur'an, such as verse 2:239. Since that verse was construed to permit a mounted soldier awaiting battle to say his prayers in the saddle instead of dismounting and going through the prescribed ritual as he should normally do, it was concluded, by analogy, that necessity may cause the impermissible to become permissible *(al darurat tubihu al-mahzurat)*. The same principle can be found in other verses of the Qur'an, such as the ones permitting a Muslim to eat forbidden food such as pork or do an impermissible thing if that is the only way to preserve his or her life.[65] The key question here is, of course, what constitutes a legitimate necessity of the degree which justifies deviation from or relaxation of the strict rules of Shari'a?

Urf or customary practice is recognized, within limits, by the Hanafi and Maliki schools but rejected by the Shafi'i school.[66] According to the Hanafi school, for example, *urf* or custom may prevail over *qiyas* but never over a *nass*, a text of the Qur'an or Sunna.

The paramountcy of *nass* is in fact the common limitation on all the minor techniques as well as *ijma* and *qiyas*. *Ijtihad* in general is believed to be permitted only in matters not covered by clear and definite *nass* or text of Qur'an or Sunna.

THE ROLE OF *IJTIHAD*

Ijtihad literally means hard striving or strenuousness, but technically it means exercising independent juristic reasoning to provide answers when the Qur'an and Sunna are silent. Sunna is reported in support of *ijtihad* as a source of Shari'a.[67] As noted earlier, the concept of *ijma* (consensus) appears to have come about as a result of the exercise of *ijtihad*, in the sense that the *ijtihad* of the founding jurists led them to the conclusion that the consensus of the community in general, or that of the Muslim scholars in particular, should be made a source of Shari'a. Moreover, the content of *ijma*, that is, the principles and rules that are now accepted as part of Shari'a through *ijma*, may have been initially conceived through the *ijtihad* of one or more Companions or early jurists. *Qiyas* (analogy) may also be seen as a technique of *ijtihad*.

Moreover, the exercise of *ijtihad*, in a broader sense, is relevant to the interpretation of the Qur'an and Sunna. Whenever a principle or rule of Shari'a is based on the general meaning or broad implications of a text of Qur'an or Sunna, as opposed to the direct ruling of a clear and definite text, the link between the text and the principle or rule of Shari'a is established through juristic reasoning. It is hard to imagine any text of the Qur'an or Sunna, however clear and definite it may appear to be, that does not need this type of *ijtihad* for its interpretation and application in concrete situations.[68]

In this way, it would seem clear that *ijtihad* was a fundamental and very active concept in the formulation of Shari'a during the eighth and ninth centuries A.D. As Shari'a matured as a legal system, and the need for developing fresh principles and rules was perceived to be diminishing, room for *ijtihad* was seen to be narrowing to the point of extinction. This phenomenon is known in the history of Islamic jurisprudence as the closing of the gates of *ijtihad*.[69] The gates are believed by the majority of Muslims to have remained closed since the tenth century A.D. up to the present time. Some recent and contemporary Muslim scholars have been demanding the reopening of the gates of *ijtihad*.[70] The crucial question being addressed in the present study is whether opening the gates of *ijtihad* and exercising it within the framework of the existing principles of Shari'a will suffice. Will the exercise of *ijtihad* today resolve the fundamental problems with the public law of Shari'a highlighted in this study without challenging the whole structure of Shari'a as established by the founding jurists?

According to its textual and logical rationale under historical Shari'a, *ijtihad* was by definition restricted to matters not governed by clear and definite texts of Qur'an or Sunna. Moreover, under historical formulation of *usul al-fiqh* (the rules governing the derivation of principles of Shari'a from their sources), *ijtihad* is not possible even in a matter settled through *ijma*.[71] It is my thesis that both limitations on *ijtihad* have to be modified. Partial support for this proposition can be found in the fact that Umar, the second caliph and one of the leading Companions, had exercised *ijtihad* in matters that were actually governed by clear and definite texts of Qur'an and Sunna.[72]

For example, verse 9:60 of the Qur'an clearly and definitely specifies the items of expenditure or the beneficiaries of state funds, to include *al-mu'alafati qulubuhum*, those whose hearts and allegiance to the Muslims need to be won over or retained through the provision of material incentives. The Prophet paid this share throughout his life. Thus, these people had a legal right to their share of public funds on the authority of clear and definite texts of both Qur'an and Sunna. Nevertheless, Umar refused to pay this share on the grounds that it was previously paid at a time when Muslims were weak and in need of the support of such people, and since that was no longer the case, payment would be discontinued. Another significant example of exercising *ijtihad* in a matter governed by clear and definite texts is to be found in Umar's refusal to distribute lands captured during the conquests of Iraq and Syria as part of *ghana'im* (spoils of war) to which Muslim combatants were entitled under verses 59:6–10 of the Qur'an. When challenged by those who maintained that the Prophet distributed such lands as spoils of war throughout his life, Umar justified his refusal to follow the Qur'anic verses as interpreted and applied by the Prophet by arguing that to do so would deprive the state of essential resources necessary for maintaining its armies to defend its territories.[73]

It has been suggested that Umar's action was justified by his perception of what constitutes the best interest of the Muslim community.[74] But this is precisely the point, namely, that here is clear and strong precedent from the earliest times of Islam that policy considerations may justify applying a rule derived through *ijtihad* even if that required overriding clear and definite texts of the Qur'an and Sunna. In my view, these examples of the action of an early and leading Companion of Umar's standing cannot be dismissed as isolated cases which were overruled by the subsequent systematic formulation of *usul al-fiqh*. I would also argue that contemporary Muslims have the competence to reformulate *usul al-fiqh* and exercise *ijtihad* even in matters governed by clear and definite texts of the Qur'an and Sunna as long as the outcome of such *ijtihad* is consistent with the essential message of Islam.

THE SHI'A PERSPECTIVES

Although several historical minorities have disagreed with the Sunni majority,[75] only one significant minority has survived, namely the Shi'a or partisans of Ali. The main subgroups of Shi'a today are the Ithna asharis, or Twelvers of Iran, the Isma'ilis, or Seventhers of India, Central Asia, Syria, and the Persian Gulf region, and the Zaydis of southern Arabia. It may be helpful to see how these groups are distinguishable from the Sunni majority and to what extent Shi'a perspectives on the sources and nature of Shari'a are conducive to resolving the public law issues addressed in the present study.[76]

The fundamental distinguishing feature of all Shi'a is the central and crucial role played by the imam, the religious and political leader of the community. In this respect, all Shi'a trace their origin to the disagreement over the choice of the first successor of the Prophet in 632 A.D. Although the majority of Muslims accepted Abu Bakr as the first caliph (followed by Umar and Uthman before Ali had his turn), a minority supported Ali from the start and were subsequently called the *shi'at* Ali, the partisans of Ali. The choice of subsequent imams among the Shi'a themselves also marks the point of departure for each of the three main surviving subsects mentioned above.[77]

The majority of Shi'a accepted Muhammad al-Baqir as the fifth imam, but a minority took Zayd, another son of the fourth imam, as their own imam. The Zaydis, as they came to be known, recognize the principle of electing the imam from among the qualified descendants of Ali. They are restrained in judging the three caliphs preceding Ali, especially Abu Bakr and Umar, because they believe that an acceptable imam has a legitimate title to the caliphate even in the face of a superior claimant (Ali).[78] The Zaydi Shi'a require that their own imam, however, be a descendant of Ali and Fatima (the only daughter of the Prophet who had children) to have the personal qualities of character, piety, and learning and to be a sovereign capable of defending the faith. Within these qualifications, a Zaydi imam enjoys "right guidance" but is otherwise an ordinary man.[79]

The majority of Shi'a took Ja'far al-Sadiq as the sixth imam, but they disagreed over the choice of the seventh imam. A minority recognized Isma'il, the eldest son of Ja'far, as the seventh imam and became known as the Seventhers or Isma'ilis, while the majority took Musa al-

Kazim as their seventh imam, followed by five more imams until their twelfth imam, Muhammad ibn al-Hasan al-Askari. When this twelfth imam disappeared, as a small boy (in a cave near Samarra, then the capital of the caliphate) in 874 A.D., this group came to believe that he was only absent *(qha'ib)* but still alive and would return at the end of time as the Mahdi-Messiah-Imam.[80] In contrast to the Twelvers, the Isma'ilis maintain that "the imam cannot completely disappear, even if to the profane eyes of the people he is invisible, *mastur* (veiled), hidden from the sight of those whose vision does not possess the penetration of the true adept. 'If the imam were to disappear from the world, even for a moment', say the Isma'ilis, 'verily, the earth would perish with all its inhabitants'."[81]

All Shi'a insist that the rightful imam be a descendant of the Prophet through his daughter Fatima and Ali. This is their fundamental doctrinal difference from the Sunni majority, who were always willing to accept a qualified leader regardless of whether he was one of *ahl al-bayt* (the Prophet's immediate family). From this fundamental difference flow other distinguishing features of the Shi'a and their theology and law. For the vast majority of Shi'a, the imam is the Perfect Man *(al-insan al-Kamil)*, who acts as a link between humankind and God. The imam "is the mysterious logical and spiritual principle which binds the whole universe together and, therefore, the final authority in both law and religion." He is infallible and incapable of error in every aspect of his life, public as well as private.[82]

The Shi'a in general accept the Qur'an and Sunna as the sources of Shari'a, subject to the following qualifications. Except for minor differences, as would arise from different styles of recitation of the Qur'an *(qira'at)* and in the order of the chapters of the Qur'an and some odd verses, the majority of Shi'a agree with Sunni Muslims over the text of the Qur'an.[83] They disagree with the Sunni Muslims, however, over the authoritative interpretation of the Qur'an. They also differ on the infallibility of the transmission of the Sunna. The Shi'a do not accept a Sunna report unless it is recorded or acknowledged by one of their own imams.[84]

Moreover, the peculiar and paramount role of the imam in Shi'a perspectives precludes the acceptance of *ijma* and *ijtihad* in the Sunni sense of these concepts. To concede infallibility to the consensus of the community in *ijma*, or to concede authority to derive rules of Shari'a by the *ijtihad* of an ordinary jurist, however learned and pious he may be, would undermine the position of the imam and his power to make law by divine ordinances.[85] For the Twelvers Shi'a, not only is the imam "the living entity of the infallible divine law, its interpreter-maker and executor," but "the Twelfth [*qha'ib* or absent] Imam's embodiment of the divine Shari'ah is . . . non-transmittable; his supreme authority as the infallible interpreter of the will of God is not open to delegation."[86] Thus the concept of law for the majority of Shi'a is "more authoritarian and far more detached from social reality than the Sunni concept."[87]

Leading historians of Islamic law differ in their assessment of the degree of similarity between Sunni and Shi'i schools of jurisprudence.[88] As Coulson rightly concludes, however, "on a purely theoretical plane, then, such coincidence as exists between Sunnite and Shi'ite jurisprudence is overshadowed and outweighed by the doctrine of the Imamate."[89] Therefore, and as far as the prospects for reform of the public law of Shari'a are concerned, it seems clear that the Shi'a perspectives only create more problems. Not only is the viability of answers based on Shi'a perspectives dependent upon acceptance by the Sunni majority of the Shi'a view of the imam and his role, but we also have to wait for the reappearance of the absent imam of the Twelvers, or acknowledgment of the veiled imam of the Isma'ilis, to hear what he has to say on the reform of Shari'a.

THE NATURE AND APPLICATION OF SHARI'A

It is certainly true that "Shari'a law had come into being as a doctrinal system independent of and essentially opposed to current [of the eighth century A.D.] legal practice."[90] Nevertheless, it is as dangerously easy to exaggerate the cleavage between the *umara* (amirs, military commanders and civil governors) and the *fuqaha* (jurists) as it is to ignore it. Although the jurists were obliged by the Qur'an to acknowledge the unity of the Islamic state, and consequently the necessity for an effective head of that state, however distasteful the individual occupant of that office may have been to them, the rulers always had to make some outward deference to Shari'a because they owed their position to the religion of Islam.[91] As a result, there has been "an uneasy truce between *ulama [fuqaha]* . . . and the political authorities *[umara]*. . . . As long as the sacred law [Shari'a] received formal recognition as a religious ideal, it did not insist on being fully applied in practice."[92]

The dichotomy between theory and practice, naturally enough, varied from time to time and from one field of Shari'a to another. The earliest stage of the Medina state is believed by the vast majority of Muslims to have reflected the strongest unity between the theory and practice of Shari'a. But that was over an extremely limited territory and for a very short period of time. Although the strict observance of Shari'a is not believed to have been a high priority with the Umayyads, their executive officials were clearly guided by it, to the extent that it had been developed by their time. In particular, increasing importance and prestige were attached by the Umayyads to the office of the *qadi* (a judge who specialized in Shari'a). This was carried further under the early Abbasids, who based the legitimacy of their challenge to the Umayyads on a claim to have greater commitment to the implementation of Shari'a. That commitment, however, "did not mean that the future course of the Islamic ship of state was to be steered by the Shari'a courts. The Abbasid rulers maintained a firm grip on the helm, and the Shari'a courts never attained that position of supreme judicial authority independent of political control, which would have provided the only sure foundation and real guarantee for the ideal of the *Civitas Dei*."[93] Subsequent stages of Muslim history reflected continuous fluctuation between greater and lesser observance of Shari'a in practice.[94]

We find that Shari'a's hold was strongest in family law and inheritance and weakest in penal law, taxation, constitutional law, and the law of war, with the law of contracts and obligations in the middle.[95] This variation in observance of the various aspects or fields of Shari'a is partly due to the greater degree of detailed regulation of these fields in the Qur'an and Sunna. The detailed provision in the Qur'an for family law and inheritance, for example, led to a stronger identification of the relevant rules of Shari'a with religious belief and practice. As a result of their primary concern with regulating the relationship of the individual Muslim with his or her God, "the jurists had formulated standards of conduct which represented a system of private, and not of public law, and which they conceived it to be the duty of the established political power to ratify and enforce."[96]

The conception of the role of the jurists and the duty of the political authorities in these terms was also reflected in the nature and degree of detail in the various fields of Shari'a. Not only did this lead to greater development of the religious and worship rituals and private and family law than the public law aspects of Shari'a, but it also led to the formulation of Shari'a principles in the form of moral duties sanctioned by religious consequences rather than legal rights and duties with specific temporal remedies. All fields of human activity were categorized in terms of *halal* or *mubah* (permissible or allowed) and *haram* (impermissible or prohibited), with intermediate categories of *mandub* (recommended) and *makruh* (reprehensible).[97]

In this way, Shari'a addresses the conscience of the individual Muslim, whether in private or public and official capacity, rather than the institutions and corporate entities of the community and the state. The other major categorization of Shari'a in terms of *ibadat* (worship rituals and practices) and *mu'amalat* (social dealings) also conforms to the fundamental nature of Shari'a as religious obligations to be reflected in private and public action from an individual private perspective.

The same individual private perspective underlies the diversity of opinions over Shari'a's ruling on any given matter. Although Shari'a professes to be a single logical whole, there is significant diversity of opinion not only between the schools but also among different jurists of the same school.[98] Because all the divergent and sometimes conflicting views are regarded as equally valid and legitimate, any Muslim has the choice of taking whatever view is acceptable to his or her individual conscience.[99] When this freedom is exercised by a judge adjudicating on the rights and obligations of litigants or an official in conducting his public functions, serious problems may arise. The same freedom has been employed by some Muslim reformers in what is known as *talfiq*, constructing a composite general principle or specific rule from a variety of sources, sometimes from more than one school of thought.[100] Such an approach is methodologically wrong because opinions and dicta of individual jurists are taken out of context and recombined according to the user's personal preference, so that an authority is sometimes used to support a conclusion unwarranted by the original author's position. Moreover, *talfiq* will not suffice as a basis or technique for modern Islamic law because the raw material of *talfiq* is the same Shari'a whose limitations have been noted in this chapter and will be illustrated in subsequent chapters.

As a result of western influence, the implementation of the public law of Shari'a has been at a very low level since the late nineteenth century. The main seats of Muslim power, in the Ottoman Empire, Persia, and India, collapsed and were co-opted into accepting the European models of the nation-state and international order and abandoning all pretense of conforming to the public law of Shari'a.[101] European legal systems became the norm in domestic law enforcement and international relations, leaving only family law and inheritance for Muslims to be governed by Shari'a.

More recently, however, almost all Muslim countries have been experiencing rising demands for a stronger Islamic identity and greater application of Shari'a. These demands have to be reconciled with the realities of the nation-state and the international order of the late twentieth century and with the expectations of the Muslims themselves to enjoy the benefits of modern notions of constitutionalism and human rights. The initial attempts to contain and reconcile these conflicting demands and expectations with the historical conception and formulation of Shari'a have failed. A new version of the public law of Shari'a has to be developed, whether through the methodology proposed in this book or by an alternative Islamic methodology which is capable of achieving the necessary balance between modernism and Islamic legitimacy.

⇗ 3 ⇖

Toward an Adequate Reform Methodology

*I*T IS MY THESIS that as long as Muslims continue to adhere to the framework of historical Shari'a, they will never achieve the *necessary* degree of reform which would make Islamic public law workable today. In this chapter I will attempt to explain and substantiate this thesis through a critique of the available literature and proposal of what I consider to be an adequate methodology for Islamic reform.

Islamic resurgence and reform are familiar themes in Muslim history. In particular, Muslim scholars have attempted to confront the challenges of Western domination and influence through an assertion of an Islamic identity since the mid-nineteenth century. In that tradition, the recent and contemporary proponents of Shari'a have proposed their models of a modern Islamic state as the basis for the fulfillment of the right of Muslims to self-determination. It is therefore important to understand these "modern" models and to assess their objectives, methods, and achievements.

It is my hypothesis that this survey and assessment will lead to the conclusion that these Shari'a models will create extremely serious problems in practice and that reform efforts *within* the framework of Shari'a have not so far achieved, and are unlikely to achieve in the future, the necessary degree of reform in the public law sphere. Stated briefly, the reason for the inevitable inadequacy of these efforts is that since they employ the reform techniques of Shari'a, they are restricted by the limitations of those techniques.

The late Sudanese writer *Ustadh*[1] Mahmoud Mohamed Taha proposed a revolutionary reform methodology, which he described as "the evolution of Islamic legislation"—in essence a call for the establishment of a new principle of interpretation that would permit applying some verses of Qur'an and accompanying Sunna instead of others. It seems to me that this approach, if accepted and implemented by Muslims today, would succeed in breaking the deadlock between the objectives of reform and the

34

limitations of the conception and techniques of historical Shari'a. The principle of *naskh* (the abrogation or repeal of certain texts of Qur'an and Sunna for legal purposes in favor of other texts of the Qur'an and Sunna) is crucial to the theoretical validity and practical viability of the evolutionary approach of *Ustadh* Mahmoud. In this chapter I will discuss the theoretical basis of the evolutionary approach, and assess its implications for the reform of Islamic public law. I will also offer a general assessment of the competing reform methodologies in an attempt to identify the one that is most likely to achieve the desired objectives of reform while maintaining Islamic legitimacy, which is necessary for practical implementation. Integral to that assessment is some consideration of the realities of discourse and implementation of Islamic law reform in the Muslim world today.

OVERVIEW OF CONTEMPORARY MODELS OF THE SHARI'A STATE

The following brief survey does not claim to cover all significant personalities and movements from all parts of the Muslim world in a comprehensive and detailed manner. It is sufficient for our limited purposes to highlight the main currents of thought relevant to objectives and methods of the modern proponents of Shari'a in relation to public law issues. One must keep the sociological and political context in mind, however, to understand the significance of the contributions made by these reforms to the field of public law.

The thirteenth-century scholar Ibn Taymiyya is often cited by the modern proponents of Shari'a in support of their position. The main features of the model of an Islamic state proposed by adherents to this line of thinking have appeared in the writings of representative contemporary proponents of Shari'a. Since there are other positions on the nature of the state for Muslim countries, we must also note the main features and implications of other possible models which purport to operate within, or at least not openly challenge, the general framework of Shari'a. Finally, the official reforms of Shari'a personal law recently implemented in many parts of the Muslim world will be noted for their public law implications and their value in indicating the limitations of reform within the framework of Shari'a.

The Proponents of a Shari'a State

Ibn Taymiyya is often cited as one of the most important pioneers of Islamic law reform. He is credited with having mounted an early and eventually significant challenge to the rigidity and futility of *taqlid*, blind imitation and following of the masters of the respective school of Islamic jurisprudence.[2] It may therefore be useful to begin with an explanation of his views, as they pertain to public law issues facing the Muslims today.[3] What is relevant to our purposes are the objectives and reform methodology of Ibn Taymiyya as the Islamic renewer and reformer *(mujadid)* often cited by the proponents of Shari'a as a model of what is needed to rejuvenate Islam today.

Ibn Taymiyya was born in 661 Hijri/1263 A.D. and died in 728/ 1328, a period of crisis and turmoil for the Muslim community.[4] He was raised and educated within the Hanbali school of jurisprudence, known for its strict rejection of personal opinion in matters of theology and law and its claims of strict adherence to the Qur'an and Sunna.

The primary attraction of Ibn Taymiyya to the proponents of Shari'a is his willingness to challenge the established order and reassert the right to exercise *ijtihad* notwithstanding the common belief that the gates of *ijtihad* have been closed since the tenth century A.D. He is believed to have undertaken the task of "a restatement of the Shari'a and a vindication of religious values."[5] Another aspect of his role as a model for Islamic resurgence is his uncompromising demand for the total application of Shari'a in public as well as private life. The object of his main work relevant to general public law issues, *Al-Siyasa al-shar'iyya fi islah al-ra'iy wa al-ra'iyya*,[6] "was to bring about a reform of the community and the state by restoring the *shari'a* to its proper place and influence and to lessen the gap between theory and practice." He maintained that the state and religion should be inseparable; otherwise discord and disorder would prevail in the affairs of men.[7]

Ibn Taymiyya is known for his emphasis on textual authority and earliest Muslim traditions over subsequent developments of the schools of jurisprudence. Although, as a Hanbali jurist, Ibn Taymiyya emphasized the Qur'an and Sunna and rejected *ra'y* (juristic opinion) as a source of Shari'a, he did recognize the authority of the *salaf*, earliest generations of Muslims.[8] Moreover, his willingness to challenge the established schools was not manifested in establishing a new school or working independently. As Schacht points out, "neither Ibn Taymiyya nor his personal disciples had ever elaborated an alternative system of positive law."[9]

In contrast to Sunni theory prevailing in his time, Ibn Taymiyya held that it was not obligatory for Muslims to maintain a universal unified caliphate. He believed it was possible for more than one imam to rule simultaneously.[10] This position would justify the existence of Islamic nation-states, as opposed to the historical universalistic Islamic state. Contemporary proponents of Shari'a find Ibn Taymiyya's position in this regard helpful in legitimizing Islamic nation-states in the modern context.

Although he pointed out that "even at the beginning there has never been a genuine election" of the ruler, he emphasized the contractual obligation of *mubaya'a* or *by'a* (the double oath of allegiance binding both the imam and his leading subjects). This contract imposed a duty of obedience on the subjects and an obligation on the imam to rule in accordance with justice and the dictates of Shari'a, including a duty to consult his subjects. Though speaking of the imam as shepherd, Ibn Taymiyya also spoke of him as the *wakil* (agent), *wali* (guardian), and *sharik* (partner) of his subjects. In his view, however, the subjects who constituted one side of the obligation of *mubaya'a* were the *ulama* (scholars and jurists) and leading members of the community, not the totality of the population of the Muslim state.[11]

Contrary to prevailing opinion of the period, Ibn Taymiyya was realistic in the qualifications he set for the imam. He criticized the excessively high, if not impossible, qualifications demanded by earlier writers as contrary to the spirit of the law. With the cooperation of *ulama* and *umara* (scholars and holders of political power), anyone who was *adl* (enjoyed full legal capacity under Shari'a) could be the imam.[12]

The modern utility of these views can be better assessed in light of the discussion of constitutional questions in the next chapter. They are noted here as elements of the appeal of Ibn Taymiyya to modern proponents of Shari'a. He offers them a model for challenging the rigidity of the established jurisprudence: a combination of commitment to the strict application of Shari'a with a view of the basis of the Islamic state in terms not unlike modern theories of social contract. His emphasis on the imam's obligation to observe the law and to consult with his subjects, albeit a selected few of them, can be expressed in modern terms as a commitment to the rule of law and "democratic" government.

Although Ibn Taymiyya had little influence during his own lifetime and for several generations to come, his ideas eventually had a significant impact through their acceptance and propagation by the eighteenth-century movements of Muhammad ibn Abd al-Wahab in Arabia and Shah Wali Allah in India.[13]

The literature on the modern application of Shari'a is too extensive to review in detail. Given the vitality of discourse over the application of Shari'a in Pakistan, the views expressed in that country may be taken as fairly representative of the debate elsewhere in the Muslim world. Pakistani thinking on the subject may be reviewed through the extensive survey undertaken by Ishtiaq Ahmed.[14] The proponents of Shari'a include those identified by Ahmed as Absolutists,[15] Mawdudi, Asad, Perwez, Hakim, and Javid Iqbal.[16]

It would be better to begin our survey of the views of the proponents of a Shari'a state with their view of the law applicable in their model state because that is crucial to their position on the key public law issues relevant to the present study. On this question we find that the Pakistani proponents of a Shari'a state are committed to the Qur'an and Sunna as the sole source of law but differ with regard to Islamic jurisprudence.[17] Whereas the Absolutists and Mawdudi see the whole of Shari'a and jurisprudence as directly applicable, Asad, Perwez, Hakim, and Javid Iqbal speak of the Qur'an and Sunna as the basis of the law with room for contemporary human discretion in its interpretation and application.

On the status of non-Muslims, the Absolutists see the Shari'a as dictating the creation of a state for Muslims as the sole citizens, with non-Muslims having no political rights.[18] Mawdudi and Asad accept the first part of the above proposition but allow non-Muslims very limited participation in politics. Perwez, Hakim, and Zafar also see the state as only for Muslims, but whereas Hakim sees a role for non-Muslims in policy implementation, Perwez and Zafar do not discuss the status of non-Muslims. Javid Iqbal seems to believe in Muslims as the primary nation, with non-Muslims as part of a broader Pakistani nation. The views expressed by those who did address the issue are consistent with a variety of preexisting views within Shari'a.

The same cannot be said, however, of all the views expressed on the status of women in the respective models. The Absolutists and Mawdudi agree in their advocacy of the segregation of women, but whereas the Absolutists would exclude women from public life altogether, Mawdudi would allow them limited participation without violating the segregation imperative.[19] Both positions are consistent with commonly accepted Shari'a. In contrast, the position of the others — allowing women participation in public life on an equal footing with men — is in accord with the aspirations of many contemporary Muslims but cannot be accepted as the correct view of Shari'a. As will be explained in subsequent chapters, some of the restrictions imposed on women are based on clear texts of the Qur'an and Sunna.

Finally, there is the question of the relationship of the Islamic state with non-Muslim states of the modern world. Once again, we will find it useful to see the views expressed by our selected subjects on the first question of the law applicable. Standing by their strict commitment to Shari'a, the Absolutists see peace with the non-Muslim world as temporary and confrontation as unavoidable.[20] Mawdudi is also consistent with Shari'a in seeing the possibility of negotiating peace with non-Muslims while admitting the inevitability of confrontation if Shari'a is the law of the land. The others, however, are ambivalent and not fully consistent with Shari'a in their positions. They all seem to believe, whether expressly or by implication, that peace with the non-Muslim world is desirable, but they differ on whether confrontation is likely. Asad perceives the concept of *jihad* as justifying the use of force only in self-defense, a position that does not accurately reflect Shari'a, as will be seen in Chapter 6. To Hakim, ideological confrontation with atheism and polytheism is necessary, a position which is hard to reconcile with his view that peace is desirable. Perwez does not address the question, but it seems that peace with non-Muslims follows from his general reasoning. To Javid Iqbal, peace with non-Muslims is desirable. Again, as in the case of women, all four authors need to reconcile their position on the Qur'an and Sunna as the law of the land with their views on international relations.

Like Pakistan and Iran, the Sudan has had recent experience with the application of the public law of Shari'a. It may therefore be pertinent to discuss the position of the proponents of Shari'a in that country. For this purpose, the example of Hassan al-Turabi, the leader of the Islamic National Front in the Sudan, is instructive. Turabi presents a significant example of the activist proponent of Shari'a because his legal training at the University of Khartoum, followed by specialized training in public law at British and French universities, makes it reasonable to assume that he is familiar with the basic issues of constitutionalism, criminal justice, and international law. Since 1964, Turabi has been the leader of the movement working for the immediate and total application of Shari'a in the Sudan. Although the Muslim Brothers constitute the hard core of this movement, it encompasses a range of "Islamic" elements, hence its political name, the Islamic Charter in the 1960s and the Islamic National Front in the 1980s.[21]

It is therefore remarkable and very significant that a trained modern public lawyer who has successfully led this movement for nearly twenty-five years into national and regional prominence and political power has avoided expressing the objectives of the movement in concrete constitutional and legal terms. Except when squarely confronted and forced to give a categorical answer,[22] Turabi always spoke in general terms about the right of Muslims to self-determination through the application of Shari'a and the need for reform and flexibility in relation to the Islamic tradition without addressing the specific implications of his position for women and non-Muslims.[23] A good example of his style of generalization and evasion is his short essay "The Islamic State."[24]

In that essay, Turabi explained his conception of an Islamic state. His various assertions suffer from two very serious weaknesses. First, he does not cite a single authority in the Qur'an or Sunna, or even from the established Islamic jurists, to support any of his bold assertions. Since most of these assertions are simply untrue, or at least disputed by serious scholars of Islam, the lack of reference to evidence in their support repudiates the credibility of his entire thesis. For example, he stated that "whereas the Prophet was appointed by God, *the caliph was freely elected by the people who thereby have precedence over him as a legal authority. . . . The caliphate began as an elected* consultative institution. Later it degenerated into a hereditary, or usurpatory, authoritarian government. This pseudo-caliphate *was universally condemned by* jurists, although many excused its acts on the grounds of necessity or tolerated them in the interest of stability."[25] As I have shown in chapter 2, and shall further explain in the next chapter, the italicized parts of the above-quoted statement are simply untrue, or at least seriously disputed by scholars. It is therefore crucial to cite authority for such propositions if they are to be taken seriously and assessed objectively by others.[26]

Second, Turabi's assertions regarding the structure and powers of an Islamic state are rendered hopelessly vague and contradictory because they are stated to be subject to Shari'a without specifying a particular school of Islamic jurisprudence or particular source of the Shari'a rules in question. To demonstrate this point, I will quote a few of these assertions and then show their irredeemable vagueness and contradiction.

An Islamic state, according to Turabi, "is subject to the higher norms of the *shariah* that represent the will of God." "The caliph, however, or any similar holder of political power, is subject to the *shariah* and to the will of his electors." "A modern Islamic government could, subject to the *shariah*, establish and enforce further norms of law and policy derived from the *shariah*." "Subject to the *shariah* and *ijma* it is up to a Muslim government today to determine its system of public law and economics." "The ultimate common aim of religious life unites the private and the social spheres; and the *shariah* provide an arbiter between social order and individual freedom." "Whatever form the executive may take, a leader is always subject both to the *shariah* and to the *ijma* formulated under it." "Any form or procedure for the organization of public life that can be ultimately related to God and put to his service in furtherance of the aims of Islamic government can be adopted unless expressly excluded by the *shariah*."[27]

All these assertions are hopelessly vague and liable to create intolerable abuse and corruption because of the uncertainty and controversial nature of the relevant rules of Shari'a. There are numerous disagreements between Muslim jurists, especially with reference to many public law issues. Therefore, to speak in categorical terms of Shari'a as a definite and well-settled code of law which directly limits the power of the caliph, or as the arbiter between social order and individual freedom, is grossly misleading.

Of particular interest to the subject matter of the present book are Turabi's views on the status and role of women and non-Muslims in an Islamic state. On the subject of women, he stated:

Nor is an Islamic democracy government by the male members of society. Women played a considerable role in public life during the life
of the Prophet; and they contributed to the election of the third caliph.
Only afterwards were women denied *their rightful place* in public life,
but this was history departing from the *ideal*, just like the development of classes based on property, knowledge *(ilm)*, or other status.
In principle, all believers, rich or poor, noble or humble, learned or
ignorant, men or women, are equal before God and they are his vice-
gerents on earth and the holders of his trust.[28]

But because he does not cite any source or authority for his conception
of the "ideal," we have no means of knowing what is women's "rightful
place in public life" under that ideal. He does not say, for example, whether,
in his conception of an Islamic state, women can be elected to public office
of authority. To Muslim jurists, it did not follow from the equality of "all
believers" before God that men and women should be equal before the
law. As we shall see in subsequent chapters of this book, there are many
features of inequality between men and women under Shari'a. By speaking of women's "rightful place in public life" without explaining it, or at
least referring the reader to a source that provides an explanation, Turabi
evades the issue.

Turabi's treatment of non-Muslims fails to address their status as
citizens of the state. He does not tell us, for example, whether they have
legal equality or whether they can hold public office, which involves exercising general authority over the population, including Muslims.[29] Some
indication of the lack of legal equality for non-Muslims under Turabi's
model of an Islamic state can be seen in his above-quoted statement in
which he speaks of equality for "believers." Furthermore, Turabi admits
that "there may be a certain feeling of alienation because the public law
generally will be Islamic law. However," he continues, "the public law of
Islam is one related rationally to justice and to the general good and even
a non-Muslim may appreciate its wisdom and fairness."[30] Does this mean
that the appreciation of the wisdom and fairness of the law by the general
population is the criterion of its validity? If that is the case, what if the
non-Muslim "citizens" of an Islamic state did not accept the wisdom and
fairness of a particular rule of Shari'a? Can they change the rule or at least
exempt themselves from its application? As we shall see in subsequent
chapters, Shari'a's clear and categorical answer to both questions is no.

Turabi says that "if there is any rule in the *shariah* which they
[non-Muslims] think religiously incompatible, they can be absolved from
it."[31] This statement is both inaccurate and misleading. It is inaccurate in
that the incompatibility of a rule of Shari'a with the religion of a non-

Muslim subject is determined by Shari'a and those Muslims who apply it, and not by the non-Muslim subject. Thus, whereas non-Muslims may be exempt by Muslim authorities from Shari'a's prohibition of intoxicating beverages because Shari'a itself accepts this exemption, they may not be exempt from, say, the amputation of the right hand as punishment for theft because that exemption is not allowed by Shari'a. This inaccuracy in Turabi's statement is misleading in that it gives the sense that non-Muslims have a choice in the public law enforced against them by the authorities of an Islamic state under Shari'a whereas in fact they have no such choice.

So much space has been devoted here to a critique of Turabi's short essay because of his leading role in the national and international movement to implement the public law of Shari'a and the likelihood of his coming to power in the Sudan. Since Turabi's outstanding intellectual and political abilities make him an effective spokesman for the contemporary proponents of Shari'a, it is fair to judge their model for an Islamic state by his work.

Proponents of a Secularist Model

In contrast to those who demand that Shari'a should be the total and comprehensive law of the land, many Muslims have called for the establishment of a secular state. But even secularist Muslims would have to confront the constitutional and human rights implications of Shari'a as personal law for Muslims. Moreover, unless one is advocating the abandonment of Islam itself, Shari'a will continue to be extremely important in shaping the attitudes and behavior of Muslims even if it is not the public law of the land. So long as the Muslim population continues to associate its religious beliefs with the historical Shari'a at the psychological and private levels, Shari'a will have a strong impact on the nature and policies of the state.

It has been suggested that "because Islamic religious doctrine has traditionally claimed full jurisdiction over questions of social morality without always providing practical answers, modern Muslim thinkers have been faced with two broad alternatives. Either they can try to breathe new life into inherited doctrines and adapt them to current needs, or they can seek their inspiration elsewhere. Increasingly, it is the latter course that has been followed."[32] The efforts of some of the leading nineteenth-century Islamic modernists have reinforced the tendency toward secularization in the Muslim world. For example, as Albert Hourani has shown, Muhammad Abduh's efforts to demonstrate that Islam can be reconciled with modern thought unintentionally opened the door to the flooding of Islamic doctrine and law by innovations of the modern world: "He had intended to build a wall against secularism, he had in fact provided an easy bridge by which it could capture one position after another. It was not an accident that, as we shall see, one group of his disciples were later to carry his doctrines in the direction of complete secularism."[33]

One significant intellectual impetus toward secularization was the 1925 publication of Ali Abd al-Raziq's book *Al-Islam wa Usul al-Hukm*.[34] In that book, Abd al-Raziq argued that there was no Islamic authority for the concept of caliphate in the classical and historical sense.[35] He went further by arguing for the much more drastic proposition that Islam has no political component and that the Prophet had purely religious and spiritual and not political leadership.[36] According to Abd al-Raziq, the Prophet could not possibly be succeeded in his religious authority, which was terminated by his death. Therefore, what followed in the establishment of the Islamic state since Abu Bakr, the first caliph, was a different and purely political form of leadership and authority.[37] Thus Abd al-Raziq not only argued for the establishment of a secular state, but he also maintained that the "Islamic" state was in fact, and from the beginning, secular and not religious. The obvious implication of this thesis was that modern Muslim societies were completely free to organize their government in whatever manner they deemed fit and appropriate to their circumstances.

It is clear that Ali Abd al-Raziq made a forceful and coherent argument in the best style of classic Islamic scholarship. His effective deployment of Islamic history and sources led many modern Muslim thinkers to resonate strongly with his thesis. In my view, however, his thesis does not resolve the problems raised by some clear and definite texts of Qur'an and Sunna on the status and rights of women and non-Muslims. Regardless of whether the state is characterized as Islamic or secular, the question remains, Are Muslims bound to apply the detailed rules applicable to women and non-Muslims by the express terms of the Qur'an and Sunna? Some of these rules have extremely serious constitutional, human rights, and international implications. Yet Abd al-Raziq's thesis does not explain how to avoid the application of those rules of Shari'a even in an allegedly "secular" state.

The admirable objectives of Abd al-Raziq and other Muslim intellectuals in his tradition are unlikely to be achieved through this line of thinking. It is true that, by modern standards, there are serious inadequacies in the public law of Shari'a. By the same standards, historical Muslim experience was obviously unsatisfactory. From this point of view, it is tempting to attempt to disassociate those historical principles and experience from Islam as a religion. Such an effort, however, is unlikely to succeed. As correctly stated by Fazlur Rahman, "the difficulty before the real secularist [in the Muslim world] is to have to prove the impossible, namely that Muhammad, when he acted as a law giver or political leader, acted extra-religiously and secularly."[38] Besides the practical difficulty of making a plausible argument along these lines, I would submit that to do so is to deny the Muslims extremely valuable cultural resources necessary for the development of their self-identity. It is unlikely that the majority of Muslims would permanently accept the secularization of their public life.[39] A better approach, I suggest, is to judge the public law of Shari'a and the historical experience of Muslims by the standards prevailing at the time Shari'a was being developed and implemented and to seek the development of alternative *Islamic* principles of public law for modern application. That is the objective of this book.

For a variety of reasons, secularization has temporarily prevailed, thereby relegating Shari'a to the private domain in the majority of Muslim countries since the end of World War I. As clearly shown by the persistent and mounting demands for the application of Shari'a in public life, especially in countries hitherto thought to be thoroughly secularized,[40] however, the realistic prospects of the secular option are increasingly diminishing. In any case, even if Shari'a is applied as personal law for Muslims, we would still have to face the constitutional and human rights implications of that personal law.

As will be shown in subsequent chapters, some of the Shari'a rules on family law and inheritance violate the fundamental and constitutional rights of women. It may therefore be pertinent to review the methods and results of official reforms in Shari'a personal law recently introduced in many Muslim countries to assess their adequacy in meeting objections from the constitutional and human rights point of view.

Official Law Reforms

The governments of the majority of Muslim countries have undertaken two types of reform since the mid-nineteenth century. The first involved replacing Shari'a with secular legislation in commercial, civil, constitutional, and penal matters. In most parts of the Muslim world, only family law and inheritance for Muslims were left to the jurisdiction of Shari'a. The second reform was undertaken in respect to the Shari'a principles and rules as applied to family law and inheritance for Muslims.

In "reforming" Shari'a family law and inheritance, official authorities in many Muslim countries have resorted to the following techniques:[41]

1. *Takhsis al-qada* (the right of the ruler to define and confine

the jurisdiction of his courts) was used as a procedural expedient for confining the application of Shari'a to matters of personal law for Muslims. The same expedient was also used to prevent the courts from applying Shari'a in specified circumstances without attempting to change the substance of the relevant Shari'a rules. For example, to discourage child marriage, an Egyptian law in 1931 denied matrimonial relief through the courts by precluding the courts from entertaining any claim of marriage if the husband had not reached the age of eighteen or the wife the age of sixteen at the time of litigation.

2. *Takhayyur* (the selection of any opinion within the particular school of Islamic jurisprudence and not necessarily the dominant opinion within the given school) was extended to allow selection from other Sunni schools. This device was used in the Sudan by issuing judicial directives allowing the courts to deviate from the rules of the Hanafi school, otherwise recognized as the official school for personal law matters of Muslims. Also known as *talfiq* (patching), this technique was used to combine part of the doctrine of one jurist or school with part of the doctrine of another jurist or school. In this manner, the authorities constructed a provision that would not have been approved, in its entirety, by any of the jurists or schools of the past, although each of its component parts could claim the most impeccable ancestry. An example of this practice can be found in the Egyptian law of 1925 regulating and restricting a husband's freedom to divorce his wife by limiting the formula by which divorce can be effected. A more extended use of this device was made in Article 37 of the Egyptian Law of Testamentary Dispositions of 1946, which adopted a principle of Shi'i origin without clear acknowledgment that it was doing so.

3. A form of reinterpretation was used to restrict the male freedom of divorce and polygamy. For example, the Tunisian Law of Personal Status of 1956 provided that no divorce would be effective except by consent of the court and allowed the court to require the husband to pay a sum of money as compensation if the court felt that the husband unjustifiably repudiated his wife or in any way caused her hardship by such divorce. In countries such as Syria and Iraq, reinterpretation was used to require approval by the court of any polygamous marriage to ensure satisfaction of the Qur'anic requirement of justice among cowives.

Reinterpretation was carried to an extreme by the Tunisian law of 1956 that prohibited polygamy altogether on the grounds that it was no longer acceptable and that the Qur'anic requirement of justice among cowives is impossible for any man, except the Prophet, to achieve in practice.

4. *Syasa shari'ya* (the discretion of the ruler to implement administrative regulations which are beneficial and not contrary to Shari'a)

was also used to introduce some reforms. For example, to enforce the general principle of Shari'a requiring a wife to obey her husband, Shari'a allows the husband to bring an action for *ta'a* (obedience by the wife). At the same time, Shari'a strictly defined the circumstances under which custody of the children should go to the wife or husband. To terminate obedience actions while securing the husband's interest in custody of his children, Article 145 of the Syrian Law of Personal Status of 1953 provided that if a wife became disobedient and her children were more than five years old, the court could place them with whichever of the spouses it deemed fit, having full regard to the welfare of the children and to the circumstances of the case.

5. In India and other former British colonies, reform was undertaken through judicial decisions in the manner used in the common law tradition.[42] Such reform through judicial decisions was not envisaged as a mechanism for challenging or changing those principles or rules of Shari'a based on clear and definite texts of the Qur'an and/or Sunna. The High Court of Lahore stated this limitation clearly in *Khursid Jan* v. *Fazal Dad*: "If there is no clear rule of decision in Qur'anic and Traditional [Sunna] Text . . . a Court may resort to private reasoning and, in that, will undoubtedly be guided by the rules of justice, equity and good conscience."[43] The court was asserting only the right to differ from the views of established jurists, not the right to refuse to apply a rule of Shari'a based on clear and definite texts of the Qur'an and/or Sunna.

Although these techniques of personal law "reform" can be seen as modifying aspects of the interpretation and application of Shari'a, it is my submission that such modifications provide nothing more than temporary and insufficient relief. As we shall see in subsequent chapters, many seriously objectionable aspects of Shari'a personal law remained despite these reforms. More important, as long as the underlying Shari'a principles remain intact, the temporary and insufficient relief that is introduced through these devices is subject to loss when there is a forceful reassertion of Shari'a. In light of recent Islamic resurgence, that prospect is very real. In any case, none of these reform techniques has been applied to the fundamental public law issues discussed in this book.

CRISIS AND INADEQUATE RESPONSE

John Voll has identified three themes of *tajdid-islah* (renewal-reform) in the major eras of premodern and modern Islamic history. These themes are the call for a return to, or strict application of, the Qur'an and Sunna;

the assertion of the right to exercise *ijtihad* (independent juristic reasoning) rather than *taqlid* (the unquestioning imitation and following of established jurists and their respective schools); and the reaffirmation of the authenticity and uniqueness of the Qur'anic experience. Strict application of the Qur'an and Sunna was the reformers' response to a variety of perceived crises or problems. The reformers maintain that "the Muslims, as individuals and as part of a community, must adhere in a strict and relatively literal way to the Qur'an and the Sunna of the Prophet. Anything that works against or dilutes that adherence approaches ungrateful unbelief and needs to be eliminated by the processes of *tajdid* and *islah*."[44]

According to Voll, *ijtihad* was a basic corollary of the first theme of strict application of the Qur'an and Sunna. If the Qur'an and Sunna are the essential and perfect sources of judgment and guidance, other sources may be helpful but are by no means binding. In addition to the call for a return to the Qur'an and Sunna, the renewer-reformer "claims the right of *ijtihad*, with the possible rejection of existing institutions and traditional interpretations."[45]

Reaffirmation of the uniqueness and authenticity of the Qur'anic message was the third theme of renewal-reform in Voll's analysis. Although the renewer-reformer claimed the right to exercise *ijtihad* to determine the proper application of the Qur'anic message in changing circumstances, he need not, and must not, borrow from non-Islamic traditions as a way of adding to basic Islamic principles.[46] In this respect, Voll distinguished and contrasted the renewal-reform tradition with other great modes of Islamic expression which have shown a willingness to accept or engage in great cultural syntheses in a conscious way. Of special interest to the subject of the present book is the mystic mode.[47] *Ustadh* Mahmoud, whose reform methodology will be explained later in this chapter, had a strong mystic orientation. Voll described the mystic mode as contemplative, exhibiting "a greater conscious willingness to recognize the universality of authentic religious experience. The mystic mode thus tends to create rather than oppose syntheses."[48] I would agree with this characterization of the mystic mode. It may be necessary, however, to add that, in creating syntheses, the mystics believe themselves to be as keen as the reformers-renewers in claiming to be "working to create a society based on a rigorous application of what they believe to be the essential heart of the Islamic message."[49] In other words, the mystics do not see their efforts at syntheses as in any way contrary to the Muslim belief that the Qur'an and Sunna are complete as guides for humanity and that they apply to all times and places. As we shall see, the modern mystic *Ustadh* Mahmoud Mohamed Taha shared the belief of the renewers-reformers that "*ijtihad*, to be legitimate, is to be solely an interpretive effort rather than an effort to supplement an already complete guidance framework [of the Qur'an and Sunna]."[50]

Subject to this last qualification, I find Voll's characterization of the main themes of Islamic renewal-reform accurate and very helpful in assessing the objectives and methods of contemporary reformers who fall within that tradition. This tradition is significant because it is the primary force behind the current efforts to apply Shari'a in the public affairs of Muslim countries. In view of their political activism and recent successes (notably in Iran, Pakistan, and the Sudan), the proponents of Shari'a present, in my view, the clearest and greatest danger in creating the problems to be discussed in the subsequent chapters of this book.

My analysis would exclude the secularist approach in the Muslim context from the renewal-reform tradition because secularism is not an *Islamic* response to the challenges facing Muslim societies. It is true that the secularist line of thinking was born out of Muslim desperation in trying to reconcile Shari'a with the needs and aspirations of modern Muslim societies.[51] Nevertheless, and by definition, secularism is not an Islamic response. While fully accepting that many aspects of Shari'a are untenable and unworkable today, I do not believe that secularism is the answer.

It is true that an Islamic approach would have to reflect *some form* of the three elements indicated by Voll—strict application of the Qur'an and Sunna, exercise of *ijtihad*, and reaffirmation of Islamic authenticity. At issue here, however, is the meaning and implications of these criteria of an Islamic approach in the modern context. In my view, these elements should be understood in light of the following considerations.

To speak of the application of the Qur'an and Sunna is necessarily to speak of their *interpretation* and application through some *human* agency.[52] In verse 29:49, the Qur'an describes itself as clear signs or meaning in the hearts and minds of those [human beings] who have been granted knowledge. Ali, the fourth caliph, is reported to have stated the common-sense proposition that the Qur'an does not speak but that men [and women today] speak for the Qur'an. The same is no doubt true about the Sunna. Thus, to demand the strict application of the Qur'an and Sunna requires the provision of an applicable interpretation of these fundamental sources of Islam in the concrete realities of social, economic, and political life of the Muslims today.

Moreover, the authenticity of the Islamic message and rejection of alien ideas are also points of interpretation. To assert a purely Islamic approach and reject what is alien presupposes a clear definition of what is Islamic and at least by implication what is alien and un-Islamic. This is obviously a complex question which has engaged many Islamic modernists and their critics.

A possible criterion for judging the Islamicity of any proposition is that it be consistent with the *totality* of the Qur'an and Sunna. The problem with this criterion is that certain verses of the Qur'an and Sunna are apparently inconsistent with others. For example, whereas the earlier Qur'an of the Mecca stage instructs the Prophet and his followers to practice peaceful persuasion and allow others freedom of choice in accepting or rejecting Islam, the Qur'an and Sunna of the Medina stage clearly sanctioned, and even required under certain conditions, the use of force to compel the unbelievers either to embrace Islam or to suffer one of the options provided for under Shari'a, which included death, enslavement, or some other unpleasant consequence. An apostate, that is, a Muslim who repudiates his faith in Islam, is punishable by death under Shari'a.[53]

To reconcile these apparent inconsistencies, the founding jurists engaged in a process of *naskh* (abrogation or repeal) of certain texts of the Qur'an and Sunna to produce a coherent and comprehensive system of Shari'a which was consistent with the totality of the Qur'an and Sunna. Thus, to justify compulsion as opposed to freedom of choice in religion, and to give legal efficacy to verses sanctioning the use of force against non-Muslims and renegade Muslims, the founding jurists deemed that the verses enjoining freedom of choice and peaceful persuasion were abrogated or repealed by the verses authorizing compulsion and use of force. It is my thesis that since the technique of *naskh* has been employed in the past to develop Shari'a which has hitherto been accepted as the authentic and genuine Islamic model, the same technique may be employed today to produce an authentic and genuine modern Islamic law.

This brings us to the second element in Voll's analysis, the exercise of *ijtihad*, which is more conveniently treated here in light of the fact that the application of the Qur'an and Sunna as well as the maintenance of Islamic authenticity necessarily involve human interpretation. It is true that the modern proponents of Shari'a often speak of *ijtihad* as the answer to all the problems facing the modern application of Shari'a. Given the fundamental nature and limitations of *ijtihad* within the framework of Shari'a, as explained in Chapter 2, this approach is unlikely to lead to sufficient reform in the specific problems of modern public law raised in this book.

Ijtihad within the framework of Shari'a is inadequate because most of the problematic principles and rules of Shari'a in the fields of constitutional law, criminal justice, international law, and human rights are based on clear and definite texts of the Qur'an and Sunna. As explained earlier, the founding jurists of Shari'a maintained that *ijtihad* is never to be exercised in matters governed by clear and definite texts of Qur'an and Sunna. Verses of Qur'an and Sunna which authorize compulsion and the use of force were deemed legally binding by the founding jurists be-

cause they were revealed during the stage of Medina and were left operative by the Prophet at the time of his death in 632 A.D.[54] Therefore, these
principles and rules cannot be amended or changed through the exercise
of *ijtihad* as originally defined under Shari'a.

Although I completely disagree with those proponents of Shari'a
who insist on its application regardless of the problems that may create
for women and non-Muslims,[55] I respect their consistency and candor.
Those proponents of Shari'a who claim that such problems can be resolved
through the exercise of *ijtihad* within the framework of Shari'a are, at best,
engaged in wishful thinking. Given the fundamental conception and detailed rules of Shari'a, it is clear that the objectionable aspects cannot
possibly be altered through the exercise of *ijtihad* as defined in historical
Shari'a for the simple reason that Shari'a does not permit *ijtihad* in these
matters because they are governed by clear and definite texts of the Qur'an
and Sunna.

To emphasize the above points, let us take, for example, the
analysis and suggestions made by John Esposito at the end of his survey
of reform efforts in Pakistan.[56] Esposito referred to a distinction between
Shari'a and *fiqh* (opinions and commentaries of Muslim jurists) which is
frequently made by modern Muslim authors to make their task of criticizing what they describe as *fiqh* appear less drastic than criticizing Shari'a
itself.[57] Because the public law principles and rules discussed here are based
on clear and definite texts of the Qur'an and Sunna, they are necessarily
part of Shari'a and not merely *fiqh*. Consequently, the distinction between
Shari'a and *fiqh*, to the extent that it is possible, is irrelevant when we
speak about principles and rules of Shari'a proper.

Esposito suggested that

> a basic concern for Muslim legal reformers must be *Qur'anic* exegesis.
> This approach can be seen in the writings of contemporary thinkers
> such as Subhi Mahmasani and Isma'il al-Faruqi who focus on the im-
> portance of ascertaining the motive, intent or purpose behind *Qur'anic*
> values as applied to newly encountered social situations in the first
> centuries of Islamic legal history. The fundamental questions today
> are the same as those facing the early jurists: "What is the morally
> [sic] imperative which the Holy Qur'an has brought from God? How
> does it read when translated into the language of obligation pertinent
> to the concrete situations of real life?"[58]

Such questions are routinely raised by modern Muslim writers who
claim that methodological and other reforms are possible. The decisive
test is, of course, what results has the particular author produced? Neither
of the authors cited by Esposito (Subhi Mahmasani and Isma'il al-Faruqi)

nor any other author operating within the framework of Shari'a has succeeded in proposing concrete changes in the principles and rules of Shari'a
which are based on clear and definite texts of the Qur'an and Sunna, such
as the status of women or of non-Muslims.

According to Esposito, *istihsan* (juristic preference) and *istislah*
(public good) are two modes of *ijtihad* which would be particularly useful
today.[59] There is nothing new in this proposal, which was made, in its
boldest form, by Najm al-Din al-Tawfi, who died in 1316 A.D.[60] Modern
authors have warned against the unacceptably generalized citation and use
of these major principles of Islamic jurisprudence.[61] In any case, the question is what type and degree of reform can be, and has been, achieved
through these techniques? Since these minor sources of Shari'a are subject
to the clear and definite texts of the Qur'an and Sunna, they cannot be
used in ways that violate or contravene any clear and definite text of Qur'an
and Sunna.

Esposito also cited efforts to transform historical notions of *ijma*
into modern legislative processes.[62] Although skeptical of the propriety
of calling the proposed process *ijma,* and doubtful of its acceptability by
the majority of Muslims, Esposito is nevertheless of the view that the ideas
expressed by the modern Muslim authors who support the use of this technique "can provide a viable means for Islamic legal reform . . . by equat-
ing reform legislation with a collective *ijtihad* alone and not with an *ijma.*"[63]
With all due respect, I must once again emphasize that it makes no difference whether the effort is characterized as *ijtihad* or *ijma* as long as one
is operating within the framework of Shari'a and in relation to a principle
or rule based on a clear and definite text of the Qur'an or Sunna. The
most problematic principles and rules of Shari'a relevant to public law issues are of this type and remain beyond any reform methodology within
the framework of Shari'a.

In sum, a legitimately Islamic response to the challenges facing
modern Muslim societies will have to be based on the Qur'an and Sunna,
which would necessarily mean an interpretation of these fundamental
sources of Islam in a way that is consistent with the totality of their content and message. The existing system of Islamic law, which is Shari'a,
raises serious problems with modern constitutional, penal, and international law and current standards of human rights, especially in relation
to the status of women and non-Muslims. Moreover, when we judge by
concrete results rather than the rhetoric of contemporary Muslim writers,
we find that the internal mechanisms of adjustment and reform within
the framework of Shari'a, including *ijtihad,* are inadequate in resolving
the problems raised by the modern application of Shari'a. Nevertheless,
an Islamic way has to be found out of this deadlock.

THE EVOLUTIONARY APPROACH

It may be helpful to begin by quoting Fazlur Rahman's characterization of the difficulty facing Islamic modernism: "The disadvantage of the Muslim society at the present juncture is that whereas in the early centuries of development of social institutions in Islam, Islam started from a clean slate, as it were, and had to carve out *ab initio* a social fabric—an activity of which the product was the medieval social system—now, when Muslims have to face a situation of fundamental rethinking and reconstruction, their acute problem is precisely to determine how far to render the slate clean again and on what principles and by what methods, in order to create a new set of institutions."[64]

Strictly speaking, Islam did not start with a clean slate because it did not come into existence in a religious, social, economic, and political vacuum. By its own terms, Islam was a continuation and the culmination of the Abrahamic tradition. Moreover, Islamic law in Shari'a adopted and modified many aspects of pre-Islamic Arabian custom and practice. Nevertheless, the early Muslims did have the mental attitude and the psychological orientation for starting with a clean slate in the sense that they believed that they had the principles and methods "to carve out *ab initio* a social fabric." It is this mental attitude and psychological orientation which has been lost and must be regained today if the Islamic venture is to continue with its fundamental mission.

One possible way of regaining that creative initiative, an Islamic way out of the deadlock in Shari'a law reform, is that prescribed by the late Sudanese author *Ustadh* Mahmoud Mohamed Taha.[65] The basic premise of *Ustadh* Mahmoud is that a close examination of the content of the Qur'an and Sunna reveals two levels or stages of the message of Islam, one of the earlier Mecca period and the other of the subsequent Medina stage.[66] Furthermore, he maintained that the earlier message of Mecca is in fact the eternal and fundamental message of Islam, emphasizing the inherent dignity of all human beings, regardless of gender, religious belief, race, and so forth. That message was characterized by equality between men and women and complete freedom of choice in matters of religion and faith. Both the substance of the message of Islam and the manner of its propagation during the Mecca period were predicated on *ismah*, freedom of choice without any form or shade of compulsion or coercion.

When that superior level of the message was violently and irrationally rejected and it was practically demonstrated that society at large was not yet ready for its implementation, the more realistic message of the Medina stage was provided and implemented. In this way, aspects of the message of the Mecca period which were inappropriate for practical implementation within the historical context of the seventh century were suspended and replaced by the more practical principles revealed and implemented during the Medina stage. *Ustadh* Mahmoud, however, maintained that the suspended aspects of the Mecca message were not lost forever as a source of law. Rather, they were postponed for implementation under appropriate circumstances in the future. Otherwise, he argued, the superior and eternal aspects of Islam would have been irredeemably lost.

It is central to *Ustadh* Mahmoud's thesis that the shift was in response to the dictates of the time. Since the earlier superior message was inappropriate for practical application under the circumstances of the seventh century, it may be queried, why did God reveal it and instruct the Prophet to propagate it in the first place? Was God unaware of the dictates of the time when He revealed the earlier message to the Prophet and instructed him to propagate it? In response to this logical question, *Ustadh* Mahmoud strongly rejected any implication of lack of knowledge on the part of God and explained that there are two reasons for the revelation of the inapplicable message of Mecca. First, and in accordance with Muslim belief, the Qur'an is the final revelation and the Prophet Muhammad is the final prophet. Consequently, the Qur'an had to contain, and the Prophet had to propagate, all that God wanted to intimate to posterity, that which was intended for immediate application as well as that which was to be applied under appropriate future circumstances. The second reason has to do with the dignity and freedom which God bestowed on all human beings. In accordance with that dignity and freedom, God wished human beings to learn through their own practical experience with the inapplicability of the earlier message of Mecca, which was then suspended and replaced by the more practical message of Medina. In that way, people would have stronger and more genuine conviction of the practicability of the message that was propagated and eventually implemented during the Medina stage.

To appreciate the logic of *Ustadh* Mahmoud's argument, we should recall the main historical events of early Islam and cite a few examples to illustrate his thesis and its implications for the modern public law of Islam. For the first thirteen years of his mission, between 610 and 622 A.D., the Prophet was instructed by the Qur'an to propagate Islam in and around Mecca through exclusively peaceful means in accordance with the principle of complete freedom of choice. Thus, verse 16:125 of the Qur'an instructed the Prophet to "invite [all people] to the path of your Lord with wisdom and good preaching; and argue with them in ways that are best and most gracious: For your Lord knows those who stray from His path and those who are the guided ones." Verse 18:29 also instructed the Prophet to "tell [them] that this is the truth revealed by your Lord; let him who wishes to believe do so, and he who wishes to disbelieve do so [also]. . . ." Numerous other verses of the Qur'an of the Mecca period instruct the Prophet in similar manner.

The substance of the message of Mecca emphasized the fundamental values of justice and the equality and inherent dignity of all human beings. For example, the Qur'an during the Mecca period always addresses the whole of humanity, using phrases such as "O, children of Adam" and "O, humankind." Moreover, all humankind was described in terms of honor and dignity, without distinction as to race, color, gender, or religion. Thus, in verse 17:70 God tells how He has "honored the children of Adam; provided them with transport on land and sea; given them good and pure things for sustenance; and preferred them over many parts of Our [His] Creation." Similarly, verse 49:13 provided "O, humankind, We have created you into male and female, and made you into peoples and tribes so that you may be acquainted [and cooperate] with each other; the most favored by God among you are those who are righteous and pious."

In response to this humane and enlightened message of Islam, propagated in ways fully consistent with its precepts of human dignity and freedom, the Arabs of Mecca and their allies persecuted the Prophet and his followers and conspired to kill him. As a result, the Prophet and his Companions were forced out of their homes and had to migrate to Medina in 622 A.D., where they were able, with the help and support of the tribes of the Medina area, to establish an independent political community. As will be explained more fully in Chapters 4 and 6, the content of the message shifted with the migration to become more specifically addressed to the Muslims as a community of believers who were authorized by the Qur'an to use force, first in self-defense and retaliation for the injustice done to them by the unbelievers and subsequently in propagating Islam and spreading the domain of the Muslim state.[67]

Another example of the shift in the content of the message after the migration to Medina is that the Qur'an of Medina and accompanying Sunna began to distinguish between men and women, Muslims and non-Muslims, in their legal status and rights before the law. All the verses (and related Sunna) that constituted the basis of discrimination against women and non-Muslims were of the Medina and not the Mecca stage. For example, chapter 4 of the Qur'an, known as *Surat al-Nisa* (the chapter on women), which contains most of the detailed rules of marriage, divorce, inheritance, and the like, with their discriminatory impact on women, was revealed during the Medina stage. In particular, verse 4:34 of this chapter was taken by the founding jurists as providing for the general principle of *qawama* (the guardianship and superior status of men over women), thereby sanctioning further discrimination against women whenever the Qur'an was not explicit on the matter.

Verse 4:34 states that "men have *qawama* (guardianship and authority) over women because of the advantage they [men] enjoy over them [women] and because they [men] spend their property in supporting them [women]." This general principle was taken by the founding jurists as authority for a wide variety of rules of public law. For example, women are disqualified from holding general public office involving the exercise of authority over men because, in accordance with verse 4:34, men are entitled to exercise authority over women and not vice versa.[68]

The overlap between the two stages of Mecca and Medina led to a gradual rather than an abrupt change in the content of the message. In the same way that the use of force was sanctioned in a gradual, progressive manner, sanction for noncompulsion and the use of peaceful means continued to appear in the Qur'an during the early Medina period. For example, verse 2:256, "there is no compulsion in religion, the right path has been determined and set aside from the wrong path," was revealed in the early Medina period. Nevertheless, the overwhelming impact of the Qur'an of Medina has been to sanction, if not positively command, the use of varying degrees of coercion on non-Muslims to induce them to convert to Islam.[69]

As a result of this shift in the content of the message and the method of its propagation, some people ostensibly converted to Islam without genuine inner conviction. This phenomenon is most clearly demonstrated by the frequent Qur'anic reference to *al-munafiqwn* (the hypocrites) in Medinese revelation whereas there is no mention of them in the Qur'an of Mecca. Given the lack of any degree or form of coercion during the Mecca period, people had the complete freedom to embrace Islam or refuse to do so. With the gradual loss of that freedom during the Medina period, some unbelievers showed outward belief to avoid the negative consequences of disbelief.

According to *Ustadh* Mahmoud, "the Meccan and the Medinese texts [of the Qur'an] differ, not because of the time and place of revelation, but essentially because of the audience to which they are addressed. The phrase 'O believers' [frequently used in the Qur'an of Medina] addresses a particular nation, while 'O humankind' [characteristic of the Qur'an of Mecca] speaks to all people."[70] This shift in audience was dictated by the violent and irrational rejection of the earlier message. In support of his argument that the message of Islam can, and in fact was, adjusted to the needs and capabilities of its audience, *Ustadh* Mahmoud often quoted verse 16:44: "We have revealed *(anzallna)* to you *al-dhikr* [the Qur'an] so that you may explain to people what has been brought down

(nuzila) to them; and that they may reflect." Ustadh Mahmoud finds the
fact that the verb used in connection with revelation to the Prophet (anzallna) is different from the one used with reference to people in general
(nuzila) clearly indicates that the Prophet was instructed to explain and
apply that part of the revelation which suited the needs and capabilities
of people at that time.[71] To the same effect, Ustadh Mahmoud used to quote
a text of Sunna in which the Prophet is reported to have said, "We the
Prophets have been instructed to address people in accordance with their
own level of understanding."

The main implication of Ustadh Mahmoud's argument for the purposes of the present study is that the public law of Shari'a was based on
the Qur'an and related Sunna of the Medina period rather than that of
the Mecca stage. As will be explained in the next section of this chapter,
this was done by the founding jurists through the process of naskh, by
holding the subsequent texts of the Qur'an and Sunna of the Medina stage
to have repealed or abrogated, for the purposes of the positive law of
Shari'a, all previously revealed inconsistent texts of the Mecca stage. The
question that would then arise is whether such naskh is permanent, thereby
rendering the earlier texts of Mecca inoperative for posterity. According
to Ustadh Mahmoud, this cannot possibly be so because if that were the
case, there would have been no point in having revealed the earlier texts.
He also argued that to deem naskh to be permanent is to deny the Muslims the best part of their religion. In other words, he maintained that naskh
was an essentially logical and necessary process of implementing the appropriate texts and postponing the implementation of others until the right
circumstances for their implementation should arise.

With regard to the public law issues discussed in the present book,
Ustadh Mahmoud proposed the evolution of the basis of Islamic law from
the texts of the Medina stage to that of the earlier Mecca period. In other
words, the evolutionary principle of interpretation is nothing more than
reversing the process of naskh or abrogation so that those texts which were
abrogated in the past can be enacted into law now, with the consequent
abrogation of texts that used to be enacted as Shari'a. Verses that used
to be enacted as Shari'a shall be repealed, and verses that used to be repealed shall be enacted as modern Islamic law. Since this proposal would
found modern principles of public law on one class of Qur'an and Sunna
texts as opposed to another class of those texts, the resultant body of law
would be as Islamic as Shari'a has been. It is true, as stated by Erwin I. J.
Rosenthal, that "Islam without a Shari'a (not necessarily the classical medieval Shari'a) is not historical any longer."[72] I submit that a system of
public law based on the Qur'an and Sunna, albeit "not necessarily the
classical medieval Shari'a," would be the modern "Shari'a." To understand

this proposal better, and to assess its theoretical validity, we need to examine the nature and implications of *naskh* in Islamic jurisprudence.

ON THE NATURE AND IMPLICATIONS OF *NASKH*

Naskh is a vast and highly complex subject in Islamic theology and jurisprudence.[73] At least two types of *naskh* were accepted by the majority of Muslim jurists, *naskh al-hukm wa al-tilawa* (abrogation of both the ruling and wording of the text) and *naskh al-hukm duna al-tilawa* (abrogation of the ruling but not the wording of the text).[74] The first type of *naskh* relates to a few verses that were at one point stated by the Prophet to be part of the Qur'an, though later the Prophet himself said that they were not to be considered as such. We are not concerned here with this phenomenon because it is not, strictly speaking, a legal issue. The verses in question are held by Muslims to be nonexistent for any purpose. Rather, we are concerned with the second type of *naskh*, in which the text remains part of the Qur'an but is deemed inoperative for legal purposes.

The principle of this type of *naskh* has been accepted by the vast majority of Muslim jurists who have disagreed on such questions as whether a particular verse has or has not been abrogated by other verses and whether Sunna may abrogate the ruling of the Qur'an, and vice versa, but who never disputed the principle of *naskh* itself.[75] Without this device for reconciling apparently contradictory verses of the Qur'an, it would have been impossible to develop Shari'a as a coherent and internally consistent legal system.[76] For example, whereas many earlier verses of the Qur'an emphasized freedom of choice and noncompulsion, subsequent verses and Sunna texts clearly sanction the use of force against non-Muslims for the purpose of converting them to Islam.[77] To the founding jurists, the only way to reconcile these apprently contradictory sources was to deem the earlier verses to have been abrogated, for legal purposes, by the subsequent verses and Sunna. This principle is a common legal device used by the jurists of many legal systems up to the present time. The legally operative intention of the legislature is taken to be manifested in its latest sources, and earlier, apparently inconsistent, manifestations of that intention are normally deemed to have been superseded, to the extent necessary to remove the inconsistency, by the subsequent expression of legislative intent.

It must be emphasized, however, that whereas the principle of *naskh*, in the sense relevant to the present discussion, had already appeared toward the end of the first century of Islam, its status and role during the earliest period are not clear. It seems, for example, that it had a limited sense for some of the Companions of the Prophet, who took the subsequent verse of the Qur'an as creating an exception to, particularizing a meaning of, or clarifying the earlier verse rather than totally abrogating it. More significantly, it is clear that the theory of *naskh* as developed and applied by the jurists "cannot go back to the Prophet because we do not find any information from the Prophet as to the existence of the abrogated verses in the Qur'an in this sense [of abrogation of the ruling of a verse which remained part of the text of the Qur'an]."[78] This is probably why we find such wide differences of opinion among the Companions as to which verse is abrogated and which remained binding and operative.

Despite its ambiguity, the principle of *naskh* was recognized by the jurists and constituted the cornerstone of their conception of Shari'a. The crucial question for our purposes is whether the abrogation of earlier texts of the Qur'an by subsequent ones is final and conclusive or whether it is open to reconsideration. If one is dealing with secular legislation, the matter would be resolved by resorting to the legislature for clarification of its legislative intent. This is not possible in the context of Islamic law because the legislature is God, who has already, according to Muslim belief, severed His direct communication with humankind by sending the final prophet and concluding all revelation in the Qur'an. Thus whatever guidance one may obtain from the legislature in the Islamic context has to be derived from the Qur'an and the Sunna of the Prophet.

It should be recalled that internal reform within the framework of Shari'a is inadequate to deal with public law issues. Since *ijtihad* under Shari'a cannot be exercised in matters governed by clear and definite texts of the Qur'an and Sunna, none of the objectionable principles and rules relating to the status of women and non-Muslims such as those stated in subsequent chapters of this book can be varied or changed through a modern exercise of *ijtihad* in the historical sense of the term. Unless a new principle of interpretation is introduced to allow modern Muslims to modify or change these aspects of the public law of Shari'a, only two other options remain: either continue to disregard Shari'a in the public domain, as used to be the case for the majority of modern Muslim states, or proceed to enforce Shari'a principles regardless of constitutional, international law, and human rights objections.

I find the first option objectionable as a matter of principle and unlikely to be realistically available for much longer in practice. It is objectionable as a matter of principle because it violates the religious obligation of Muslims to conduct every aspect of their public as well as private lives in accordance with the precepts of Islam. Moreover, in view of the mounting Islamic resurgence, this option is unlikely to continue to be available for much longer in practice. I also find the second option morally repugnant and politically untenable. It is morally repugnant, in my view, to subject women and non-Muslims to the indignities and humiliation of the application of Shari'a today. I believe that the public law of Shari'a was fully justified and consistent within its own historical context. But that does not make it justified and consistent with the present context. Furthermore, given the concrete realities of the modern nation-state and present international order, these aspects of the public law of Shari'a are no longer politically tenable.

It is in light of this fundamental dilemma that the question is raised, What makes the early process of *naskh* so final and conclusive? Why should modern Muslims be denied the opportunity to rethink the rationale and application of *naskh* so they can implement verses of the Qur'an which have hitherto been deemed abrogated, thereby opening up new possibilities for developing alternative principles of Islamic public law?

Several modern Muslim writers have addressed this question. Some of them have attempted to harmonize and reconcile apparently contradictory verses;[79] others have rejected the theory of *naskh* altogether.[80] The crucial question facing both approaches is what to do with the subsequent clear and definite text if the earlier text is to be deemed binding and operative. For the reconciliatory approach, as long as both sets of contradictory verses remain legally operative and binding, reconciliation is impossible. For those who reject *naskh* altogether, the question becomes, Which set of verses represents the law of Islam on a given subject?

Ustadh Mahmoud argued that it is possible, indeed imperative, to rethink the rationale and application of *naskh* to achieve the necessary degree of Islamic law reform. He said:

> The evolution of Shari'a, as mentioned above, is simply its evolution by moving from one text [of the Qur'an] to the other, from a text that is suitable to govern in the seventh century, and was implemented, to a text which was, at the time, too advanced and therefore had to be abrogated. God said: "Whenever We abrogate any verse *(ayah)*[81] or postpone it *(nunsi'ha),*[82] We bring a better verse, or a similar one. Do you not know that God is capable of everything?" [the Qur'an 2:106]. The phrase, "When we abrogate any verse" means cancel or repeal it, and the phrase "or postpone it" means to delay its action or implementation. The phrase "We bring a better verse" means bringing one that is closer to the understanding of the people and more relevant to their time than the postponed verse; "or a similar one" means reinstating the same verse when the time comes for its implementation. It is as if the abrogated verses were abrogated in accordance with the needs of the time, and postponed until their appropriate time

comes. When it does, they become the suitable and operative verses and are implemented, while those that were implemented in the seventh century become abrogated. . . . This is the rationale of abrogation. . . . [In other words, it was not intended to be] final and conclusive abrogation, but merely postponement until the appropriate time.

In this evolution we consider the rationale beyond the text. If a subsidiary verse, which used to overrule the primary verse in the seventh century, has served its purpose completely and become irrelevant for the new era, the twentieth century, then the time has come for it to be abrogated and for the primary verse to be enacted. In this way, the primary verse has its turn as the operative text in the twentieth century and becomes the basis of the new legislation. This is what the evolution of Shari'a means. It is shifting from one text that served its purpose and was exhausted to another text that was postponed until its time came. Evolution is therefore neither unrealistic or premature, nor expressing a naive and immature opinion. It is merely shifting from one text to the other.[83]

This long statement of *Ustadh* Mahmoud is quoted in full here because it not only explains the application of his evolutionary approach as a principle of interpretation which does not violate the Islamic authenticity of the law, but also because it shows the criterion he would apply for identifying which verses are to be implemented today and why they should be implemented. Umar, the second caliph, did in fact exercise *ijtihad* by refusing to implement clear and definite texts of the Qur'an and Sunna when he felt that the ruling of those texts had exhausted its purpose. This early strong precedent should give support at least to the initial proposition that it is possible to suspend the application of a clear and definite verse of the Qur'an under appropriate circumstances. The contribution of *Ustadh* Mahmoud is the comprehensive framework he provided for identifying which verses to implement and which to repeal in the modern context.

ASSESSMENT AND PROSPECTS

The record of significant Islamic reform in the public law field is best described as one of frustration and disappointment. If we look at the work of Ibn Taymiyya, we find that the model offered is nothing more than the strict model of the Shari'a state. As we shall see in subsequent chapters, that model raises very serious constitutional and other public law problems. In resolving these specific problems, neither the substance nor the form of the work of Ibn Taymiyya is in any way helpful for the modern application of Islamic law.

In the modern era, both Jamal al-Din al-Afghani and Muhammad Abduh emphasized the need to incorporate modern philosophical and scientific disciplines to show that Islam is not inconsistent with modernity.[84] Yet the "founders" of Islamic modernism are somewhat disappointing in their attempts to generate concrete results for public law purposes. Abduh seems to have had more lasting influence, but the ambivalence of his position provided common ground for opposing points of view. On one hand, his position could be used to justify free adoption of Western ideas and institutions without regard to Islamic values. On the other, it could be used to justify rigid reassertion of the early Shari'a state. In his own work he failed to carry his argument to its logical conclusion by constructing out of conflicting viewpoints of reform a synthesis acceptable to both groups of his followers.[85]

Fazlur Rahman has pointed out that the *ulama*, those trained in *fiqh* (the historical jurisprudence of Shari'a), are incapable of contributing to the process of modernization because their education and orientation not only restricted them to the traditional confines but prevented them from even perceiving the problem. He concludes that this is why modernism (insofar as it existed at all) has been the work of "lay" Muslims with a liberal education. Given the common conception that the Islamic credentials of "lay" modernists are perceived to be somewhat suspect, Fazlur Rahman seems to think that these "lay" modernists "could not lay the foundations of a new Islamic theology."[86]

This psychological dimension to the defeat of most modern Muslim intellectuals who conceded too much "religious" authority to the proponents of Shari'a is extremely significant. Most contemporary Muslim intellectuals, educated in the liberal tradition of modern universities, seem to lack the necessary self-confidence to challenge the aggressive proponents of Shari'a.[87] This is particularly sad and disappointing because Islam, at least in the Sunni tradition, does not recognize the distinction between "clergy" and "lay" Muslims. There is no basis for the authority which Muslim intellectuals concede to the *ulama* and the proponents of Shari'a.

Nevertheless, this psychological factor has very real and serious consequences. On one hand, the majority of those intellectuals who retained their religious commitment to Islam have tended gradually to gravitate to conservatism and at least acquiesce in the call for a Shari'a state.[88] On the other, many Muslim intellectuals who oppose the Shari'a model for an Islamic state tend to seek an alternative model outside Islam. Lacking the self-confidence to challenge the "experts" of Islam on their own ground, many Muslim intellectuals tend to gravitate toward secularism.

As has already been suggested, real secularism is unlikely to receive broad and lasting support in the Muslim world. It may be true that although there is little explicit secularism in the Muslim world, there are powerful practical secularist trends in contemporary Muslim political life.[89] Nevertheless, in view of recent developments, I would suggest that secularism is increasingly on the defensive and is actually receding, even at the undeclared practical level. In essence, by conceding religious authority to the proponents of Shari'a, secularist intellectuals are conceding defeat without a fight. Consequently, the end result of opting for secularism in the Muslim world is the same as that of gravitating toward conservatism. Both, in the end, bolster the ascendance of the proponents of a Shari'a state.

I have already noted several examples of the inherent contradiction of attempting significant reform within the framework of Shari'a. I will now add a few more examples because of their value in illustrating the internal consistency and efficacy of the reform methodology proposed by *Ustadh* Mahmoud.

Some modern Muslim intellectuals have argued, at least implicitly, for a distinction between the moral precepts and the specifically legal prescriptions of the Qur'an.[90] These Muslim intellectuals would argue, for example, that although the Qur'an accepted slavery as a formally legal institution, its intention was clearly to abolish slavery once conditions permitted. Unless an effective legislative mechanism for realizing this "original" intent of the Qur'an is initiated, however, the previously implemented "transitional" principle of legalized slavery will remain intact.

It has also been argued that since verse 4:3 of the Qur'an required justice among cowives as a condition of polygamy, and since verse 4:129 stated that such justice is impossible to achieve in practice, it follows that the intention of the Qur'an was to abolish polygamy. This line of thinking suffers from the same difficulty noted in the preceding paragraph. The proponents of this view have to find a way to deal with the full text of verse 4:129, which reads as follows: "You will never be able to be fair and just as between women [cowives], even if it is your ardent desire: But do not turn away completely [from one of your wives] so as to leave her [as it were] hanging in the air. If you come to be friendly, understanding and practice self-restraint, God is Oft-forgiving, Most Merciful." Thus the full text of the verse cited by modernist Muslim intellectuals in support of restricting polygamy allows for an exception that permits polygamy.

Iqbal engaged in the same flawed logic when he relied on part of verse 2:228 without dealing with the rest of the verse. The relevant portion of the verse may be translated as follows: "And women shall have rights equivalent to the rights against them, according to equitable prevailing practice *(al-ma'aruf)*, but men have a degree [of advantage] over them [women]. And God is Exalted in Power." Iqbal used the first part of this verse to argue that men and women should have absolute parity today.[91] But because he did not explain how this can be consistent with the remainder of the verse, his argument is bound to fail.

Given the full text and context of the verses in question, a new principle of interpretation has to be employed for polygamy to be *legally* restricted and for men and women to have absolute parity *by law*. This new principle of interpretation, in my view, is the evolutionary principle proposed by *Ustadh* Mahmoud. According to this principle, the exception under verse 4:129 was made to permit the practice of polygamy, which was necessary at that stage. In the historical context of Shari'a, women were dependent on men for their security and economic well-being. Since men were in short supply because of the ravages of war in the seventh century, it was better for a woman to share a husband with other cowives than to remain a destitute and defenseless spinster. Similarly, the part of verse 2:228 to the effect that men have a degree of advantage over women has to be seen in historical context. Although that degree was reflected in the legal status of men and women in the previous context, it should have no legal consequences in the modern context. Differences in physical and spiritual abilities exist among men and among women as well as between men and women. Such differences, however, do not justify legal discrimination. This principle could not have been appreciated and implemented in the context of seventh-century Arabia, but it can be appreciated and implemented today.

Ahmad Hasan rejected the principle of *naskh* (in the sense that some verses of the Qur'an are deemed to have abrogated and barred the application of others) as inconsistent with the eternal validity of the Qur'an. "The mere existence of the abrogated verses as part of the text of the Qur'an," he maintained, "is not the sign of eternity unless they carry a practical value. The concept of the eternity of the Qur'an presupposes that all its laws should remain effective in the Muslim *Ummah* [nation] for ever." He then contended that since the Qur'an was revealed piecemeal over twenty-three years, each revelation generally came down in the context of specific social conditions. Thus, he reasoned, to implement the Qur'anic rulings in different times and places, one must study the historical context of each revelation and then the Qur'an in its totality must be implemented. He then offered the generalization that the Qur'anic injunctions were revealed in a given situation only to suggest that "instead of abrogating the previous rulings by the subsequent ones, it seems proper to implement them in the conditions similar to those in which they were revealed." The example he used to illustrate his argument deserves to be quoted in full because of its special significance to the subject of the present book:

> There are many passages in the Meccan *surahs* [chapters of the Qur'an]
> that ask the Muslims to be patient and to tolerate the aggression of
> the infidels [16:126–27]. On the contrary, the Medinese *surahs* consist
> of a few verses that call upon the Muslims to launch an attack on the
> infidels and kill them wherever they are found [5:9]. There is apparently
> a contradiction between these two sets of verses. It seems that the com-
> mentators [on the Qur'an] could not reconcile them and, therefore,
> held that the former had been abrogated by the latter. But the ques-
> tion arises: Are the Meccan verses in question actually abrogated?

Ahmad Hasan argued that the different rulings belong to different situations in that the Meccan verses were revealed in a situation when the
Muslims were weak and could not retaliate, whereas the Medinese verses
containing the command of *jihad* belong to a period when the strength
of the Muslims had grown considerably. He then concluded: "From this
it may be inferred that, in the first place, if the Muslims anywhere are weak,
they may tolerate the aggression of the non-Muslims *temporarily*. But
simultaneously they are duty-bound to make preparations and make themselves powerful. Secondly, when they grow powerful they are required to
live in a state of preparedness and to shatter the power of the enemies of
Islam."[92]

Thus, unfortunately (and despite his rhetoric about historical context and social conditions), Ahmad Hasan has arrived at exactly the same
position held by the founding jurists of Shari'a, but in an opportunistic
and unprincipled manner. Since the Muslims cannot be bound by contradictory rulings, the early jurists were logical in applying the principle of
naskh to abrogate the earlier verses of the Mecca period and implement
the subsequent verses of the Medina period. In contrast, Ahmad Hasan
maintains that the Muslims are bound by one set of verses or the other,
depending on the state of their strength or weakness in relation to the
"enemies of Islam." In this way, Ahmad Hasan renders the Qur'anic message not only into unprincipled and opportunistic terms, but also comes
to a conclusion that is incredibly naive. If his suggestion is correct, why
should the non-Muslims wait for the Muslims to become powerful enough
to attack them as and when they are able to do so? The inevitable result
of this thinking is to make international peace and coexistence utterly impossible, a result no rational human being would want to contemplate,
let alone accept as a religious imperative.

Incidentally, it is interesting to note the change in Ahmad's
language. Initially he paraphrases verse 9:5 accurately in that it calls upon
Muslims to launch an attack on the infidels and kill them wherever they
are found. Later on, he speaks of Muslims living in a state of preparedness
and to shatter the power of the "enemies of Islam." This shift in his lan-

guage is indicative of his lack of conviction in what he preaches, a common phenomenon with the proponents of Shari'a. Because he knows that the clear and definite meaning of verse 9:5 and the rest of chapter 9 of the Qur'an are both morally and politically untenable today, he seeks to modify that in his own language in the hope of making it more acceptable. As will be clearly demonstrated in Chapter 6, the Qur'an, Sunna, and the totality of Muslim practice during and following the Medina stage indicate a view of international relations based on the Muslim right, indeed duty, to attack non-Muslims to force them either to embrace Islam or to submit to Muslim sovereignty. This duty to attack non-Muslims is a fundamental principle of Shari'a, irrespective of "aggression" by the non-Muslim side, or their being "enemies of Islam."

Special consideration should be given to Fazlur Rahman as a major contemporary Muslim scholar.[93] Despite his valuable contribution to the clarification of the issues and presentation of the problems of modern Islamic reform, Fazlur Rahman, too, did not have the answer to problems raised by this book. This is particularly disappointing because he has often touched upon, but never fully developed, a very promising line of inquiry. He has pointed out, for example, that "the essential point, however, which the modernist did not clearly formulate is that the Qur'an although it is the eternal Word of God, was, nevertheless, immediately addressing a given society with a specific social structure. . . . Therefore, a legal and a moral approach were both equally necessary."[94] Unfortunately, he failed to follow through with the question which logically arises from this view, namely, whether the legal shall remain legal, and the moral remain beyond the realm of legal requirement, forever, or whether it should be possible, at some point, to enact the moral approach into law and, consequently, set aside the corresponding legal principle of the past. The logic of his remark about the need for a legal as well as a moral approach in relation to slavery and the status of women would lead to the conclusion that the Islamic moral precepts against slavery and in favor of equality for women should be translated into legal principles once the "specific social structure" of Muslim society had changed to the degree necessary for implementing the moral imperative. If this is not yet true of Muslim society, or rather societies, in relation to women, it is undoubtedly true in relation to slavery. Yet, as will be explained in Chapter 7, slavery remains lawful under Shari'a and shall remain lawful unless we find an adequate and systematic reform methodology to implement the original intention of the Qur'an.

In terms of this methodology, Fazlur Rahman proposed that "the entire body of the *Shari'a* must be subjected to fresh examination in the light of the Qur'anic evidence. . . . A strict methodology for understanding and interpreting the Qur'an should be adopted."[95] To this end, he suggested a threefold approach:

> "(a) A sober and honest historical approach must be used for finding the meaning of the Qur'anic text. . . . First of all, the Qur'an must be studied in chronological order. An examination of the earliest revelations to begin with will bestow an accurate enough perception of the basic impulse of the Islamic movement as distinguished from measures and institutions established later. . . . (b) Then one is ready to distinguish between Qur'anic legal dicta and the *objectives* and *ends* these laws were expected to serve. . . . (c) The objectives of the Qur'an must be understood and fixed, keeping in full view its sociological setting, i.e. the environment in which the Prophet moved and worked.[96]

The reason why Fazlur Rahman did not develop these ideas to their logical conclusions may be his view that "although this method of interpretation of the Qur'an and the Sunna seems to be the most satisfactory and perhaps the only possible one — it is honest, true and practical — there is no reason to believe that Muslims are ready to accept it."[97] Because of this evaluation of Muslim attitudes, Fazlur Rahman has focused on "the only real remedy of the situation . . . [namely] a basic reform of the modern educational system" to impart "genuine Islamic values in schools and colleges beside other subjects."[98] But as an examination of his specialized book on the subject reveals,[99] there is no escape from the fundamental question: what are the "genuine Islamic values" to be imported in schools and colleges? Do they include, for example, Shari'a principles on the status of women and non-Muslims? If not, how can we achieve the sufficient and yet legitimate degree of reform in these and other issues of public law?

Fazlur Rahman preached that "the thinking Muslim has to go right behind the early post-Prophetic formative period itself and to reconstruct it all over again."[100] *Ustadh* Mahmoud Mohamed Taha has done precisely that and come up with the reform methodology briefly explained above. He actively advocated this methodology for reform from the early 1950s until his death in 1985 because he realized that Muslims would never be ready for the "honest, true and practical" approach, indicated by Fazlur Rahman, unless it was presented to them in a clear and systematic manner. The case for reform must be articulated and continuously pressed until it is accepted and implemented.

The internal consistency and efficacy of *Ustadh* Mahmoud's approach will become clearer in subsequent chapters. The key to the approach, however, is the candid and specific proposition that Muslims should shift the legal principle of Islamic law from one text of the Qur'an to the other, from a text that was suitable to govern in the seventh century, and was implemented, to a text that was, at the time, too advanced and therefore had to be abrogated in effective legal terms.

However coherent and effective this approach may be, it still has to face the question of practical acceptability raised by Fazlur Rahman. In this regard, it may appear that the prospect of wide acceptance and implementation of *Ustadh* Mahmoud's evolutionary principle by the majority of Muslims in the near future does not seem to be promising. This is not only because the principle itself presents such a drastic break with the long tradition of Islamic jurisprudence but also because it raises the prospect of serious challenge to the vested interest of powerful forces in the Muslim world. Moreover, the repressive and authoritarian nature not only of the vast majority of political regimes in power throughout the Muslim world but also of social and intellectual attitudes can hardly be conducive to the free and open discourse necessary for the advocacy of new and revolutionary ideas.

Muslims throughout the world are experiencing a severe state of confusion and crisis. Islam is being asserted as a source of identity and practical ideology in the face of political frustration, economic deprivation, and social disorganization. Yet when the so-called Islamic alternative in the form of Shari'a has been attempted in countries like Iran, Pakistan, and the Sudan, it has created more problems than it has solved. Thus, although an Islamic solution is indicated by the objective circumstances of the Muslim world, Shari'a does not appear to be that solution. Paradoxical as it may seem, the very rise of the so-called Islamic fundamentalism has exposed the inadequacy of Shari'a as the basis of the model modern Islamic state proposed by that movement. As long as the Shari'a state remained a romantic ideal, to be cited as the miraculous cure for all the ills of Muslim societies, it was immune to effective challenge. But once the proponents of Shari'a had to face the specific requirements of practical and just government in the modern world, the inadequacy of their model was exposed for all to see.

It is my belief that conducive conditions for candid and orderly debate will materialize and that significant and lasting change will occur by overcoming the negative atmosphere and lack of candid and orderly debate. As long as Muslims perceive criticism of Shari'a to be heretical, the proponents of Shari'a will continue to manipulate the sentiments of the masses of Muslims against the modernist elements. Moreover, as long as secularism remains the only alternative to Shari'a, the proponents of Shari'a will be able to enlist Muslim public opinion to their side. In demonstrating that the public law of Shari'a is not really divine in the sense of being the direct and invariable will of God, this book hopes to help many Muslims overcome the perceived barrier of "heresy" and undertake candid and orderly debate on the modern applicability of the public law of Shari'a. Furthermore, by providing a viable basis for an alternative interpretation of the sources of Islam, this book hopes to demonstrate that secularism is not the only alternative to Shari'a.

≯ 4 ≮

Shari'a and Modern Constitutionalism

𝒯HE STRUCTURE AND ORGANIZATION OF THE STATE, the manner of distribution and exercise of its powers and related matters, is the logical starting point for our discussion of the public law of Islam. It is within this structure and organization and through the distribution and exercise of government powers that the relationship between private persons and the official organs of the state (the subject matter of domestic public law) is legally determined. This is the framework for official action affecting individual and collective fundamental rights and liberties within the state and for the conduct of international relations between states. Besides the discussion in this chapter on the constitutional dimension of fundamental rights and liberties, a specialized treatment of these rights and liberties (in the context of the administration of criminal justice and of their international protection as human rights) is offered in Chapters 5 and 7.

Since the founding jurists and subsequent generations of early scholars did not think in terms of "positive law," as distinguished from religious and ethical matters, let alone in terms of constitutional law as such, it is necessary to establish our criteria for identifying those principles and rules of Shari'a which are taken here to be relevant to constitutional law issues.

MODERN CONSTITUTIONALISM AND ITS RELEVANCE
TO THE MUSLIM CONTEXT

The following conception of modern constitutionalism and its necessary implications reflects, in my view, the consensus of public opinion today, both within and outside the Muslim world. Since this concept and its necessary implications have received their best articulation and application in Western countries, Western authors on the subject are cited in the following pages. This does not mean that Western constitutionalism is the ideal to be copied by the Muslims or the peoples of any other part of the world. It is my submission that Western achievement in this regard is to be appreciated as a contribution to the totality of human experience and knowledge from which the Muslims and other peoples may adopt and adapt as they deem fit in light of their own religious and cultural traditions. The following general exposition of constitutionalism is offered in this light and should be considered as such.

General Considerations

Human society needs some form of authority/government which has the necessary powers to maintain law and order and regulate political, economic, and social activities. In the course of time, however, it came to be realized that to avoid the dangers of the corruption and the abuse of power and to ensure that the powers of government were properly employed to achieve their legitimate objectives through their prescribed methods, the structure and functioning of government must be regulated by clearly defined and strictly applied rules. This body of rules, as enacted and applied within the context of a given state, is called the constitution of that particular state. In the formal sense of the term, the constitution of a state is the body of rules and regulations which create the various organs of government and determine their relationship to each other and the relationship between these organs and their private human subjects, whether in their individual or collective capacities.[1]

In this formalistic sense, a constitution has been defined as "the organic and fundamental law of a nation or state; establishing the character and conception of its government; organizing such government, and regulating, distributing, and limiting the functions of its different departments, and prescribing the extent and manner of the exercise of sovereign powers."[2] Constitutionalism is the theory or principle of constitutional government, or adherence to that theory. In a similar vein, another source defined constitutionalism as the principle "that public authority is to be exercised according to law; that state and civic institutions, executive and legislative powers, have their source in a constitution, which is to be obeyed and not departed from at the whim of the government of the day; in short, a government of law and not of men."[3]

Although useful at one level, these definitions of constitutionalism do not tell us enough. Every organic law that contains the elements of regulation, distribution, and limitation of the powers and functions of government, and every government in accordance with formal law, however oppressive and unjust that law may be, would satisfy these minimal definitions. By the same token, any government that adheres to its own constitution would qualify as constitutional government. We need to know more about the political function of a constitution and about the law enacted thereunder if we are to be able to judge the justice, appropriateness, and expediency of a given constitution and the government established and conducted in adherence thereof.

It is generally accepted, I believe, that constitutionalism is more than government in accordance with any "constitution." A constitution properly so called must not only enforce effective limitations on the powers of government and impose positive obligations on it but must do so to achieve certain objectives. It has been said that a constitution is "that assemblage of laws, institutions and customs, derived from certain *fixed principles of reason, directed to certain fixed objects of public good,* that compose the general system, according to which the *community has agreed to be governed.*"[4] This basically valid definition needs to be understood in light of the following considerations.

The specific dictates of reason and objects of public good vary over time and place. Thus some of what has been indicated by medieval principles of reason and objects of public good may no longer be valid today. For example, whereas the right to participate in government used to be restricted to certain privileged classes or groups of people, it is generally accepted today that this right should be exercised by the entire adult population of the state. Therefore, the community whose consent legitimizes the constitutional order is now the totality of the population and not a specific segment thereof.

Moreover, whereas the process by which the dictates of reason and objects of public good are modified and adjusted over time is essentially internal to the society in question, this process is influenced by the experience and achievements of other societies. Although this has always been the case throughout the history of human civilizations, it is particularly true in the present interdependent and effectively unified modern world. It is therefore my submission that both the internal and external indicators would now confirm that constitutionalism should not only link ends and means in a rational and effective manner, thereby always pursuing desirable ends through legitimate means, but must also do so in certain ways. Both ends and means of constitutionalism, I suggest, should be conducive to the realization of the proper balance between complete individual liberty and total social justice.

The existence and probable continuation of the nation-state as the most viable form of large-scale social and political organization is taken for granted in this study. Regardless of its precise origins in intellectual and political developments since the European Renaissance and despite the processes by which this model was adopted or impressed upon other peoples of the world, the fact remains that the nation-state has become universal. Muslims throughout the world have inherited this form of government from their colonial experiences and have continued to operate their own nation-states voluntarily for decades after gaining independence. Notwithstanding the historical Muslim ambivalence toward the concept of a nation-state, the institution is now firmly and irrevocably established throughout the Muslim world.[5] In light of this crucial development, it is now imperative to assess any given constitution, whether of a Muslim or non-Muslim state, according to its ability to achieve the proper balance between individual liberty and social justice in the context of the modern nation-state. In particular, I believe that the modern nation-state should be predicated on the principle of the equality of all its citizens before the law, without discrimination on grounds such as race, color, gender, language, religion, or political or other opinion. A constitution that sanctions discrimination among the citizens of the state is not worthy of the name, and a government adhering to such an instrument of oppression and humiliation of its own subjects should not be accepted as a constitutional government.[6]

Representative government based on universal suffrage is often mentioned as a sign of constitutionalism; this is a necessary, but insufficient, condition. As recent history has clearly shown, universal suffrage can create and support tyranny of the majority or of a minority or of even one man.[7] It is therefore important to emphasize that the processes of government must be controlled by higher and more fundamental principles, which guarantee the rights of individuals and minorities against the will of the majority by invalidating any legislative or executive action that is inconsistent with those principles.[8] The terms *majority* and *minority* can be problematic because the numerical majority may not necessarily be the political majority. What is important here is the principle of protecting the rights of whoever is subjected to or threatened with oppression or discrimination, be it a majority, a minority, or a single person.

In anticipation of the need for adjusting and adapting in response to changing circumstances, it is always necessary to provide some mechanism or procedure for amending the constitution. Provided that the amendment mechanism or procedure is satisfied from the *formal* point of view, the constitution can be lawfully changed, even if the amendment repudiates the most fundamental aspects of constitutionalism.[9] To safeguard against this danger, we need to develop sufficiently strong and vivid national consensus on the fundamental principles of constitutionalism to ensure that the ends are not defeated by the means or that substance is not lost in spite of the survival of the form.

It may be useful to conclude this general outline by indicating what this concept is not intended to achieve. The formulation of policies and enactment of laws and regulations and the implementation of all of these to promote the objectives of justice, individual liberties, social equality, political stability, economic growth, and distribution of wealth involve continuing and delicate adjustment of competing interests and shifting priorities. The principle of constitutionalism does not purport to settle these interests and priorities once and for all. Rather, constitutionalism merely provides the framework, institutions, and mechanisms for the constant mediation and resolution of the outstanding issues within the context of a given nation-state.

Historical Antecedents and Cultural Legitimacy

Every state in the world today may be said to have a constitution in the minimal sense of rules and regulations which create the various organs of government and determine their relationship to each other and between them and their subjects. Minimal constitutionalism may also be said to have existed in the historical experience of several ancient and intermediate civilizations.[10] When we focus on the definition of constitutionalism and its necessary implications in accordance with the criteria suggested above, however, none of the historical civilizations and very few, if any, contemporary states would qualify as a constitutional system in the full and specific sense of the term.

The "constitutions" of historical civilizations were deficient not only because they failed to provide for the full range and scope of fundamental and welfare rights and lacked effective remedies for the enforcement of rights but also because the "citizens" who enjoyed rights that were provided for did not include substantial groups (such as women and slaves) who would qualify as citizens in the modern sense. These defects, especially the exclusion of groups such as women from the effective exercise of sovereignty, and the very existence of slavery, are fatal from the point of view of modern constitutionalism.[11]

The vast majority of contemporary states, I believe, are lacking in sufficient safeguards of either civil and political or economic, social, and cultural rights. Nevertheless, a few contemporary states may actually guarantee both sets of rights to a sufficient degree and scope as to satisfy the standards of constitutionalism. As it happens, however, the majority of these states fall within the Western democratic socialist tradition. The association between constitutionalism and this Western tradition is not sufficient justification, in my view, for either accepting or rejecting constitutionalism. Acceptance or rejection of constitutionalism and its necessary implications should be based on rational and objective arguments. I believe that at least two arguments, one moral and the other empirical, can be cited in support of the universal validity of the principle of constitutionalism and its application to non-Western cultural traditions.

The moral justification is simply the principle, common to all cultural and religious traditions of the world, that one should treat others as one would like to be treated by them.[12] One should place himself or herself in the shoes of the other person and decide whether he or she would accept being in that position. If one would not accept for himself or herself living in a state that does not conform to the principle of constitutionalism as defined above, or would not accept being denied any of the necessary implications of that principle, one cannot morally defend the imposition of the same upon any other person. I maintain that every human being would demand for himself or herself all the benefits of constitutionalism and must therefore concede the same benefits to all other human beings.

The empirical argument in support of the universal validity of the principle of constitutionalism is the fact that it has been the free choice of the vast majority of peoples throughout the world. Most peoples of Africa and Asia did not enjoy the essence of constitutionalism, namely, the right to self-determination, during colonial rule.[13] Upon gaining independence, almost all of these previously colonized peoples decided to assert constitutionalism as an ideal they were seeking to achieve.[14] This phenomenon cannot be explained away as simply a relic of colonialism because it has persisted for several decades after independence and often after the countries in question have enacted more than one version of their own independent constitutions. However elusive it may have been to achieve in practice, constitutionalism continues to be the free choice of the vast majority of the peoples of the world, including the Muslims.

It is no doubt true that, in making transcultural analyses of concepts such as constitutionalism, one has to be aware of the dangers of oversimplification and the assumption of either too much or too little common ground. On one hand, one should be careful to scrutinize the assumption that "the theoretical model necessary for trans-cultural qualitative judgement on law, constitutions, politics and judicial behavior already exists in refined form in the Western World." On the other hand, one should also scrutinize "the contrary assumption that each cultural system is so unique and separate from the world community that virtually all apparent similarities unearthed by careful country-specific, and comparative legal studies must be regarded as illusory or insignificant."[15]

In response to the caution against the assumption that the necessary model already exists in the Western world, I do not assume that the theoretical model for transcultural qualitative judgment on constitutions is the existing Western model. The model I propose is the one briefly outlined earlier in this section, which does not rely for its validity on its existence anywhere in the world today. It is my thesis that this is the model we should be pursuing, regardless of who else is pursuing it or has already achieved it. Nevertheless, the achievements of both Western and non-Western civilizations are instructive in the construction and implementation of modern Islamic constitutionalism.

The caution regarding the assumption of uniqueness of cultural systems should be qualified by noting that a cultural or religious tradition may claim some degree of uniqueness and separateness. This would operate in terms of the tradition's own internal criteria, but within the framework of the universal validity of a given moral and political principle such as constitutionalism. We may then consider the validity of such a claim of uniqueness and may find it appropriate to grant it some degree of satisfaction without violating our fundamental position on the principle in question. In other words, we may examine a claim to an alternative view of constitutionalism, and assess it in light of the above-noted arguments of moral and empirical universality of constitutionalism and its necessary implications, before accepting or rejecting it. To do this in relation to Islam as reflected in Shari'a, I will now survey the relevant principles of Shari'a to determine their consistency or inconsistency with modern constitutionalism.

ASSESSMENT OF THE HISTORICAL SHARI'A STATE
AS CONSTITUTIONAL GOVERNMENT

The founding jurists of Shari'a did not think in terms of positive law (as distinguished from religious norms and ethics), let alone distinguish constitutional and other public law issues and address them as such. It is therefore necessary to use the concept and implications of constitutionalism outlined above in both identifying and evaluating the relevant corresponding principles of Shari'a.

The most authoritative source of constitutional theory under Shari'a is the model of the Medina state, as established by the Prophet himself in 622 A.D. and implemented by his four successors (al-khulafa al-rashidun).[16]

Whether characterized in modern terminology as a theocracy or a nomocracy,[17] the Prophet's Medina state had a specific de facto organization that was supposed to be copied after his death, subject to modifications necessitated by the termination of divine revelation.[18] In accordance with this view, the ruler of the Muslim community after the Prophet was called *Khalifat Rasul al-Allah*, the caliph (successor) of the Messenger of God, the Prophet.[19] For the Sunni majority, therefore, the caliph was the successor to the role of the Prophet as supreme political ruler of the Muslim community, without succeeding him in his role as prophet and recipient of divine guidance.[20]

When we look at the Medina model, we find that the caliph was either selected by a small group of Muslims or appointed by the preceding caliph and was then confirmed by the general Muslim population through a mass oath of allegiance *(by'a).*[21] The vagueness of the basis of political legitimacy and the informality of the procedure under the Medina model permitted the appointment of the caliph to degenerate into direct hereditary monarchy, whereby *by'a* for the next caliph was secured during the lifetime of the existing caliph.[22]

This historical model has been cited by some Muslim scholars, at various stages of Muslim history, as the ideal they hope to reestablish. Despite widespread call for reform and reformulation, no significant change has so far been introduced in this aspect of Shari'a. Therefore, unless and until such change has been specifically and expressly introduced by the modern proponents of a Shari'a state, it is reasonable to assess this historical model in terms of modern constitutionalism because it is the one the proponents of Shari'a propose to implement today.

The Sources and Nature of the Powers of the Ruler

It is not meaningful to speak of the Prophet's rule in terms of constitutionalism. That term implies legal limitations on the powers of the ruler and his political accountability to a human entity other than himself, whereas the Prophet was to the Muslims the agent of God, and his words and deeds were the only criteria of validity and legality. In constitutional terms, the Prophet was the original human sovereign and founder of the Islamic state. Yet he was succeeded by men who enjoyed the same degree of political power without having his corresponding religious authority.[23] Although the caliph's right to rule was supposed to be based on popular belief in the caliph's moral integrity and faithfulness to the teachings of the Prophet, there was no way for verifying that basis of political legitimacy once the initial appointment and confirmation of the caliph, *by'a* (oath of allegiance), was made and no way for withdrawing support and allegiance at any subsequent stage. In other words, the authority of the caliph was supposed to be derived from popular support without any principle and mechanism by which that popular support could have been freely given, restricted, or withdrawn. This is, I maintain, one of the fundamental sources of constitutional problems with the Shari'a model of an Islamic state.

The second source of difficulty has to do with the nature and scope of the Prophet's powers, which were inherited by his successors, the caliphs. During the first ten years of the Medina state, the Prophet was the sole recipient and interpreter of divine revelation and the ultimate executive and judicial head of the community. From the constitutional and legal point of view, the Prophet was the sole human sovereign of the Medina state, holder of ultimate and absolute legislative, executive, and judicial powers. It is no doubt true that the Muslims submitted to the Prophet's rule spontaneously and voluntarily, out of their profound allegiance to his magnetic and overwhelming personality and their deep appreciation of the validity of his objectives and the subtlety of his methods. This, however, should not be allowed to cloud the constitutional nature of his rule. In my view, the failure of subsequent generations of Muslims to appreciate the peculiar and special nature of the Prophet's role and their attempt to confer the same role on his successors, the caliphs,[24] are the causes of much of the confusion and many of the problems of Islamic political theory.

It may well have been that the first four caliphs did not wish to succeed to the precise nature and full scope of the powers of the Prophet,[25] but the fact remains that they were perceived to have done that. Moreover, and given the pre-Islamic and early Islamic nature of political and social institutions, it may well have been that such degree of succession was natural and expedient. Nevertheless, when the model so established was taken by subsequent generations of Muslims to be the most authoritative model of an Islamic state, it became impossible to reconcile Shari'a with constitutionalism. Subsequent generations of Muslim jurists and scholars may have been aware of the problems created by that model,[26] but they continued to rationalize and defend it for generations, and often centuries, after the fact.[27]

As a result of the entrenchment of the model by which the caliph succeeded the Prophet as supreme ruler, not limited by any human person or body of persons, it became impossible to structure and limit the powers of the ruler as required by constitutionalism. As the ultimate agent of divine sovereignty,[28] the ruler determines which view or interpretation of Shari'a is the authoritative and operative one and decides how to implement it in practice. Although he might delegate some of his legislative, executive, and judicial powers, he retains the power to overrule the policies and decisions of any of his deputies and judges.[29]

Some scholars have expressed the view that since God Himself is the legislator in Islam, there can be no room for legislation or legislative powers under Shari'a.[30] This position is incorrect, in my view, because human judgment has always been exercised in determining the applicable principles and rules of Shari'a. Both the Qur'an and Sunna had to be interpreted to develop legal principles and rules. The nature and extent of the legislative function under Shari'a was correctly stated by a contemporary Muslim scholar as follows:

> Without in any way trespassing upon the function reserved exclusively for God of *making* law, the need has existed and remains for a temporal authority which understands or *interprets* Divine law or *elaborates* its details. This is so because often the *shari'a* states a principle *simpliciter* and leaves it to human beings to work out the legal details and regulations that flow from the principle. Or, *shari'a* may specifically release to the sphere of human reason and understanding the setting up of regulations in certain matters. Then again, the very existence of different schools of Islamic law shows that a great deal of Islamic law is interpretative and derivative from *shari'a* in nature, and that for such interpretation, derivation and elaboration a legislative temporal authority should be identifiable, which authority would be *in pari materia* with the legislative branch of the constitutional state of contemporary political science.[31]

This is the sense in which there is a legislative function under Shari'a. According to the historical model, that function was under the ultimate control of the caliph, although he could rely on the opinions of his judges and other jurists. For example, whenever there is a difference of opinion among the jurists, which is usually the case, "it is the acknowledged right of the ruler to impose that one opinion among conflicting authorities which he considers best suited to the case in point."[32]

Popular Participation in Government

Much is made by some contemporary Muslim authors of the notion of *shura*, whereby the ruler is supposed to consult with the leading members of the community on the affairs of the state.[33] The problem with *shura* as a constitutional principle, however, is that, by virtue of its original concept and authority in the Qur'an as well as its historical practice, it has neither been comprehensive in scope nor binding in effect.[34] In their desire to construct a modern constitutional principle out of historical Shari'a, many modern Muslim authors have distorted the historical facts to fit their view. Although it is correct to say that popular participation in government and the accountability of the rulers to the ruled *ought* to be binding Islamic constitutional principles, it cannot be credibly maintained that they have always been so. If the binding nature of *shura* was already established by Shari'a, it would not be necessary to argue for this position now, several centuries after the fact.

According to verse 3:159 (the first of two verses of the Qur'an which mention the term *shura*), the Prophet is enjoined to deal gently and kindly with the believers and to consult them in public affairs, but once he is resolved, he should proceed to execute his decision in reliance on God. Although he did consult in some situations, and sometimes followed the advice given to him, it was neither seen by the founding jurists as being contemplated by this verse, nor was it the invariable practice, that the Prophet always consulted his Companions and implemented their advice.[35] In any case, given the Prophet's religious role and the nature of his relationship with his followers, it is inconceivable that he was bound to consult his Companions on public affairs and was bound to accept the advice he received. Whatever obligation to consult his Companions the Prophet may have had, it was an obligation to God and not to his human subjects. This makes the whole process religious and moral rather than legal and constitutional in nature.

Verse 42:38 (the other verse of the Qur'an which mentions *shura*) describes the believers as a community who decide their affairs in consultation among themselves. It does not say, nor has it been interpreted by the leading jurists to mean, that the majority view should prevail.[36] In fact, there was never any procedure or mechanism for consultation, and no legal consequences followed from the failure of the ruler to consult his subjects or to follow the advice that was given to him. Since the days of the first caliph, Abu Bakr, the ruler decided on his own discretion whether to consult his subjects and whether to act on the advice he was given. Abu Bakr went against the view of the vast majority of the leading Companions when he decided to fight the Arab tribesmen who rebelled after the Prophet's death *(al-murtadin)*. Umar, the second caliph, also went against the view of the vast majority of leading Companions over the distribution of lands taken as spoils of war in southern Iraq.[37]

The modern proponents of *shura* (as a constitutional principle requiring the ruler to consult and be bound by the advice he receives) also cite other verses of the Qur'an, such as verses 3:110, 3:112, and 22:41, which describe the Muslims as "commanding good and prohibiting evil."

Although these verses may be interpreted today as supporting the duty to command good and prohibit evil in *government*, hence enjoining participation by implication, this cannot be presented as the historical interpretation of the verses as understood by the founding jurists.

Another source of confusion over the constitutional nature of an Islamic state under Shari'a is the view that the caliph was not a despotic and absolute ruler because, like every other Muslim, he was bound by Shari'a. But since the caliph himself was the ultimate authority on what the rule of Shari'a was and how it should be applied in any given case, that is, he was the ultimate legislative authority in addition to being the ultimate judicial and executive authority, his limitation by Shari'a was of little practical value.[38] The status of the jurists who were technically competent to determine Shari'a was always advisory. Once again, it should be emphasized that the modern possibility of establishing an independent and constitutionally sanctioned authority which is capable of declaring and implementing the law against the executive ruler should not be confused with the position under historical Shari'a.

The dangers of abuse and corruption of powers is present as long as the caliph, or a corresponding modern chief executive, is the ultimate authority in determining what is the relevant principle of Shari'a, whether through his own knowledge or by selecting from among the available opinions of qualified jurists. Investing that power in a jurist (or body of jurists), as has been attempted recently in Iran, simply transfers the problem to being one of abuse and corruption of powers by this supervisory body. The crucial question would then become how is that jurist (or body of jurists) selected, and to whom and how is he (or are they) accountable? If this jurist (or body of jurists) is guaranteed independence as expert(s) of Shari'a, his (their) rulings would be binding on the executive without being politically responsible for the consequences of the prescribed course of action. Yet to make him (them) accountable either to the caliph or to the population at large is inconsistent with the rationale of his (their) role, which is to ensure the government's compliance with Shari'a regardless of the will of the caliph or of the general population.

To illustrate this point in a modern context, we can refer to the 1979 Constitution of the Islamic Republic of Iran. The stages of the revolution and its power structure have been documented and analyzed by a number of scholars.[39] What is significant from the point of view of the present chapter is the fundamental principle of *wilayat al-faqih*[40] (guardianship of the jurist(s) of Shari'a). Since the essential function of the Islamic state is to implement or enforce Shari'a, it follows that the most qualified jurist(s) should stand guardian over the constitution to ensure its continued compliance with the dictates of Shari'a.[41] In accordance with this principle, Article 4 of the Constitution provides that all laws and regulations should be based on Islamic principles. "This principle will in general prevail over all of the principles of the Constitution, and other laws and regulations as well. *Any judgment in regard to this will be made by the clerical members of the Council of Guardians.*"

This and other related provisions of the Iranian Constitution reflect the ambivalence of the Shari'a model to the principle of sovereignty, as explained below. On one hand, Article 2 of the Iranian Constitution states that the Islamic republic is a system based on belief in "1) one God (There is no God but one) and the exclusive sovereignty of God, the acceptance of His rule, and the necessity of obeying His commands." On the other hand, the "exclusive" sovereignty of God translates in the Constitution into guardianship by the clergy. The question would therefore arise, Why speak of the exclusive sovereignty of God when we know that in practice it will have to be exercised by men?

It is my submission that this devious terminology is intended to avoid the obvious objection against making men above the constitution. Therefore, the logic upon which the Islamic constitution is predicated is that since Muslims accept the ultimate sovereignty of God, they must accept the practical sovereignty of men who speak for God. This logic, however, is based on two premises, one unverifiable and the other false. The unverifiable premise is that a man knows (or a group of men know) the will of God. The false premise is that when the capacity to "discover" the will of God is vested in a group of men, they will speak with one voice. The fallacy of this assumption is admitted, for example, by the express terms of Articles 5 and 107 of the Constitution of Iran, which provide for the possibility of disagreement among the clergy on the fundamental question of the appointment of the jurist leader who shall have the ultimate mandate for state affairs.

Sovereignty

The general constitutional assessment of the Shari'a model set out above clearly indicates the need to clarify two related concepts underlying modern constitutionalism, namely, sovereignty and citizenship. These concepts (which go to the heart of political philosophy) cannot be discussed in depth here. Nevertheless, we need to be clear on the position taken in the present study in relation to these central concepts.

Sovereignty has somewhat varied connotations in international law, constitutional law, and political philosophy, but it always signifies the highest governmental or legal authority.[42] It has been defined as "the supreme power by which any citizen is governed and is the person or body of persons in the state to whom there is *politically no superior.* [Sovereignty is] the necessary existence of the state and that right and power which necessarily follow. . . . [By] sovereignty in its largest sense is meant supreme, absolute, and uncontrollable power, the absolute right to govern. The word which by itself comes nearest to being the definition of 'sovereignty' is will or volition as applied to *political affairs.*"[43]

The debate over the concept of sovereignty is best understood in historical context because it originated out of the search, since the sixteenth and seventeenth centuries, for a purely secular basis for authority within the state.[44] Apparently opposing views on the subject may be reconciled if we allow for the fact that some authors were speaking of sovereignty in the context of the danger or reality of an emergency or civil war, while others were addressing the issues in normal political conditions.[45] This contextual factor may account for differences over how sovereignty may be exercised at any given point. It may therefore be useful to conceive of sovereignty as permanently residing in one person or body of persons who may delegate its exercise to another under certain circumstances and for specific purposes.

Questions such as who is the permanent holder of sovereignty, whether it has been delegated, to whom, to what extent, and for which purposes can be discussed and definitively answered only within the context of a given state and in light of its own political philosophy or ideology as reflected in its constitutional order. I believe, however, that there is a broader context, derived from a prevailing sense of justice and expediency, which may be used as a foundation for some general hypothesis on where sovereignty *ought* to reside, to whom it may *legitimately* be delegated, and so forth. Since sovereignty signifies the power to determine policy and enforce it through the law and other institutions, it can only be justly and expediently based on the consent of the whole of the population purported to be so governed. It is both morally repugnant and practically difficult to coerce people into enforcing policies and complying with laws against their own free will. That does not mean that each person should have an individual impulsive choice of the policies he or she may freely wish to enforce and of laws with which he or she may capriciously wish to comply. Rather, it means that each and every subject of the state must have a way of *significantly* influencing the processes of determination of policy and the legislation of laws. To be able significantly to influence these vital processes, each and every person must have an equal and unimpaired opportunity to become, or choose those who may become, makers and enforcers of policy and law.

Moreover, since policy making and legislation are all-pervasive and continuous processes, each and every subject of the state must be able *significantly* to influence these vital functions *whenever and at whatever level* he or she may deem that to be necessary. Therefore, every subject of the state must be entitled, as of right, to express approval or disapproval of policy and legislation and be afforded the opportunity to seek to change them in association with others. Equally important is the ability of each and every subject of the state lawfully to challenge any policy or law through legal as well as political means. These ideas are relevant to all the necessary implications of constitutionalism discussed below.

It would seem that one of the main issues underlying all the problems with constitutionalism under Shari'a is a certain ambivalence regarding sovereignty. Although it is the profound Muslim belief that ultimate sovereignty resides with God,[46] this in itself does not indicate who is authorized to act in the name of the ultimate sovereign. During the lifetime of the Prophet, the answer to this question was obvious and beyond dispute.[47] Once the Prophet had passed away, the right of any person to claim the position as the human agent of the divine sovereign came into question. The claim of the caliphs, whether implicit or explicit, that they were acting merely as instruments of the will of God as expressed in Shari'a begs the question of how the caliph is to be appointed and made accountable for his conduct. To implement modern constitutionalism we must answer the following fundamental questions: Can the notion of a human agent of the divine sovereign (whether a caliph or his modern equivalent) be reconciled with constitutionalism? How is that agent to be selected and appointed? How can that agent be accountable for his discharge of the terms of that agency?[48]

The argument that the agent of the divine sovereign is the *Umma*, the totality of the Muslim population of the state, rather than an individual person or body of persons, seems to offer some possibility of resolving the problem.[49] If the *Umma* is the collective agent of the divine sovereign, it would be entitled to appoint its representatives for discharging the duties of government and hold them accountable to itself as the human "principal," the original agent of divine sovereignty. Besides the more fundamental objection noted in the next paragraph, it should be emphasized that Shari'a did not provide for the implementation of this concept of responsible representative government.[50] Shari'a never provided clear mechanisms and procedures for the selection of the caliph by the community at large, for his accountability while in office, or for his removal in an orderly and peaceful manner. That is not to say that these mechanisms and procedures cannot be developed today. Rather, it is simply to note that they are not already in existence.

The more fundamental problem with this notion of the *Umma*

as the human sovereign is that it excludes non-Muslim citizens of the state. As we shall see below, Shari'a excludes non-Muslims completely and restricts the participation of Muslim women in conducting the affairs of the state. This is obviously inconsistent with the modern constitutional requirements of equality and nondiscrimination among citizens.

Citizenship

The second underlying notion which is problematical under Shari'a is citizenship. Who does the phrase "each and every subject of the state," frequently used in the preceding discussion of sovereignty, include? No state can be reasonably expected to confer the full range of civil and political, economic and social rights upon aliens who happen to be temporarily within its territory. Nor can any state be reasonably entitled to claim the corresponding duty of allegiance from whosoever happens to be within its territory. Consequently, constitutional and legal systems would normally distinguish between those who are so entitled, and so bound by a duty of allegiance to the state, and those who are not. What ought to be the criteria for making this distinction among persons subject to the jurisdiction of the state?

Citizenship has always been associated with the balancing of rights against, and duties toward, the community. "This," it has been suggested, "explains the fact that everywhere the personal concept of citizenship preceded the development of the territorial concept which, with the rise of the modern nation state, has come to prevail in international law."[51] Whereas the personal concept of citizenship would confer this status on the basis of some personal attribute or quality such as religion or ethnicity, the territorial conception of citizenship, which has now become the norm, confers the benefits and burdens of citizenship on all those born and permanently resident within the territory of the state, as well as those naturalized under the relevant provisions of the law of the land. It is morally repugnant and politically inexpedient, I submit, to deny full citizenship to any person who was born and permanently resident within the territory of the state unless such person opts for and acquires the citizenship of another state. Any state would, of course, have full discretion to determine whether and under what conditions it may allow the naturalization of persons born in another country. I will concentrate on the legal status and rights of those who are citizens by virtue of both birth and permanent residence within the territory of the state.

The right of *all* citizens continuously and significantly to influence the formulation and execution of public policy and the enactment of public laws is the moral and pragmatic justification for the sovereignty of the state. For this right to be meaningful and effective, all citizens must enjoy the freedom to seek and exchange information on public issues and to cooperate with other citizens in furtherance of their shared view of the common good. The underlying idea may be expressed in terms of the *right* and *opportunity* for the minority, even of one person, to *seek* to become the majority and thereby succeed in having his or her views formulated into policy and enacted into law. The principle of majority rule cannot be maintained unless the minority has the legal right and practical opportunity to become the majority so that its views may one day prevail.

It would seem logically to follow from this premise that the majority and minority should not be constituted on the basis of permanent incidental factors such as race or gender, which an individual is unable to change. Neither should an individual be forced to abandon an essential attribute of his or her human liberty and dignity such as his or her freely held religious or other belief to be part of the majority. Policy and law must therefore always be founded on a rational basis which can be equally appreciated and supported by all citizens, regardless of race, gender, or religion or other belief. Otherwise, we cannot expect to maintain allegiance to the state and its laws from those who are confined to an eternal submission to the will of the majority, with no prospect of becoming the majority themselves.

The possibilities of alternative interpretations of the historical Muslim constitutional experience are useful only if they are combined with some revisions of specific aspects of Shari'a, as well as supplementing its deficiencies in providing mechanisms for genuine representation and accountability. In particular, the conception of the *Umma* as the collective original agent of the divine sovereign, and as such the only human sovereign, can provide a viable foundation of constitutionalism only if the composition of the *Umma* under Shari'a is revised to include all citizens on the basis of complete equality, with no discrimination on grounds of religion or gender.

In conclusion, it is important to reiterate the caution against confusing historical Shari'a with the possibilities of reform which can be implemented in the future. The present possibility of reinterpreting Islamic sources in ways that support modern constitutionalism should not lead one to think that these ways were used in the past. After analyzing the historical Islamic state in terms of a double-contract theory, one forming society and the other enthroning a king (caliph) to rule, Khadduri concluded that "the early Caliphate state, which was based on a double-contract theory, was obviously democratic; but its development under the impacts of Byzantine and Persian traditions gradually transformed it into an autocratic institution. The Muslim jurist-theologians, who on the whole tended to give an *apologia* of its historical development, failed to formulate a critical political philosophy which would point out the inherent justice and democratic spirit of the early contractual basis."[52] I would suggest, however, that the early caliphate developed into an autocratic institution more because of features inherent to Shari'a than because of the impact of Byzantine and Persian traditions. In other words, the "inherent justice and democratic spirit" of the Medina model of an Islamic state were outweighed by undemocratic features of the same model which were justified by the historical context, including the Byzantine and Persian traditions. The challenge facing the Muslims today is how to formulate a critical political philosophy that can overcome those elements of historical Shari'a that are inherently inconsistent with modern constitutionalism.

CONSTITUTIONAL ASSESSMENT OF OTHER RELEVANT ASPECTS OF SHARI'A

In my view, the inherent problems with the Shari'a state as the ideal to be pursued by Muslims today are more serious than the problems of realizing that "ideal." Even if that ideal were realized in practice today, it would still fall short of the standards of modern constitutionalism. Some of these inherent problems can be explained as follows.

The Constitutional Status of Muslims

Those subjects of the state who are formally identified as Muslims are the only full citizens of an Islamic state under Shari'a, with a theoretical entitlement to the full range of civil and political rights,[53] subject to the following limitations. First, any person who is formally identified as a Muslim may not become an apostate, whether by converting to another religion or by becoming an unbeliever. One may be deemed to be an apostate whenever the authorities hold him or her to be guilty of maintaining views and opinions incompatible with the basic tenets of Islam, regardless of his or her own view of their relationship to Islam.[54] In other words, belief in Islam is determined objectively by the authorities, and not subjectively by the person concerned.[55]

An often-cited justification for penalizing apostasy is the claim that such apostasy will undermine the integrity of the Muslim community and security of the Islamic state. One author, for example, started with the premise that the Islamic state is a doctrinal or ideological state designed to uphold and promote the values of Shari'a. He defined the nation as a human society based on common beliefs. Consequently, he maintained that all individual rights and freedoms are limited by the principle prohibiting deviation from the ideology of the state or advocacy of a different ideology because this would amount to an act of civil disobedience and a call to rise against the state in order to abolish its Islamic character. He stated that those who renounce Islam, its ideology, and its law have no choice but to refrain from identifying with that state and society and must seek to identify with another state and society.[56]

This line of reasoning is, in my view, both false with reference to apostasy and objectionable from a constitutional point of view. It is false with reference to apostasy because private apostasy per se is punishable by death under Shari'a, regardless of whether or not the apostate publicized his or her views or advocated them.[57] Moreover, and even if we accept, for the sake of argument, the claim that Shari'a punishes an apostate by death only if he publicized and advocated his views, such a principle would violate the fundamental constitutional freedoms of belief, expression, and association. Whereas a Christian, for example, would be encouraged to convert to Islam and preach his new faith to others, a Muslim who converts to Christianity would be punished by death, regardless of whether he preached his Christian faith.

In a thoughtful study, S. A. Rahman, a former chief justice of Pakistan, argued that the death penalty should not be imposed for peaceful apostasy per se.[58] He did not consider the other civil and personal law consequences of apostasy.[59] One may accept or reject the validity of Rahman's argument for abolishing the death penalty for peaceful apostasy within the framework of Shari'a. As a constitutional matter, however, the point to emphasize is that Shari'a not only punishes a Muslim apostate but also subjects him or her to a number of other negative civil and personal law consequences.[60] This is inconsistent with the constitutional freedoms of belief, expression, and association.

The second limitation on the civil and political rights of Muslims has to do with the freedom of women to exercise their rights. Although Muslim women are entitled to hold any opinion deemed to be within the basic tenets of Islam, Shari'a's restrictions on their right to appear and speak in public and associate with Muslim men in furtherance of their opinions[61] impose severe limitations on the civil and political rights of both Muslim women and men.

Third, besides the above-noted restrictions on their right to participate in public life, Muslim women are also disqualified by Shari'a from holding any public office that involves the exercise of authority over Muslim men. This general principle of Shari'a is said to be based on verse 4:34 of the Qur'an, which states that men are the guardians and protectors (*qawamun*) of women. Thus, for example, while the Shafi'i school disqualifies women from holding any judicial office whatsoever, the Hanafi school allows them to be judges in civil cases only.[62]

The reasoning of the Hanafi school in allowing women to hold some judicial office is based on another disqualification of Muslim women, namely that since they are accepted as competent witnesses in civil and commercial transactions, they may act as judges in similar cases. The underlying disqualification, as we shall see in the next chapter, is that whereas women may testify in civil and commercial matters, as provided in verse 2:282 of the Qur'an, they are not accepted as competent witnesses in the more serious *hudud* criminal offenses. Moreover, according to the rule based on this verse, it takes two women to make a single witness in cases in which the testimony of women is accepted at all.

Although there were sociological and political justifications in the past for restrictions and disqualifications imposed by Shari'a over women, such justifications, I believe, are no longer valid. Moreover, it is inadequate to say that these disqualifications were frequently disregarded in practice. It is both wrong and dangerous to argue that legal discrimination is less objectionable because it will not be strictly enforced in practice. It is wrong for society to maintain a law it does not intend to enforce because people can no longer take the law as a reliable guide to permissible and impermissible conduct. To maintain a law without intending to enforce it is dangerous because it leaves too much discretion in the hands of those charged with enforcing the law, enabling them to select cases for enforcement based on selfish and other corrupt purposes.

The Constitutional Status of Non-Muslims

Shari'a does not conceive of the permanent residence of unbelievers, as identified by Shari'a itself, within the Islamic state except under temporary license *(aman)* which defines the terms and conditions of their presence. Unless they have been granted the equivalent of the status of *dhimma*, to be explained below, unbelievers have no civil and political rights whatsoever under Shari'a, even if they happened to be born and permanently resident within the territory of the Islamic state.[63] Consequently, such subjects of the state, even if allowed security to their persons and property under *aman*, have no right to participate in the public life of the community at large. They may not have even communal autonomy in their private affairs unless they have been granted the status of *dhimma*.

Initially, the status of *dhimma* was offered to those subjects of the Islamic state who were identified by Shari'a as believers in one of the heavenly revealed scriptures *(ahl al-kitab)*.[64] As the criterion by which *ahl al-kitab* were identified was gradually relaxed by the Muslim jurists,[65] the status of *dhimma* was applied to unbelievers who were allowed to stay within the territory of an Islamic state for more than one year. Whoever is granted the status of *dhimma* is entitled under Shari'a to protection of his or her person and property and to practice his or her religion in private in exchange for payment of poll tax *(jizya)*.[66]

Jizya was not imposed on non-Muslims until late in the Medina stage.[67] Muslim scholars usually emphasize that though subject to *jizya*, non-Muslims are not subject to payment of religious tax *(zaka)*, which is required by Shari'a from Muslims alone.[68] Moreover, they argue that *jizya* was required from non-Muslims in exchange for protection by the Muslims because they were exempt from fighting in Muslim armies.[69] This is not an accurate statement of the position under Shari'a, which disqualifies non-Muslims rather than exempting them from having to fight in defense of themselves. Exemption implies request, or at least the choice of the person being so exempt, whereas under Shari'a non-Muslims have no choice in accepting the status of being defended by the Muslims in exchange for payment of *jizya*.[70] As to the first point that *jizya* is in lieu of *zakat*, this is also unsatisfactory in modern constitutional terms. *Jizya* was intended, by the terms of the Qur'an itself, to signify submission and humiliation of the non-Muslims who had to pay it.[71] It was clearly perceived as such by both sides.[72]

A community of *dhimmis*, that is, a community enjoying a compact of *dhimma* with the Muslims, is entitled under Shari'a to govern itself in personal and private matters, while remaining subject to the jurisdiction of the Islamic state in public affairs.[73] Shari'a prescribes that jurisdiction in all the public affairs of the state must always remain within the exclusive domain of Muslims.[74] Consequently, *dhimmis* have freedom of opinion or belief, expression, and association within their own community and only in relation to private practice of their religion and to the conduct of their personal affairs within the framework of the particular community of *dhimmis*.[75]

Equality before the Law

All the above-noted aspects of historical Shari'a in relation to women and *dhimmis* violate the constitutional principle of equality before the law. Further examples of inequality and discrimination on grounds of gender and religion under Shari'a can be listed under this heading.

First, as we shall see in the next chapter, Shari'a penal law discriminates among citizens according to gender and religion. For example, *diyia* (monetary compensation paid to surviving blood relatives of a victim of certain types of homicide) for killing a woman or *dhimmi* is less than that for killing a Muslim male.[76] Moreover, the reputation of a *dhimmi* is not valued in the same way as the reputation of a Muslim. Thus, one of Shari'a's requirements for imposing the *hadd* for *qadhf* (the strictly prescribed punishment for unproved accusation of fornication) is that the person accused of fornication without proof must be a Muslim.[77] Although a lesser punishment may be imposed at the discretion of the authorities for *qadhf* of a *dhimmi*, the humiliating and discriminatory implications of the distinction have obvious psychological and social consequences.

Second, Shari'a law of evidence discriminates among witnesses on grounds of gender and religion. The testimony of women and *dhimmis* is inadmissible in the more serious criminal cases of *hudud* and *qisas*, to be explained in the next chapter. In civil matters, the testimony of Muslim women is accepted, but it takes two women to make a single witness.[78] None of these restrictions applies to the testimony of a Muslim male, who is always a fully competent *(adl)* witness under Shari'a unless disqualified by his specific personal conduct.

The details of these two types of discrimination on grounds of gender and religion will be discussed in greater detail in Chapter 5. As we shall see, there are some differences of opinion among the various jurists and schools of jurisprudence over the precise scope of these and other discriminatory principles and rules of Shari'a. Nevertheless, all schools and jurists agree that women and *dhimmis* are not treated in complete equality with Muslim men in the administration of criminal justice.

Finally, the personal law of Shari'a presents a third source of discrimination against Muslim women and *dhimmis*. According to Shari'a family law, for example, a Muslim male can marry up to four wives and divorce any of them at will without having to justify or explain his decision to any person or authority. In contrast, a Muslim woman is confined to one husband at a time and can obtain a divorce only through the courts on very strict grounds or through the consent of the husband.[79]

Another example of discrimination against Muslim women in Shari'a family law is the general right of the husband to exercise guardianship and control over his wife to the extent of chastising her in a variety of ways, including beating her "lightly" if he deems her to be "unruly" *(nashidh)*.[80] The mere existence of this license for the husband to discipline his wife by beating her is totally incompatible with the human dignity of all women, whether or not a particular woman is likely to become victim of such humiliation.

Shari'a's prohibition of marriage between a Muslim woman and a non-Muslim man while permitting a Muslim man to marry a *kitabiya*, for example, a Christian or Jewish woman,[81] is an example of discrimination on grounds of both gender and religion.

Another example of discrimination against Muslim women is to be found in the Shari'a law of inheritance *(mirath)*. The general rule of *mirath* is that a female is entitled to half the share of a male who has the same degree of relationship to the deceased.[82]

Modern Muslim writers seek to defend Shari'a on all of these features of discrimination against women and *dhimmis* by citing historical sociological and political justifications. Although the acceptance or rejection of a given justification as valid is a subjective matter, generally prevailing notions of justice and reasonableness have a role to play in the process. For example, whereas slavery may have been accepted as justifiable in the past, no one would claim that it is now. It is my submission that these elements of discrimination against women and non-Muslims cannot be accepted as justifiable by the standards of justice and reasonableness prevailing today.

Enforcement Mechanisms and Remedies

The question of remedies is of vital importance to every aspect of constitutionalism. Not only the rights and liberties of individuals and groups of persons, but also every other aspect of the most basic and fundamental regulations of the incidence, transfer, and exercise of power are rendered meaningless without effective remedies to ensure compliance and further development of these rights and regulations. For every right, guarantee, or regulation, there must be a clear and effective method of enforcement and implementation short of revolutionary force. It has been said that the lack of such remedies was the fundamental weakness of all medieval European constitutionalism.[83] This was also true of the historical Muslim experience.

Although judicial remedies against the abuse and excess of powers are of primary importance for constitutionalism, they are neither sufficient where they do apply nor appropriate to every conceivable violation of constitutionalism. Judicial remedies need to be supplemented by a variety of structural and institutional devices and to be supported by an enlightened and active public opinion expressing a political culture that is conducive to constitutionalism. The human factor of individual judgment and discretion in government is not only unavoidable but desirable. At one level, general policies and formal enactments find their proper interpretation and application in daily life through such judgment and discretion. At another level, officials charged with supervising the interpretation and implementation of policies and laws and adjudicating in cases of dispute also have to exercise judgment and discretion in holding officials bound and accountable to the legal limits of their powers. To facilitate the proper exercise of judgment and discretion at both levels of the processes of government, the constitution must provide for a clear structure of powers as well as for open and accessible channels and mechanisms of communication and mutual limitation among officials. This will enhance the efficacy of public action to ensure compliance with the letter and intent of the constitution and other laws of the land.

In accordance with this line of thinking, it has been devised that the legislative, executive, and judicial functions should be exercised by separate agencies, acting in accordance with different procedures, preferably conducted by different persons or bodies. Under such a scheme, it would be much more difficult for any of the three organs to exceed or abuse its powers or to conspire with another organ to that end. The purpose of separation of powers is thus to minimize the risk of collusion between those who provide legal authority for action (the legislature), those who interpret and act upon such authority (the executive), and those who may have to adjudicate in case of conflict or dispute (the judiciary).

Too rigid a separation, however, may lead to the undesirable result of weakening and hampering effective government, which may be desperately needed in times of crisis.[84] To guard against the dangers of such rigidity, attempts have been made to make the three organs mutually dependent and generally to seek to maintain a balance between the benefits of separation of powers and the dangers of obstruction and hindrance of the smooth operation of government.

In any case, objections to an overly rigid separation are not an argument for the complete fusion of powers in one person or body of persons. In particular, the separation and independence of the judiciary is a vital component of constitutionalism. Without an independent, fair, and strong judiciary to enforce judicial remedies and render credibility to extrajudicial devices, the whole scheme of constitutionalism would collapse.[85]

These notions of separation of powers, and especially the independence of the judiciary, appear to be successful in their countries of origin, the liberal democracies of the West. Although that success may recommend separation of powers and independence of the judiciary for constitutionalism elsewhere in the world, one should be careful to distinguish the principal and essential purpose of these devices from their specific form and practice in any particular political and cultural context. What needs to be achieved is the fundamental objective of structuring and limiting the powers of government in terms of their legitimate rationale and justification. Whatever device is capable of achieving this objective is welcome, provided it is well suited to the cultural tradition of the state in question.

Shari'a neither established a regular and effectively enforced procedure for the appointment and subsequent accountability of the caliph or his equivalent, nor did it seek to impose legal limitations on his powers. For all practical purposes, the caliph combined all ultimate legislative, executive, and judicial powers and was not accountable to any human agency. Coulson characterized the situation under Shari'a as follows:

> Concentrating upon the ideal of a government wholly in accordance with the letter and the spirit of the divine law, the jurists completely subordinated the principle of the individual liberty to that of the public interest and welfare. For under this ideal form of government, they argue, all men will naturally receive their due rights. The supreme paradox, which leads to an outright nullification of this pious ideal, lies in the fact that the Shari'a fails to provide any guarantee that government will, in practice, assume this ideal form, and that, far from ensuring the existence of practical remedies against the ruler's abuse of his recognized powers, it simply counsels acceptance of such abuse.[86]

Therefore, from the legal constitutional point of view, Shari'a's theoretical limitations on the caliph, or his modern equivalent, were not very meaningful because there was no regular and orderly way of enforcing them.[87] Muslim scholars have debated for centuries whether it is permissible to depose the caliph once he has been duly appointed. Both sides in the controversy have cited Qur'anic and Sunna texts in support of their positions.[88] In any case, and even if we assume that the right to depose a caliph who violates Shari'a exists, there is no mechanism or procedure by which the issue could be resolved in a peaceful and orderly manner.[89] It is precisely for this reason that almost all leading historical Muslim scholars who addressed constitutional issues have emphasized the duty to obey the ruler, however evil and wrongdoing he may be.[90]

Some contemporary Muslim authors have attempted to create an effective enforcement mechanism for the limitation of the caliph by the terms of Shari'a. Taj al-Din al-Nabhani, for example, suggested that a caliph who violated Shari'a ought to be deposed through a legal ruling issued by a legal body/court. Should the caliph refuse to abide by the ruling of this court, the Muslims would be required to depose him because their original approval of his appointment would no longer be binding on them.[91] Such efforts are clearly based on the principles of modern constitutionalism and will have to be promoted if those principles are to be implemented. For example, there must be clear provision for the independence and efficacy of the body/court that may depose the ruler. It should not be left to the discretion of the ruler himself whether to comply with a decision to depose him.[92]

THE SHARI'A STATE IN CURRENT MUSLIM THINKING

As illustrated by the extensive survey of current Muslim thinking on an Islamic state offered in Chapter 3, the major constitutional problems of Shari'a remain unresolved. The main features of one of the better works by a proponent of Shari'a, Muhammad Asad's *Principles of State and Government in Islam*, emphasize the inadequacy of this approach in light of the foregoing discussion of the principle of constitutionalism and its implications.

　　Although he maintained that the Qur'an and Sunna did not lay down any specific form of state and that Shari'a did not elaborate a detailed constitutional theory, Asad nevertheless held that any form of an Islamic state must be in full agreement with the explicit, unequivocal Shari'a relating to communal life. He stated early in his book that *"Shari'ah* cannot be changed because it is a Divine law; and need not be changed because all its ordinances are so formulated that none of them ever conflict with the real nature of man and the genuine requirements of human society at any time: simply because it legislates only with regard to those aspects of human life which by their very nature are not subject to change." He then says that Shari'a consists of either general principles, within which detailed rules can be introduced through *ijtihad*, or detailed rules in matters not affected by changes caused by man's social development. He also envisaged room for *ijtihad* in matters not covered by Shari'a.[93]

　　In accordance with his view that the Qur'an and Sunna do not lay down any specific form of state and that Shari'a does not elaborate in detail a constitutional theory, he maintains that there are many forms for the Islamic state so long as it is in full agreement with the explicit, unequivocal Shari'a law relating to communal life.[94] Thus, placing his model squarely within the confines of Shari'a, he proceeds, in subsequent chapters, to state and defend what he calls the political laws of Shari'a in relation to a variety of public law issues. I will focus on some key issues.

Since he took the purpose of an Islamic state to be not "self-determination" for a racial or cultural entity but the establishment of Islamic law as a practical proposition in human affairs, it is obvious, he says, that only a person who believes in the divine origin of that law — in a word, a Muslim — may be entrusted with the office of head of state.[95] But this logic would disqualify non-Muslims from holding any office involving the interpretation and application of Shari'a and not only the office of head of state. Moreover, since he holds that the rules of Shari'a are unchangeable, such disqualification will have to apply because it is provided for by Shari'a.

On this issue, however, he avoided the situation of women. He maintained that apart from the stipulation that the *amir* (ruler or head of state) be a Muslim and be mature, wise, and superior in character, Shari'a does not specify any further conditions for eligibility to the office. This statement is not accurate because, according to Shari'a, the imam or ruler must be a man. Again, though he notes that the *majlis* (elective assembly charged with legislative functions) must be representative of the entire community, both men and women, he does not expressly say whether women may be elected to that body.[96]

In case of disagreement between the *majlis* and executive organ, says Asad, the fundamental difference is to be referred to a body of arbiters, who, after an impartial study of the problem, would decide which of the two conflicting views is closer to the spirit of the Qur'an and Sunna. The same "impartial supreme tribunal," he maintains, would have the power to veto legislation and administrative acts that offend against texts of the Qur'an and Sunna. Members of this supreme tribunal, says Asad, must be selected through consultations between the executive and *majlis*, and be guaranteed security of tenure and other safeguards.[97]

Throughout his model, Asad is strongly concerned with constitutional questions relating to the nature and powers of the various organs of the state. Thus, in various chapters of his book, he deals with issues such as government by consent and council and the relationships between the executive and the legislature and between citizens and government.[98] This concern is no doubt encouraging because it indicates a commitment to constitutionalism. But Muslims with this commitment should realize that it is impossible to achieve constitutionalism through the application of Shari'a.

Muslims like Asad are at least sensitive to the issues and can appreciate the arguments made in this chapter. Unfortunately, we have to deal with others who may not be able to conceive the issues. This is likely to be the case among Muslims who continue to adhere to the old highly specific model of an Islamic state. A good example can be found in a document produced by al-Azhar Islamic University of Cairo in 1978 and entitled "Proposal for the Islamic Constitution."[99]

Article 1(b) of this proposed draft of the "Islamic Constitution" specifies that Islamic Shari'a is the source of all legislation. Article 4 states that the people shall supervise the imam, his deputies, and all governors and hold them to account in accordance with the provisions of Shari'a. These articles set the tone for the rest of the constitution. Many of the specialized provisions are specifically linked or made subject to Shari'a.

Chapter 2 of al-Azhar's proposed draft constitution, dealing with the foundations of the Islamic society, describes these foundations in terms of Shari'a, including the role of women, the content of education, and public conduct. To ensure that all aspects of society are in accordance with Shari'a, Article 17 states that in all situations, not only the objectives but also the methods adopted for their implementation must be in complete accord with the provisions of Shari'a.

The Islamic economy is the subject of chapter 2 of the proposal. Article 19 guarantees freedom of trade, industry, and agriculture within the provisions of Shari'a; Article 20 provides that the state shall plan for economic development in accordance with Shari'a. All specific provisions are derived from Shari'a, such as prohibition of *ribba*, interest on capital in all commercial and other transactions, the collection and distribution of *zaka*, Islamic religious tax, and the like.

Individual rights and liberties are also described in accordance with Shari'a. Article 29 provides that freedom of religious belief and opinion, freedom of expression and association, personal liberty, and freedom of movement are all natural rights guaranteed by the state within the limits of Shari'a. According to Article 37, the right to work and earn an income and the right to own property may not be interfered with except in accordance with Shari'a. Women may work, says Article 38, within the limits permitted by Shari'a. All other individual rights and liberties are either made subject to Shari'a or derived from its provisions, with Article 43 concluding the chapter with the requirement that all rights may be exercised only in accordance with Shari'a.

Chapter 5 of the proposal is devoted to the imam and starts with Article 44, which provides that the imam must be obeyed even when one disagrees with him, unless, says Article 45, he orders one to do something that is expressly prohibited by Shari'a. Article 47 requires that all candidates for the office of imam must be Muslim males, of the age of majority and sound mind, pious and knowledgeable of Shari'a. The drafting committee was divided over the issue, says proposed Article 48, of whether women should be allowed to vote for the imam or merely be permitted to request to be allowed to vote when qualified. Since Article 49 permits one to object to the appointment of a given person as imam before the imam's confirmation, *by'a*, it follows that no such objection is allowed after confirmation.

All the remaining articles of the proposal, dealing with the judiciary, *shura* (consultation), and government and general and transitional provisions, are either derived from Shari'a or made expressly subject to its provisions. A footnote to chapter 7 on *shura* provides that this chapter is to be omitted in countries that do not have councils of *shura*. This footnote reflects the view of al-Azhar that *shura* is neither obligatory nor binding on the ruler under Shari'a.

In view of the various constitutional problems of Shari'a, it is clear that any blanket incorporation of Shari'a in a constitutional document is unsatisfactory. In fact, al-Azhar's proposed constitution explicitly illustrates several of the points made. Two general points should be noted. First, the main question is not whether Shari'a requires a specific form of government; rather, it is whether Shari'a does or does not apply. If Shari'a is to apply, then all its features that discriminate against women and non-Muslim citizens will necessarily follow regardless of the form of government.

The second point illustrates the first. It is very interesting that a draft constitution produced in Egypt, a country with a significant non-Muslim minority, did not contain a single word about the status and rights of non-Muslim citizens. We are not even told whether these non-Muslims are citizens. The reason for this serious omission is clear enough. The document could not specify the rules of Shari'a on non-Muslims and yet claim to be a proposal for a constitution. It is for this reason that the document referred all relevant matters to Shari'a, in full knowledge of the status and rights of non-Muslim subjects under Shari'a.

A MODERN CONCEPTION OF AN ISLAMIC CONSTITUTIONAL STATE

The main commonly accepted features and implications of constitutionalism were explained at the beginning of this chapter. In my view, the best statement of these features and implications by an Islamic scholar is to be found in the work of the late Sudanese Muslim reformer *Ustadh* Mahmoud Mohamed Taha. According to *Ustadh* Mahmoud, constitutionalism is founded on two fundamental principles. First, every individual person is an end in himself/herself and must never be used as a means to another end. Second, society is the most effective means for achieving the ends of individual liberty and dignity.[100] Accordingly, the objectives and methods of constitutionalism must achieve the proper balance between the need of the individual for complete individual liberty and the need of the community for total social justice.[101]

To this end, the constitution must impose institutionalized and effective limitations on the powers of government in order to protect each and every individual subject of the state against interference with his or her personal liberty and autonomy. Yet the constitution may regulate and limit personal liberty in the interest of total social justice because the latter is an essential and indispensable means for achieving the former. It must be emphasized, however, that such regulation and limitation must be strictly justified with reference only to and through such methods as are fully consistent with the fundamental objectives of maintaining and enhancing the life, liberty, and dignity of every subject of the state. In other words, we must always keep in sight the proper relationship between the end of constitutionalism, enabling every person to achieve complete individual liberty, and its essential and indispensable means, enabling the community to achieve total social justice.

Consequently, and to make the protection and exercise of personal liberty meaningful, the constitution must strive to provide for all necessary support for human life and material welfare through education, work opportunities, health, and other essential services. Constitutionalism encompasses, in my view, not only limitations on the powers of government but also the imposition of positive obligations on the government to maintain and enhance the life, liberty, and dignity of its citizenry.

It is obvious that various cultural and ideological traditions in the world today differ in their ranking of individual liberty and social justice. Moreover, such differences may exist within the same country or cultural and ideological tradition.[102] These differences among and within cultural and ideological traditions, I submit, do not dispute the equal importance of both aspects of constitutionalism. Rather, they merely pertain to the methods by which both aspects may be realized, the assumption being that one aspect will naturally flow from, or be achieved through, realizing the other. I believe that both aspects must be combined and pursued at the same time, one being the fundamental end and the other the essential and indispensable means. Otherwise, constitutionalism will not inspire the degree of national consensus and popular support it needs to thrive and develop.

To insist that both aspects of constitutionalism must be pursued simultaneously and with equal vigor is not to say that they ought to be so pursued through identical methods. The need for appropriate methods, however, should never be used as a pretext for undermining or postponing the realization of one aspect of constitutionalism or the other.

It is hoped that the discussion so far in this chapter has clearly shown that this conception of constitutionalism is unattainable under Shari'a. Without a new principle of interpretation capable of evolving an alternative conception of the public law of Islam, only two options would be open to modern Muslims: either abandon the public law of Shari'a or disregard constitutionalism. Whereas the first option appears to be unrealistic in view of the common belief of Muslims that they have a religious obligation to implement Islam in their public life, the second option is morally untenable and politically unacceptable in the context of the modern nation-state.

Fortunately, there is an Islamic alternative to the public law of Shari'a through the reform methodology proposed by *Ustadh* Mahmoud Mohamed Taha. When we apply this reform methodology to the constitutional problems of Shari'a explained in this chapter, we will find that all the problematic principles of Shari'a are based on texts of the Qur'an and Sunna of the Medina stage. The historical conception of the Shari'a state was developed during the Medina period, since the Muslims were not a political community and did not establish a state during the Mecca period. If we are to take the Medina model as one that was dictated by the political and social realities of the seventh century in accordance with the suggestion of *Ustadh* Mahmoud, we would not be bound to implement it under radically different modern conditions.

Moreover, all the objectionable aspects of Shari'a on the status and rights of women and non-Muslims noted in this chapter are also based on texts of the Qur'an and Sunna of the Medina stage. Again, by the same principle of interpretation proposed by *Ustadh* Mahmoud, the relevant Medina texts can now be superseded by those of the Mecca stage. The status and rights of women may be used as an example of the working of this principle.

It should be recalled that the fundamental principle of the subordination of women to men, which is taken as authority for disqualifying women from holding public office involving the exercise of authority over men, is that of the *qawama*, the guardianship and authority of men over women by virtue of the Medinese verse 4:34 of the Qur'an. The relevant part of this verse may be translated as follows: "Men have *qawama* (guardianship and authority) over women because of the advantage they [men] enjoy over them [women] and because they [men] spend their property in supporting them [women]." According to *Ustadh* Mahmoud, the *qawama* of men over women is made conditional, by the express terms of the verse, upon the security and economic dependence of women over men. Because this is no longer the case in a society in which both men and women are dependent for their security on the rule of law and women are, as a general rule, more capable of being economically independent, the rationale of *qawama* has been repudiated in practice.

When we take this analysis together with the general principle of the equality of men and women to be found in the Qur'an of the Mecca stage, argued *Ustadh* Mahmoud, we can only conclude that men and women must be equal today as a matter of law. This is the necessary first step in the long process of achieving such equality in practice.

Thus, through a combination of contextual analysis of the Medinese texts and invocation of more fundamental Meccan texts, *Ustadh* Mahmoud argued for the complete equality of men and women, Muslims and non-Muslims, thereby establishing the essential premise of modern constitutionalism as an Islamic principle.

This approach is Islamic because it applies the Qur'an and Sunna in supporting the principle and detailed rules of constitutionalism. Although Islam as a religion speaks of duties owed by the believer to God, Islamic law shall translate those into rights of human beings through the rational thinking and practical experience of the believers. The Qur'an does not mention constitutionalism, but human rational thinking and experience have shown that constitutionalism is necessary for realizing the just and good society prescribed by the Qur'an.

An Islamic justification and support for constitutionalism is important and relevant to Muslims. Non-Muslims may have their own secular or other justifications. As long as all are agreed on the principle and specific rules of constitutionalism, including complete equality and nondiscrimination on grounds of gender or religion, each may have his or her own reasons for coming to that agreement.

⟫ 5 ⟪

Criminal Justice

$\mathcal{T}$HE ADMINISTRATION OF CRIMINAL JUSTICE presents the most visible and controversial issues of the current debate over the application of Shari'a. Numerous problems of substantive law, evidence, and procedure are raised by the prospects of implementing this branch of Shari'a. These problems must be resolved at both the theoretical and practical levels *before* Islamic criminal law is implemented. As will be illustrated by the recent experience of the Sudan later in this chapter, the premature and arbitrary application of the penal law of Shari'a can only lead to extreme hardship and drastic political repercussions.

CRIMINAL JUSTICE IN THE MODERN NATION-STATE

The state seeks to maintain law and order and preserve security through the power to impose criminal punishments affecting the life, liberty, and property of the individual. The imposition of criminal punishment involves not only the possible loss of life, liberty, and property for the individual but also severe social stigma and psychological pain and suffering. That such drastic consequences can be justified as necessary for discharging the vital function of protecting public and private security should not obscure the very serious risks of abuse and manipulation of this power.

It is not surprising, therefore, that the administration of criminal justice has been singled out for special limitations and rigorous scrutiny under national constitutions and international instruments. It is significant, in my view, that the vast majority of modern Muslim states have adopted this special approach to criminal justice in their own national constitutions.[1] A large number of them have also subscribed to the relevant international instruments. Nevertheless, as I will demonstrate in this chapter, these constitutional and international standards for the administration of criminal justice are not fully consistent with Shari'a on the subject.

The following constitutional and international standards are derived from what I would call the consensus of the international community, as reflected in national constitutions and international instruments of high political and moral (if not legal) authority and weight such as the Universal Declaration of Human Rights of 1948[2] and the International Covenant on Civil and Political Rights of 1966.[3] The vast majority of Muslim countries have supported the Universal Declaration, either when it was adopted in 1948 or in subsequent United Nations resolutions and declarations.[4] Moreover, many Muslim countries are parties to the Civil and Political Rights Covenant of 1966 and are bound by it as an international treaty.[5]

One of the reasons Muslim countries are obligated to respect the standards set by international documents, especially in relation to the administration of criminal justice, is that they must protect the rights of aliens within their borders. All of these states have a significant number of aliens, some of whom are non-Muslims,[6] who are subject to the criminal jurisdiction of the country. Criminal jurisdiction is not confined to nationals of the country and normally includes whoever happens to be within the territory of the state, even if they are there for a short time. Thus, even Saudi Arabia, which purports to restrict its citizenship to Muslims alone,[7] has a significant and highly influential number of non-Muslims subject to its criminal jurisdiction. Under contemporary economic and political conditions, no country in the world is religiously monolithic, however traditional and "closed" it may wish to be.

Most of the constitutional and international standards of criminal justice pertain to the procedural aspects of the process in that they require minimum safeguards for a fair and valid determination of guilt or innocence.[8] These safeguards are predicated on the fundamental assumption of innocence and a requirement of proof of guilt by the accuser. Consequently, the accused person should not be required to prove his or her innocence. On the contrary, he or she must be afforded every opportunity to confront his or her accuser and challenge the evidence presented in support of the accusation as well as presenting his or her own rebuttal of the charge. Moreover, and in view of the increasing technicality of substantive and procedural criminal law, the accused person is generally said to be entitled to the benefit of expert legal advice in confronting the case for the prosecution and presenting his or her own defense. All of this is part of the general concept of a fair trial, which also includes safeguards as to the composition and independence of the tribunal and the way the hearing is conducted, as well as opportunities for postconviction appeal or review by a higher tribunal.

Furthermore, and to minimize hardship and avoid the dangers of the abuse of the criminal process in relation to an accused person, who is presumed to be innocent until proven guilty, procedural safeguards are generally required before the trial stage.[9] Thus, for example, no person is to be arrested, nor may his or her person and property be searched, without sufficient cause. Even when an arrest is justified, an arrested person should not be kept in pretrial custody except as strictly required by the efficiency and integrity of the investigation and trial of the accusation. Moreover, and in view of both the presumption of innocence and requirement of proof by the accuser, an accused person should not be subjected to torture to induce a confession of guilt.

Although constitutional and international standards usually relate to procedural matters, there are two matters often covered by these standards which are not strictly procedural, namely, what are generally known as the principle of legality and the question of punishment and treatment of convicted persons. In essence, the principle of legality is designed to give the public at large sufficient prior notice of what is prohibited by the criminal law so that they may behave accordingly.[10] It is generally deemed to be unfair for the state to punish those subject to its criminal jurisdiction for violating the law without having given them sufficient opportunity to comply with its dictates. Consequently, the legislature must define offenses in the clearest and most precise terms and the state publicize penal legislation before imposing punishment in accordance with its terms. As a corollary to the same principle, it is sometimes said that the courts must give the strictest or narrowest possible interpretation of penal legislation. In accordance with the individual's fundamental freedom of action and presumption of innocence, one should not be penalized except for conduct he or she can reasonably and realistically be deemed to have known to be prohibited under penalty of criminal punishment.

Constitutional and international standards are normally silent on what conduct may be prohibited and penalized by the criminal law, but some national constitutions and international instruments prohibit cruel and inhumane punishment or treatment.[11] The problem with this purported limitation on the nature and quality of punishment or treatment of offenders, however, is the obvious difficulty of defining the standards by which the cruelty and inhumanity of punishment or treatment may be determined. This difficulty is relevant to the penological justification of punishments sanctioned by Shari'a, to be discussed below.

Finally, there is a general principle that seems to underlie the power of the state to impose criminal sanction, although it is not expressly stated in national constitutions and international instruments. It is true that each society is entitled to determine for itself the proper scope of its penal law. This power, however, presupposes a certain process of penal legislation within the framework of a legitimate constitutional order. Provided that the function of determining which conduct is to be prohibited by the criminal law and how it should be punished is undertaken by the society at large, usually through its legitimate representatives in appropriate legislative organs, the imposition of criminal sanction may be taken as a proper exercise of national sovereignty.

What is indicated by this reasoning, however, is genuine and substantive rather than merely formal legality. Even when enacted through the regular and democratic legislative process, criminal punishments must seek to conform with the widest possible consensus of the society as a whole. In particular, due regard must be given to the legitimate expectations and concerns of ethnic, religious, and political minorities. The dictatorship of the majority takes its most dangerous and offensive form when it is reflected in the criminal law. The peculiar implications of this perspective for the enforcement of the criminal law of Shari'a in a multireligious society will become clear from the discussion later in this chapter. The key point is that national sovereignty over the substance of the criminal law is not a license for the majority to impose on the minority the majority's moral values and sense of the proper scope and content of the criminal law.

The validity and purported binding nature of any of the abovementioned constitutional and international standards will have to be based on a moral value judgment. The best argument one can provide in support of these standards is that since they are the minimum standards one would demand for himself or herself, one is morally bound to concede the same standards for others.

OVERVIEW OF CRIMINAL LAW UNDER SHARI'A

The early Muslim scholars and jurists did not distinguish between the religious, ethical, and legal aspects of Shari'a, let alone identify specific legal fields. Consequently, those principles and rules of Shari'a relevant to what is known in modern terminology as criminal law, evidence, and procedure can be extracted only from general and extensive treatises of Islamic jurisprudence.

Modern writers have identified three main categories of offenses: *hudud*, *jinayat*, and *ta'zir*. *Hudud* are said to be those named offenses for which a specific punishment is strictly applied without allowing discretion to either official or private body or person. *Jinayat* cover homicide and bodily harm and are punished by either *qisas* (exact retaliation) or payment of *diya* (monetary compensation) to the victim or his or her surviving kin. The last category, *ta'zir*, refers to the residual discretionary power of the ruler and his judges and deputies to reform and discipline their subjects.[12]

In view of the indiscriminate nature of the early treatises on Islamic jurisprudence, we cannot expect specialized treatment of questions of evidence and procedure. Moreover, since some of the relevant texts of the Qur'an and Sunna specified special evidentiary requirements for specific *hudud* offenses, the jurists stated and explained those requirements as part of the ingredients of the particular offense. For example, the *hadd* (singular of *hudud*) for *zina*, fornication, requires proof through the testimony of four male witnesses to the actual act of intercourse. This requirement and its details regarding the qualifications of the four witnesses and the implications of their testimony are discussed by early Muslim jurists as part and parcel of the definition of the offense itself.

With regard to procedural and practical aspects of criminal law enforcement, Shari'a is extremely rudimentary and informal. The broad and unstructured administrative discretion of the rulers and their officials described in the preceding chapter characterized all aspects of government, including the administration of criminal justice. For example, it was left to the discretion of the caliph whether to appoint specialized judges and how to supervise or regulate their activities. Those judges who were appointed (and other officials charged with judicial or quasi-judicial functions), in turn, had broad discretion over the conduct of pretrial and trial procedure.

Given the lack of reliable specialized historical information, it is difficult to provide a detailed survey of the actual administration of criminal justice in Muslim history. Nevertheless, the following general remarks can be offered. Although Shari'a principles were supposed to be enforced whenever they applied, one can safely assume that much administrative discretion was exercised in the administration of criminal justice at the various stages of Muslim history. This must have been particularly true after the early period of the Medina state (622 to 661 A.D.) and more likely to have been the case in rural and remote parts of the Muslim states.

Whatever may have been the precise arrangements for criminal justice, and whatever may have been the degree of their conformity to Shari'a at any given period of Muslim history, it is clear that the application of Shari'a criminal law was drastically reduced by the beginning of the twentieth century. Starting with the capitulations of the Ottoman Empire in the west of the Muslim world and corresponding concessions by the Mongol Empire in the east during the nineteenth century and the gradual colonization of Muslim lands by European powers, Western criminal law replaced Shari'a at the formal as well as the practical level.[13] This diminished application of Shari'a criminal law is better understood, I suggest, as being the result not only of growing Western influence throughout the Muslim world, but also of growing Muslim awareness of the inadequacy of the relevant Shari'a concepts. It may even be suggested that Western influence was the consequence rather than the cause of the diminished role of Shari'a in the administration of criminal justice.

Since attaining independence, mainly after World War II, however, many Muslim countries experienced mounting demands for the application of Shari'a criminal law. In response to criticisms of Shari'a criminal law as archaic and inadequate, the proponents of the total and immediate application of this branch of Shari'a have resorted to "anachronistic projections of modern principles of criminal justice back into a legal order in which they were completely unknown." In so doing, Muslim writers of this group display a high degree of eclecticism, quoting major figures of historical Islamic jurisprudence along with minor ones, jurists of the main schools along with ones from minor or extinct schools, Sunni scholars along with Shi'i ones, reformers along with traditionalists.[14]

It is misleading to use material from the work of early Islamic jurists in this way without indicating the criteria for preferring the opinion of one jurist over another or stating why one rule is taken from a given jurist while other rules stated by the same jurist are disregarded. When one accepts some aspects of a jurist's position while rejecting other aspects, one must state that clearly and proceed to show how the accepted aspects remain valid and binding without the rejected aspects. Moreover, this must be done within the basic perspective of, and through the interpretation and derivation techniques employed by, the author of the original source. Otherwise, one would not be justified in relying on that source as an authority for the given proposition or part thereof.

Despite the scholarly weakness, if not intellectual dishonesty, of the proponents of the total and immediate implementation of the criminal law of Shari'a, the strong influence of their religious logic upon the hearts and minds of Muslims should not be underestimated. Ordinary Muslims are usually torn between a sense of religious duty to comply with Shari'a and the practical difficulties of performing that duty. They are therefore likely to accept a misrepresentation of Shari'a that claims to resolve any ambivalence or anxiety on the particular issue rather than face the responsibility of reinterpretation and reformulation of Shari'a itself. Nevertheless, the substance and essential validity of the objections raised by the opponents of the modern application of the criminal law of Shari'a must be admitted and addressed. It is the purpose of this chapter to do so in a preliminary and tentative fashion. This effort must be seen, however, within the context of the general thesis and main objectives of this book as a whole.

SOURCE, DEFINITION, AND PENOLOGICAL JUSTIFICATION OF *HUDUD*

Horrific images of amputations of hands and feet, crucifixion, execution, and whipping, which are the punishments specified by Shari'a for *hudud*, are the dominant popular perceptions of the application of Islamic law. Although the enforcement of these punishments appears to be the highest priority of those Muslims who advocate the total and immediate application of Shari'a, there are several serious problems with the identification and definition of these offenses. It would not be possible to discuss here the detailed ingredients of all the offenses that are usually included in this class, but we can discuss some initial and fundamental problems with respect to the source from which this class of offenses is derived, give some examples of the definitional problems associated with these offenses, and reflect on the question of the relevance of penological justifications in relation to them.

Source of *Hudud*

The main distinguishing feature of *hudud* is the invariability of punishment, that is, the requirement that the specified punishment must be imposed once the offense reaches the knowledge of the authorities and is proved in accordance with Shari'a, regardless of the wishes of the victim or the authorities. Neither the victim nor the authorities have any discretion in the matter once the offense is reported. This is the crucial distinction between *hudud*, on one hand, and *jinayat* (homicide and other bodily harm) and *ta'zir* (discretionary punishments), on the other. Although the punishments for *jinayat* are provided by express texts of the Qur'an, the same texts permit discretion as to whether to prosecute, as well as allowing a choice between exacting *qisas* (exact retaliation) or accepting *diya* (monetary compensation).

Except for the doubtful *hudud* of *sukr* (intoxication) and *ridda* (apostasy), there is no Islamic religious authority for abolishing any *hadd* offense in principle, although there may be much room for varying the general and specific conditions for the particular offense within the usually broad limits of Qur'an and Sunna. In other parts of this study, a radical approach to reforming the public law aspects of Shari'a has been suggested because Qur'anic authority can be cited for the alternative modern principle. There is no such Qur'anic authority for abolishing the *hudud* in principle. What can be done, from the Islamic point of view, is to restrict their application in practice.

One of the fundamental questions in determining the number of *hudud* and the definition of each *hadd* is the source from which they are derived: are they restricted only to those offenses for which the punishment is strictly prescribed in the Qur'an or do they include offenses for which punishment is prescribed by Sunna alone? The position taken by the majority of the founding jurists is that *hudud* are offenses for which punishment is strictly prescribed by *either* the Qur'an *or* Sunna. According to this view, *hudud* are six, namely, *sariqa* (theft),[15] *haraba* (rebellion or highway robbery),[16] *zina* (fornication),[17] *qadhf* (unproven accusation of fornication),[18] *sukr* (intoxication),[19] and *ridda* (apostasy from Islam).[20]

Some of the treatises on Islamic jurisprudence mention a seventh *hadd,* called *al-baghy,* which involves armed rebellion against the Muslim state.[21] But since the verse of the Qur'an usually cited as the source of this alleged *hadd* does not contemplate an individual punishment,[22] the independent existence of *hadd al-baghy* is doubtful. If there is to be a *hadd* punishment for violent rebellion against the state, it may be based on another source, possibly the verse on *haraba,* as will be suggested later in this section.

In view of the extreme harshness of the prescribed punishments and the negative political consequences of their enforcement, I believe that it is better, as a matter of principle as well as policy, to restrict the requirement of invariability of punishment for *hudud* to those offenses for which the Qur'an provides the specific invariable punishment. If this is to be the criterion, *hudud* would be restricted to the first four offenses, *sariqa, haraba, zina,* and *qadhf,* because these are the only offenses for which specific punishments are strictly prescribed by the clear and definite text of the Qur'an. Moreover, this restrictive view of the source of *hudud* is recommended by certain problems associated with the other two alleged *hudud, sukr* and *ridda.* With respect to *sukr* (intoxication), neither the Qur'an nor Sunna prescribed a specific punishment.[23] In view of the wide difference of opinion among Muslim jurists over many aspects of this offense, including the specific number of lashes to be administered upon conviction,[24] it is curious that the jurists have agreed on classifying the offense as a *hadd.*[25] Since the Prophet did not administer any punishment for drinking alcohol in some cases and ordered the infliction of an indeterminate number of lashes in others, it can be argued that the cases in which he did order punishment were specific instances of his exercise of the power of ta'zir (discretionary punishment) rather than prescribing a specific and invariable punishment that makes the offense a hadd.

Again, although ridda (apostasy) is condemned by the Qur'an in the strongest terms, the Qur'an does not prescribe any punishment for apostasy in this life.[26] Nevertheless, the majority of Muslim jurists have classified apostasy as a hadd punishable by death as prescribed in Sunna.[27] Such classification violates the fundamental right of freedom of religion, sanctioned by the Qur'an in numerous verses. Relying on the higher authority of the Qur'an for freedom of conscience, and arguing that the available Sunna imposing the death penalty can be explained by the special circumstances of the cases in question, some modern Muslim writers have maintained that apostasy is not a hadd.[28] This approach, however, does not address the other negative consequences of apostasy under Shari'a, nor does it preclude the imposition of another punishment for apostasy under the discretionary power of ta'zir. To remove all constitutional and human rights objections, the legal concept of apostasy and all its civil and criminal consequences must be abolished. Whatever Sunna authority may exist for penal and other legal consequences of apostasy should be taken as transitional and no longer applicable in accordance with the evolutionary principle explained in Chapter 3.

One problem with excluding Sunna as a source of hudud is that the punishment of stoning to death for zina (fornication) when committed by a married person is based on Sunna. The Qur'an specified one hundred lashes for zina, without reference to the marital status of the offender, while Sunna makes the punishment stoning to death if the offender is a married person. The use of Sunna to support the harsher punishment in this case may be distinguished from its use as a source of hudud, as such, in that zina is a hadd by virtue of the Qur'an, with Sunna merely imposing a harsher punishment under certain specified aggravating circumstances.[29]

Problems of Definition

Even when taken from the Qur'an alone, hudud raise serious problems of definition and scope. Because the Qur'an is a religious text, it gives little guidance in the relevant verses as to the legal definition and specific ingredients of each hadd. The founding jurists constructed their own understanding of each hadd through the use of Sunna and other available traditions. Since the matter can be taken to be one of juristic judgment on the authenticity and interpretation of the relevant traditions, there may still be substantial room for legislative discretion in determining the definition and ingredients of each *hadd*. This is so because the strict invariability of punishment for *hudud* presupposes the establishment of both the general and specific conditions for liability.

Legislative discretion can, of course, go either way. It can be used either to restrict or to expand the scope of the offense and its application in practice. It is submitted, however, that sound modern policy suggests a restricted rather than a broad scope for any of the *hudud*. To illustrate the definitional problem, its potential for abuse, and possibilities of a restrictive interpretation, I will discuss the *hadd* of *haraba*. The same logic would apply, I submit, to other *hudud*.

The starting point of our discussion of this *hadd* is, of course, its Qur'anic foundation, namely verse 5:33 of the Qur'an, which may be translated as follows: "The punishment of those who wage war *(uharibun)* against God and His Apostle, and strive with might to effect mischief or corruption *(fasadan)* through the land, is to be executed, or crucified or to have their hands and feet from opposite sides amputated [cross-amputation of the right hand and left foot], or be banished from the land. That is their disgrace in this life, and great punishment awaits them in the next life." This verse is cited in classical treatises as authority for the offense of *haraba*, which translates as rebellion, although the same offense is sometimes called *qat al-tariq*, which translates as highway robbery.[30] It is obvious that beyond the difference in terminology is a much more serious difference in the conception of the offense itself and of its necessary ingredients.[31] The definition of the offense and its essential ingredients clearly depend on the answer to the basic question: is this simply a property offense aggravated by the use of force against an isolated and defenseless victim, or is it a political offense, involving armed dissent, civil war, and large-scale strife with incidental loss or destruction of property? Which conduct warrants the extremely harsh punishment prescribed in the verse quoted above?

It may be argued that only armed rebellion, threatening the very fabric of society and security of the state, warrants this degree of harshness. Specific instances of homicide and bodily harm may be punishable as *jinayat* (homicide and bodily harm) and the forcible taking of property per se may be punished through the discretionary power of *ta'zir*, since it would not constitute the *hadd* of *sariqa* (theft) as defined by the jurists.[32] Moreover, property interests are also protected by the civil remedy of restitution.[33]

A possible objection to the above interpretation is that directing the offense under verse 5:33 of the Qur'an to political dissent carries a greater risk of abuse by official authorities. This danger may be reduced by restricting the *hadd* offense contemplated by the verse to violent serious rebellion and not merely to pacifist nonviolent political dissent. The key word in verse 5:33, *uharibun* (which translates as wage war), clearly indicates violent armed rebellion rather than peaceful political dissent or disagreement.

Alternatively, it may be argued that the verse is addressed to all armed attacks, whether motivated by political objectives and directed against the state or seeking unlawful gain through terrorizing private persons. This broader interpretation can be supported by the language of the verse in that highway robbery is also, in a sense, waging war against God and His Apostle and effecting mischief or corruption *(fasadan)* in the land. It can be argued that this conduct, too, threatens the fabric of society and the prospects of peaceful life under the law.

The broad scope of the term *fasadan* (mischief or corruption) mentioned in verse 5:33 opens the way to extremely broad and oppressive interpretations when used as a separate category independent from the use of force. The grammatical construction of the verse may permit the inclusion of nonviolent "mischief and corruption" if the first part, "waging war," is taken in a metaphorical sense. Such a broad and oppressive interpretation can only be excluded by a definite policy decision in favor of a restrictive interpretation.

It is not within the scope of the present book to make the policy determination upon which the choice between these, and possibly other, competing interpretations should be made. What is emphasized here is that these problems of scope and definition must receive the widest possible debate among Muslims and be resolved at the broadest and deepest political level, with due regard to appropriate policy and practical considerations, *prior* to attempting any implementation of *hudud* today. Such debate and resolution, it would seem, should take into account the penological justifications of *hudud* and the political and sociological circumstances within which they are supposed to apply.

Relevance of Penological Justification

The initial question here is whether, to what extent, or in what sense are penological and sociological justifications and political realities relevant to the conception and application of *hudud*? Is the principle of *hudud* a religious imperative or is it open to question in penological and sociological theory and practice? Assuming that the principle is a religious imperative for Muslims, is the application of *hudud* nevertheless subject to political and other considerations with respect to non-Muslims? How are both aspects of the principle and practice affected by social and political pluralism in the modern nation-state?

According to the logic of Shari'a as a religious law, once the Qur'an and Sunna speak clearly and definitely, the believer has no choice but to comply.[34] When all consideration of the relevant texts and their interpretations is exhausted, compliance with the conclusion becomes imperative for the believer. Search for rational justification may help the believer to understand the wisdom and rationale of the rule, but failure to find sufficient objective justification does not relieve him or her of the duty to comply. In this way, and as far as Muslims are concerned, penological and sociological considerations cannot affect the principle of *hudud*. In other words, the existence of *hudud* as part of the criminal law of an Islamic state is not dependent on the existence or strength of penological or sociological justifications. Nevertheless, it seems obvious to me that the practical application of *hudud* is subject to political factors, part of which is the strength of the religious commitment of the community as a whole and its sense of penological and sociological justification of these offenses.

Contemporary penological literature seeks to determine penal policy in considerations such as retribution, deterrence, and reform of the offender. The application and implications of a given penological justification are usually discussed at a theoretical level to formulate a hypothesis, which is then tested through empirical research. Underlying both levels of arguments, however, is a value judgment on the appropriateness of penalizing the particular conduct and the reasonableness and efficacy of the prescribed punishment. Whether or not it is admitted, penological debate is based on a personal or collective view of the seriousness of the conduct in question and the reasonableness of the punishment.

This is particularly true of retribution but is also relevant to deterrence and reform. Retribution, the sense that the conduct of the offender deserves to be punished in a particular way, is obviously based on a value judgment of the moral culpability of the conduct. This, in turn, is based, in part, on an assessment of the magnitude of the harm done to some individual or social interest. Considerations of deterrence, whether of the particular offender or of other potential offenders, and reform of the offender through punishment, are based on certain assumptions regarding patterns and motivations of human behavior. Nevertheless, the decision to implement a particular punishment for a given offense, even when justified as deterrent or reformative, is based on the value judgment that it is not too excessive or disproportionate to the offense. In other words, the excessive unreasonableness of a given punishment may be deemed to outweigh its deterrent value or defeat its potential for reform and therefore lead to its exclusion.

When applied to *hudud*, this analysis may lead to the following conclusions. Our independent human sense of justice may find that, for example, amputation of the right hand is excessively harsh punishment for *sariqa* (theft). Again, we may feel that stoning to death is excessively harsh punishment for *zina* (fornication) by a married person. Such views of the appropriateness of the *hudud* punishments are based on our value judgment of the moral culpability and social consequences of the conduct in question. From the religious point of view, however, a believer must hold any human value judgment to be subordinate to divine judgment as expressed in revelation. He or she should accept divine value judgment and seek to justify and understand it rather than reject it on the basis of his or her own independent human value judgment.

Given this religious imperative, a Muslim is supposed to believe that the specified *hudud* punishments are appropriate and will achieve any conceivable social and personal good because God prescribed them. From this point of view, it is futile to look for cultural indication of *hudud* punishments.[35] For the believer, the punishment is strictly prescribed because God said so.

Nevertheless, and however convincing religious logic may be to a believer, it should be conceded that it has no validity for a nonbeliever. Unless *hudud* can be justified on rational grounds, these laws cannot be reasonably enforced against non-Muslims because they would not appreciate their religious rationale and would not be able to benefit from their ultimate religious good.

Ustadh Mahmoud has maintained that the principle of *al-mu'awadah* (retribution and reciprocity), which underlies *hudud* (and *qisas*, an eye for an eye), "emanate from the fundamental source of life. These are not religious law in the common sense of the term." As such, this general principle can be appreciated by all human beings, regardless of their religion or other belief. He stated that these punishments are appropriate because they serve the interests of the aggressor as well as those of the victim and society at large. They serve the interest of the aggressor by enhancing his awareness of the magnitude of the harm he has inflicted upon the victim. Taking the example of someone who pulls out the eye of another person in a fit of anger, *Ustadh* Mahmoud explained his point as follows: "If he received retribution by being placed in the same position as his victim, and his eye is pulled out in reciprocity *(mu'awadah)* for what he had done, then two purposes would have been served at the same time. Firstly, the interest of the community would be preserved by deterring the aggressor himself, as well as deterring others by his example. Secondly, the aggressor deepens his sensitivity, by himself experiencing the pain he inflicts upon others, and thus realizes the severity of the pain and the magnitude of the loss he has caused."[36]

He justified *hudud* punishments in a similar way. Taking the example of the *hadd* punishment for *zina* (fornication), he said that since "the fornicator sought easy pleasure without regard for Shari'a [law], he [she] is made to suffer pain in order to recover his [her] senses. An individual tends to lean more towards pleasure than towards pain. By pulling the self to pain, when it succumbs to prohibited pleasure, he [she] reestablishes a certain equilibrium and avoids recklessness and folly."[37]

This reasoning may or may not be convincing to non-Muslims. It must be emphasized, however, that Muslims' belief that *hudud* are in the best interests of non-Muslims as well as Muslims is irrelevant from the point of view of non-Muslims, who do not share in that belief. Yet there is high authority in Shari'a for the enforcement of certain *hadd* punishments on non-Muslims. On the understanding that stoning to death for *zina* by a married person is part of Jewish law, the Prophet is reported to have applied this punishment to Jews under his rule in the Medina state.[38] Does this mean that enforcement of the criminal law will depend on the religion of the offender? Who has the competence to determine the religious law of non-Muslims, and according to which sources and interpretation? Is Jewish or Christian religious law, for example, to be determined by Jewish or Christian theologians from their own sources or is it to be determined by Muslims with reference to Muslim sources on what that law is supposed to be?

To exempt non-Muslims from the application of *hudud* may create other serious practical problems of enforcement, including the question of determining the religious affiliation of the offender. If *hudud* apply only to Muslims and *ridda* (apostasy) is not punishable by death, as suggested earlier, an offender may attempt to avoid a *hadd* punishment by repudiating his or her faith in Islam. Could this problem be resolved by relating the imposition of *hudud* punishments to the religious belief of the offender as it was objectively determined to have been at the time of the commission of the offense and not at any subsequent point?

Such an approach to criminal punishment may be challenged as discrimination on grounds of religion in violation of the constitutional right of equality before the law. In other words, a Muslim citizen may object to being subjected to punishments not applicable to non-Muslims. Can this objection be sufficiently answered by the voluntary nature of the negative consequences of discrimination? Can it be convincingly argued that a Muslim has voluntarily accepted being subjected to *hudud* by becoming or remaining a Muslim in the knowledge that such religious belief will make him or her subject to the prescribed punishment?

In conclusion, I would suggest that purely religious rationalization of *hudud* is insufficient justification for including these offenses and their punishments in the criminal law of a modern nation-state. Yet no effort has been made to justify *hudud* in cross-cultural, cross-religious penological and sociological terms. From an Islamic point of view, I would argue that the fundamental Islamic principles of freedom of religion and justice in government clearly indicate that Islamic penal measures should not be imposed on non-Muslims against their will.

Moreover, penological and sociological justification of *hudud* is relevant at another level. As suggested above, Muslim religious obligation to accept *hudud* in principle is consistent with efforts to restrict their practical application. A desire to restrict the application of *hudud* in practice seems to be the reason behind the elaborate technical requirements developed in historical Islamic jurisprudence.[39] Given the lack of clear definitions of individual *hudud* and clear specification of the general conditions for their application, modern efforts in this regard, I believe, should take full account of contemporary knowledge of psychology, penology, sociology, and other relevant disciplines of learning. In particular, the general orientation of such modern efforts must seek the most restrictive definitions and the strictest general conditions for the application of *hudud*.[40]

The general conclusion of this section is that there is too much uncertainty and potential for abuse for *hudud* to be enforced under the current state of Shari'a on the subject. More final and general conclusions will be offered after further discussion of other aspects of the criminal law of Shari'a.

PROBLEMS WITH SHARI'A'S CONCEPT OF *JINAYAT*

Homicide and bodily injury are covered by several texts of the Qur'an and Sunna. In relation to the question of the juridical nature of these offenses, we need only quote verses 2:178 and 5:45 of the Qur'an to illustrate the problem. These verses may be translated as follows:

> Oh believers, the law of *qisas*, exact retaliation, is prescribed for you in cases of murder: A free person for a free person, a slave for a slave, and a woman for a woman. But if any remission is made by the brother [kin] of the slain, then grant any reasonable demand, and compensate him with handsome gratitude. This is a concession and a mercy from your Lord. Whoever exceeds this limit shall receive great penalty.

> We have ordained [in the Torah] that a life [should be taken] for a life, an eye for an eye, a nose for a nose, an ear for an ear, a tooth for a tooth, and wounds [are to be punished] by *qisas*, exact retalia-

tion. But if anyone remits exact retaliation by way of charity, that will
be an act of atonement for himself. Whoever fails to judge in accordance with what God has revealed shall be of the unfair ones.

The element of discretion granted to the victim or his or her kin in both
verses excludes *jinayat* from the category of strict *hudud* where there is
no equivalent discretion. As can be expected, this discretion in *jinayat* was
previously interpreted in light of tribal customs prevailing in early Muslim
society. Both the person authorized to exercise that discretion and the appropriate compensation *(diya)* were determined by the customary tribal
practice of seventh-century Arabia. Sunna and early Muslim practice sup-
plied the details of the principle of *jinayat*.[41]

The question now is whether that body of rules is to be accepted
in its entirety or be modified with reference to modern Islamic policy considerations. Some aspects of those rules seem to be inconsistent with the
principle of equality before the law. For example, *diya* (monetary compensation) for killing a woman was deemed by the founding jurists to be
half the amount of compensation for killing a man.[42] This is partly because the first verse quoted above provides that a woman should be killed
for a woman and partly because of the general principle of Shari'a, based
on other verses of the Qur'an, that a woman has half the testimonial
competence of a man and receives half his share in inheritance.[43] The need
to remove all forms of gender discrimination has been discussed in Chapter 4. Removing such discrimination in the payment of *diya* would seem
to follow logically from the same principle.

Similar reform is needed to remove other objectionable rules of
the historical law of *jinayat*. For example, according to the majority of
the schools of jurisprudence, a Muslim may never be killed for killing a
non-Muslim. Moreover, the founding jurists have held that *diya* for killing a non-Muslim is less than that for killing a Muslim.[44] Again, this is
an example of discrimination on grounds of religion discussed in Chapter 4. The constitutional imperative established in that chapter would also
require the removal of all manifestations of such discrimination in the administration of criminal justice.

Another question that needs to be addressed is whether proceedings for homicide and bodily injury should be classified as criminal or
civil in nature.[45] It is true in principle that criminal proceedings may conclude with a finding for monetary compensation as well as imposing a
punishment on the offender. But it is nevertheless important to determine
the basic nature of the proceedings in view of the significant differences
in the rules of evidence and procedure applicable to each type of proceeding. As a matter of policy, I think it is essential to maintain those differ-

ences and their application in daily law enforcement at the pretrial, trial, and posttrial stages of the proceedings.

That the Qur'an and Sunna grant private individuals control over the initiation of proceedings for *jinayat* (homicide and bodily harm) and a choice between *qisas* or payment of *diya* does not exclude public interest, including the interest of the person accused of having committed the act. This consideration would require certain safeguards to be introduced in the modern administration of justice. For example, the discretion not to prosecute and choice of mode of punishment vested in the victim or his or her kin can be exercised through some appropriate mechanism built into the system while still allowing for public official supervision.

As a general proposition, and in view of the nature of the conduct in question and serious consequences to the accused person, it is suggested that all *jinayat* be characterized as criminal proceedings. In consequence, criminal rules of evidence and procedure should apply. Private discretion can contribute to the decision whether to prosecute and also whether to accept *diya* in appropriate cases. The courts must retain the right to rule on guilt or innocence and determine the amount of *diya* in light of established principles for the assessment of damages without being bound by archaic rules discriminating against women and non-Muslims because these rules would be unconstitutional in the context of a modern nation-state.

This suggestion raises the question of the degree of control that is allowed to private persons, whether the victim or his or her kin. In other words, who should have the final word on whether to prosecute and whether *qisas* or *diya* should be imposed in case of conviction? Is it possible to vest the power to make final decisions on these matters in official organs (prosecutorial decisions in an executive office and sentencing decisions in the courts) provided that such organs act in light of the circumstances of the offense and the antecedents of the offender? The main problem with this approach is that it may be seen as infringing on the rights of the victim or his or her kin entrenched by the clear and definite text of verses 2:178 and 5:45 of the Qur'an quoted above. There may be room for executive and judicial discretion in determining the conditions for private choice to arise, but the logic of Shari'a as a religious law would prevent the elimination of private choice because it is granted by the express terms of the Qur'an.

The answer proposed here is that official reaction to the private wishes of the victim (or his or her kin) should depend on the nature and reasonableness of those wishes. If the private person(s) wish to forfeit her (their) interest, the state may still wish to prosecute to enforce its view of the public interest. This may be done through the discretionary power of *ta'zir*. If, however, the victim (or his or her kin) insists on prosecuting under circumstances which, in official estimate, do not warrant a prosecution, the official organs could decline to prosecute on the grounds that the conditions necessary for the exercise of private discretion had not arisen. If a prosecution was warranted and conviction followed, the terms of verse 5:45 of the Qur'an would not permit denying the victim (or his or her kin) the choice between *qisas* or *diya*.

As in the case of *hudud*, the religious approach to *jinayat* raises difficulties with non-Muslims, who may not accept the religious imperative or share in the religious motivation that underlies the approach. If the non-Muslim is the victim, it may be argued that he (or his kin) may decline the option of insisting on *qisas* out of his personal convictions and receive monetary compensation instead if he wishes. The real problem arises when the non-Muslim is the offender and the victim (or his kin) is (are) Muslim(s). In such a case, the option of *qisas* would depend on the wishes of the victim (or his kin), who can cite the Qur'an in support of his or her right to do so. In light of the standards explained in Chapter 4 of this book, is it unconstitutional to discriminate between offenders on the grounds of the religious beliefs of the victim (or his kin)?

Thus the ultimate question is whether *jinayat* can be included in the criminal law of a modern nation-state without violating constitutional imperatives. Assuming that penalizing homicide and bodily harm is acceptable to all segments of the population, the question remains as to whether imposing *qisas* (exact retaliation) as punishment for the offense is equally acceptable irrespective of religious authority that is binding on Muslims alone? Another question is whether it is possible to eliminate all discrimination on grounds of gender or religion in the definition and application of *jinayat*.

DISCRETIONARY POWER OF *TA'ZIR*

As indicated earlier, historical Islamic jurisprudence vested the ruler of an Islamic state or his judges with a residual power and discretion whether to penalize and how to punish what they consider to be reprehensible conduct which is not covered by the specific categories of *hudud* and *jinayat*.[46] It was considered to be appropriate, in the historical context of the early formulation of Islamic criminal law, for the ruler and his judges to enjoy this residual discretionary power of discipline and reform.[47] The founding jurists have attempted to provide some guidelines for the power of *ta'zir*.[48] But these guidelines were so vague and purely advisory in nature that they are inadequate for structuring and controlling this power in the context of a pluralistic modern nation-state.

The largely theoretical formulation of Shari'a tended to assume an ideal state of affairs in which the ruler and his officials would feel constrained by their personal religious obligation to maintain justice and fairness in the execution of their duties. Whatever may have been their reasons, the early Muslim jursits hypothesized that there was no conflict between the individual and the state and that persons in power will naturally act in the best interest of both the individual and the community.[49] In view of the long and painful historical experience with abuses of discretion, it is now generally accepted that there is no justification for such hypotheses or assumptions. On the contrary, we must proceed on the assumption that there is at least potential conflict between the individual and the state and that no official can be entirely trusted with the task of identifying and maintaining a proper balance between individual and collective interests. In particular, we must assume that official self-restraint and subjective scruples are inadequate bases for fair and impartial government, especially in the administration of criminal justice.

One of the primary mechanisms for checking abuse of the powers of government is the principle of the rule of law whereby officials are authorized to act only in accordance with predetermined rules of law of general application.[50] As applied to the administration of criminal justice, the rule of law requires that no punishment may be inflicted except in accordance with preexisting, published, and easily understandable penal legislation. This principle also requires strict interpretation of penal legislation and the structuring of judicial discretion in sentencing to achieve the objectives of public penal policy and to avoid abuse and corruption in individual cases.

Some modern Muslim scholars maintain that Shari'a was completely consistent with the fundamental principle that there can be no punishment without prior criminal legislation. Abd al-Qadir Auda, for example, argued that the principle of legality is fully observed even in ta'zir offenses in that the discretion of the ruler and his judges is restricted by a variety of texts, general principles, and the spirit of Shari'a. It is difficult to accept this position in view of Auda's own admission that Shari'a authorizes the judge to apply in his discretion any of the punishments sanctioned by Shari'a for any act or state of affairs that affects the order or interest of the community.[51] It is precisely this wide discretion in determining, *after the fact* whether the particular act or state of affairs affects the order or interest of the community in a way that warrants punishment (and the wide range of possible punishments that may be imposed in such cases) which is objectionable from the point of view of the principle of legality.

I submit that it is imperative to eliminate the individual residual power of discretionary *ta'zir* previously enjoyed by the ruler and his judges under Shari'a. Whatever Qur'anic and Sunna authority may exist for general administrative discretion should not be interpreted to include the administration of criminal justice. The power to impose criminal punishment must lie in the community at large and must be exercised in accordance with the principle of the rule of law. It is now generally accepted that penal power should be exercised by the legislature through penal legislation of general application, which is interpreted and applied by an independent and technically competent judiciary, whose decisions are strictly enforced by the executive organ. It is true that there is some disagreement as to the exact details of the principle of separation of powers. There may also be room for cultural and ideological variations on its application to the various functions of government. These differences and variations do not affect, in my view, the universal validity of this principle as applied to the administration of criminal justice.

When exercising collective discretion on which conduct to penalize and how to punish it through the criminal process, the community as a whole, both Muslim and non-Muslim alike, must enjoy the freedoms of expression and association and effective access to the policy formulation process. Decisions should not be based exclusively on the religious sense or rationale held by Muslims as part of their faith but also on general social utility and consensus. Unless Muslims can convince all segments of the population of the need to penalize certain conduct and of the appropriateness of the particular type and degree of punishment to be imposed, the imposition of penal punishment would be tantamount to perversion and manipulation of the formal legislative process to legitimize Muslim domination of the other segments of the population.

Because of the discretionary nature of the original power of *ta'zir,* penal policy questions in this area may lend themselves more readily to compromise and consensus than in the areas of *hudud* and *jinayat.* Muslims are not generally bound by the fundamental tenets of their faith to penalize certain conduct or to inflict a given form of punishment other than in cases of *hudud* and *jinayat.* It is true that the Qur'an, in verses such as 4:15–16, authorizes some sanction against conduct other than *hudud* and *jinayat,* but it does so in very general terms permitting wide discretion in interpretation, including the use of nonpenal measures. After all, criminal sanction is not the only mechanism for enforcing morality and promoting the public good. What needs to be emphasized, however, is that in determining the scope of the criminal law, a certain level of tolerance and goodwill must prevail in the debate if it is to succeed in producing fair and widely accepted legislation and enforcement policies. Due consideration must be given to the wishes of all segments of the population in every aspect of the criminal law.

GENERAL PRINCIPLES OF CRIMINAL RESPONSIBILITY, EVIDENCE, AND PROCEDURE

Several issues pertaining to the general principles of criminal responsibility, evidence, and procedure may be discussed together because they all seem to be equally underdeveloped in Shari'a. Modern Islamic legislation may be more readily adopted in these areas not only because there is little, if any, authority against their adoption, but also because such legislation can be easily supported by general authoritative underlying principles of justice and utility.[52]

Shari'a principles of Islamic criminal law were formulated by the early jurists in the three separate categories of *hudud, jinayat,* and *ta'zir.* The ingredients of each offense were specified, and the applicable rules of evidence and procedure were discussed separately without attempting to develop general principles applicable to all offenses. This approach is too complex and fragmented to sustain a modern penal system. The development of principles of criminal responsibility, evidence, and procedures of general application is not inconsistent with the application of additional special ingredients and special rules of evidence and procedure to any specific offense or class of offenses.

In relation to the general principles of criminal responsibility, it is now commonly accepted as necessary to determine the threshold of liability in terms of mental and physical elements of crime. The complexity of criminal activity, moreover, requires general consideration of questions such as liability for attempts falling short of the complete crime, abetting another person to commit a crime, and the joint liability of a number of participants in the commission of a single crime. Again, recent experience seems to show the need to provide for general defenses and exceptions to criminal responsibility. The early Muslim jurists dealt with some of these issues in relation to some specific offenses and categories[53] but never as general principles applicable to all offenses.[54] All these aspects of modern criminal law have to be linked and rationalized, as much as possible, with reference to a comprehensive and consistent penal policy and theory of criminal responsibility in accordance with the constitutional and international standards discussed earlier in this chapter.

A few questions will illustrate the need to address these issues before implementing Islamic criminal law today. In relation to the mental element in crime, is a specific intent to be required as a general rule and how is it to be proved? Does Islamic criminal law accept implied or constructive intent or accept the notion of strict liability regardless of the mental state of mind? The question of causation is, of course, essential to the physical element of crime. How do we determine that the accused person's conduct caused the prohibited result or state of affairs? What is the effect of intervening causes or an interruption in the chain of causation?

The separate categories approach of historical Islamic jurisprudence would have all action falling short of one of the specific *hudud* and *jinayat* punishable under the residual power of *ta'zir* at the discretion of the ruler or his judges. As suggested earlier, *ta'zir* power has to be exercised collectively through the legislature. Legislation will now have to define the general principles for punishing attempts, that is, action falling short of satisfying the requirements of criminal responsibility for a specific offense. Similarly, legislation must regulate the liability of an abettor as distinguished from the liability of the direct perpetrator of a crime. For example, legislation should determine whether and how the fact that the abetted person was a minor or mentally disabled should affect the responsibility of the abettor. Legislation will also have to regulate the relative responsibility of several participants in the same criminal activity. The early Muslim jurists tended to deal with each issue in relation to the offense under discussion, as when the offense was committed by several persons acting jointly.[55] Even if we are to generalize from the rule as formulated in relation to a specific offense, we would find too much diversity of views among the jurists and too little concrete authority for their opinions to sustain a coherent and comprehensive set of general principles.[56]

Finally, in relation to general defenses and exceptions, what is the effect of mental disorder short of complete insanity? How far, if at all, are psychological or psychiatric disorders to be taken into account? What are the limits of the right to private defense? How are these limits affected by public policy considerations mandating resort to the public authorities as opposed to self-help? Is there a difference between private defense of a person and defense of purely property interests? Does the right to private defense extend to defending the person and property of others? What is the effect of the consent of the victim in running the risk of injury or even requesting it as in cases of so-called mercy killing? Should there be an exception from criminal liability for police officers as public servants acting in the course of their duties?

To illustrate the need for authoritative treatment of these issues, take the case of the effect of the consent of the victim. The idea that homicide is a civil wrong or tort rather than a crime led Muslim jurists to opposite views on the effect of consent of the deceased. The Hanafi, Shafi'i, and Hanbali schools are reported to hold that consent of the deceased precludes *qisas* (exact retaliation). Using the same logic of civil wrong, however, Malikis held that *qisas* must be enforced because the right thereto belonged to the heirs of the victim and could not be affected by the victim's consent. Zahiri and Zaydi jurists agree with this conclusion but on the different ground that the victim, by consenting to something

God had forbidden, became impious and unworthy of having his wishes respected. This latter view is accepted by some Hanafi and Shafi'i jurists. Which of these conflicting views is the correct position of Shari'a and which of the opposing grounds is its proper rationale?

The list of unresolved issues is much longer. Each of the questions raised above subsumes a number of equally important issues. None of these issues had been addressed and resolved authoritatively before the recent application of Islamic criminal law in countries such as the Sudan, in part for political reasons. But I submit that it is the nature of the criminal law of Shari'a, with its serious deficiencies and inconsistency with modern standards, that made political manipulation possible, if not inevitable. Before assessing this recent experience and concluding with a new agenda for the application of Islamic criminal law, it is important to note the other two sets of fundamental questions of evidence and procedure which are also being disregarded in the head-on rush to apply Shari'a criminal law first and ask questions later.

Although linked to the separate categories of *hudud, jinayat,* and *ta'zir,* the rules of evidence previously articulated by the early jurists raise some common problems. Discrimination against women and non-Muslims was carried into the law of evidence by denying women and non-Muslims testimonial competence in some cases or restricting their competence in others.[57] When the testimony of women is accepted, for example, it takes two female witnesses to make a single male witness. As suggested in the previous chapter, these features of discrimination against women and non-Muslims can be removed only by a fundamental revision of some of the basic assumptions and orientation of historical Shari'a. It would seem obvious that a reformulation of existing rules of evidence by basing testimonial competence on objective and fair criteria other than gender and religion is imperative for the modern application of Islamic law in general, and criminal law in particular because the most discriminatory rules apply in the criminal law area.

Resolution of other questions of evidence may not involve fundamental revision of historical Shari'a. Previous formulations of the impact of coercion on the admissibility of confessions, for example, simply reflected the views of the specific jurists or school of jurisprudence, which are not linked to the basic assumption and orientation of Shari'a as a whole as is the case with the status and rights of women and non-Muslims.[58] Again, the adoption of modern rules of evidence regulating the admissibility and weight of, for example, the opinion of expert witnesses or physical or documentary evidence does not seem to be inconsistent with general principles of Shari'a. The early jurists had no need to address these issues because they were inconceivable at the time.

There are also very few general rules of procedure for pretrial,

trial, and posttrial stages. Being consistent with the structure and functions of the state in their own historical context, the early jurists were naturally unaware of the currently much-appreciated need to regulate and control the powers of arrest, search and seizure, and so forth. For the same reason, questions of pretrial release on bail or other security and the regulation of trial procedure, sentencing process, and posttrial review and appeal were not discussed by the early jurists. Once again, it is obvious that the modern application of Islamic criminal law cannot be undertaken in a humane and effective manner without addressing and resolving all these and other related questions. As will be shown in the following assessment of recent experience of the Sudan, it is wrong and counterproductive to superimpose Shari'a principles on the preexisting secular legal system without first working out the details and possibilities of conflict.

While appearing to appreciate the need for substantial reform and supplementation of Shari'a, contemporary Muslim writers continue to be ambivalent and apologetic in this regard. Thus one author said: "Historically, aside from defining substantive crimes and their punishment, the Shari'a did not set forth a detailed system of criminal procedure since such a system falls within the province of delegated interest, i.e., those which the ruler has the authority to organize according to his personal reasoning, consistent with particular circumstances of time and place, and inspired by the spirit of the Shari'a and its general principles."[59] Nevertheless, the author went on to state in some detail what he maintained were the features of the Islamic system of criminal procedure without citing specific authority for the majority of his propositions. This is clearly an example of what Ann Mayer has described as "anachronistic projections of modern principles of criminal justice back into a legal order in which they were unknown."[60] The truth of the matter is that historical Shari'a had very little to say on these vital questions of practical law enforcement. This leaves the way open for modern formulation in light of Islamic policy considerations. A detailed system of criminal procedure must now be formulated and enacted before the application of Islamic criminal law.

Muslims should not, however, blindly copy any specific model of criminal procedure. Substantial differences between the major existing models and constant changes within each model clearly show the organic and dynamic nature of a modern legal system. There is no agreement, for example, on the precise scope and rationale of what is known as the privilege against self-incrimination, that is, protecting a person from having to answer questions that may incriminate him. Again, there is no agreement on the effect of employing illegal methods in obtaining evidence. Even within the same general legal tradition, such as what is known as the common law tradition, we would find that different jurisdictions have adopted divergent views on these issues. Moreover, each jurisdiction is constantly changing in its response to the conflicting policy considerations underlying its position.[61] It cannot, therefore, be reasonably suggested that a modern Islamic criminal law should automatically adopt the position of any of these legal systems. What is needed is a humane and systematic Islamic response to the legitimate concerns underlying these and other rules of evidence and procedure.

AN ASSESSMENT OF RECENT EXPERIENCE

To illustrate the problems discussed in the preceding sections of this chapter and to demonstrate the need for reform and further development and specification of Shari'a criminal law before its modern enforcement, I will assess the experience of the Sudan. Needless to say, problems similar to those raised by the Sudanese experience are likely to arise wherever the criminal law of Shari'a is enforced in a modern nation-state.

The most significant date for the application of Shari'a criminal law in the Sudan is September 1983. Previously, Sudanese criminal law was based on principles of English common law, as adapted through application in India and other former British colonies.[62] As has always been the case throughout Sudanese history, customary law applied, and continues to apply, in many parts of the country.

Background in Sudanese Legal History

Little specific and reliable information is available about the administration of criminal justice before the nineteenth century, but it can be safely assumed that the strong historical decentralization of government in the Sudan must have also applied to the administration of criminal justice.[63] The vast area and inaccessibility of most parts of the country, coupled with the strong tribal and ethnic organization of the population, have always supported decentralized administration through tribal chiefs and local rulers. The country was not unified into a single political entity until the Turco-Egyptian conquest of 1821.

Whatever interest the Turco-Egyptian rulers had in the affairs of native Sudanese was confined to the main towns, where Turco-Egyptian codes, by then significantly influenced by principles of European law, applied.[64] For the vast majority of native Sudanese, customary law, as influenced or modified by Shari'a in the predominantly Muslim parts of the country, applied throughout the Turco-Egyptian period.

Although the majority of the population of northern Sudan had converted to Islam by the fifteenth century, Shari'a did not apply as a comprehensive legal system except perhaps during the Mahdist state of 1884–98.[65] In particular, Shari'a criminal law did not apply before the Mahdist era except in nominal respects, and often as modified by local custom.[66] For example, *diya* was often paid in cases of homicide and other bodily injury, but the conditions for its payment and the amount paid were determined more by local custom than by Shari'a.

Muhammad Ahmed, "al-Mahdi," the divinely guided one, launched his religio-political revolution around 1881 with the declared objective of overthrowing the "un-Islamic" Turco-Egyptian rule. Consequently, al-Mahdi, and his successor al-Khalifa (caliph) Abdullahi purported to enforce a strict application of Shari'a, including its criminal law, throughout the areas under their control.[67] Because al-Mahdi deemed Islamic jurisprudence, *fiqh*, to have distorted and obscured the pure and original principles of Shari'a, the Mahdist administration prohibited all reference to the historical schools and founding jurists for the interpretation of the relevant texts of Qur'an and Sunna. Instead, al-Mahdi's decrees became the only permissible source of Shari'a besides the pure texts of Qur'an and Sunna. Thus, although it was supposed to be a period of strict application of Shari'a, the Mahdist state applied its own version of Shari'a.

Moreover, and throughout its short reign, the Mahdist state was beset by internal dissent, strife, and civil war, as well as constant external wars. Consequently, the regime never had the time and resources to develop its own institutions and regularize its administration of criminal justice. Therefore, the Mahdist experience cannot offer a reliable guide for the modern application of Shari'a criminal law.

The Anglo-Egyptian conquest of 1898 had the specific objective of obliterating all remnants of the Mahdist state. After an initial period of martial law, principles of English common law and codes based on English law as modified through application in India were introduced in the Sudan. In time, native Sudanese were trained to take over from colonial police officers and judges.[68]

Although the codes claimed general territorial application after the first few years of Anglo-Egyptian rule, they never displaced customary law in the rural and nomadic areas of the country.[69] When the "native administration" was regulated by the 1920s, the courts of tribal chiefs and native administrators were officially granted criminal jurisdiction within certain limits.[70]

With the institutionalization of the official administration of criminal justice, including the customary law component, it was not surprising that political independence in January 1956 did not bring any significant change in this field. A national debate over the future of the country's constitutional and legal orders started soon after independence,[71] but nothing was done to change the essential nature and content of the preexisting legal system until 1983.[72] Nevertheless, what may be described as the legislative coup d'état of 1983 should be seen in light of political and other developments since 1977.[73]

The Laws of 1983

We are not concerned here with the exact motivations and mechanics of the legislative coup d'état of 1983, which purported to make Shari'a the sole legal system of the Sudan.[74] Rather, we are concerned with the impact of that basic policy change on Sudanese criminal law. In accordance with the new policy of total Islamization, several basic criminal statutes such as the Penal Code, Code of Criminal Procedure, and Road Traffic Act were revised and reenacted in 1983 to incorporate principles of Shari'a.[75] The country's first Evidence Act was enacted at the same time to enforce Shari'a rules instead of the general principles of English common law of evidence.

Although some of the defects of what came to be known as the September (1983) Laws can be attributed to the haste and ambivalence with which the policy of Islamization was imposed by former President Ja'far Numayry, other defects reflect the basic problems of the modern application of the criminal law of Shari'a discussed in the preceding sections. In the following brief critique of some of the 1983 laws, emphasis will be placed on the latter type of defects because they are the ones likely to arise wherever historical Shari'a criminal law is enforced in a modern nation-state.

Except for a brief mention of Shari'a punishments for *hudud* and *jinayat* and authorization of the chief justice to issue circulars specifying the school or schools of Islamic jurisprudence to be observed by the courts and determining the amounts of *diya* to be paid in *jinayat* (homicide and bodily harm) cases,[76] the 1983 Code of Criminal Procedure was simply a reenactment of the previous "secular" Code of Criminal Procedure in its entirety.[77] None of the procedural questions raised by the modern application of Shari'a criminal law were addressed in the new code. For example, the code failed to regulate the relationship between the rights of private persons and powers of public authorities in cases of *jinayat*.

Because of the lack of a comprehensive system of substantive criminal law under Shari'a, the Sudanese Penal Code of 1983 was reduced to superimposing Shari'a rules of *hudud* and *jinayat* on the preexisting penal code. Thus preexisting general principles of joint criminal responsibility when an offense was committed by more than one person, for abetting another person in committing an offense, and for attempts to commit an offense were retained in their entirety.[78] Moreover, and in view of the lack of sufficient development of general defenses and exceptions to criminal responsibility under Shari'a, preexisting specifications of the right to private defense and other general exceptions to criminal responsibility were adopted without regard to the substantial change in the nature and consequences of criminal responsibility introduced by the enforcement of *hudud* and *jinayat* punishments.[79] For example, no regard was paid to this factor in adopting preexisting notions of the effect of the compulsion of the offender or the consent of the victim on the criminal responsibility of the offender.[80]

When Shari'a principles were introduced in relation to general principles of criminal responsibility, they had the effect of creating greater ambiguity. For example, section 49 of the 1983 Penal Code replaced the previously specified minimum age for criminal responsibility with the phrase "age of puberty." This phrase, used by historical treatises of Shari'a, creates obvious problems because puberty is a period of transition and not a specific age that can be determined by a court of law for the purposes of criminal responsibility.

Again, when Shari'a principles were enacted in section 64 of the 1983 Penal Code, specifying the punishments that may be imposed under the code, an unacceptable degree of ambiguity and broad discretion were introduced. For example, section 64(3) provided that whenever the term *imprisonment* is used by any section of the code without specifying the period, it shall mean imprisonment for any period deemed by the court to be fair under the circumstances. Similarly, section 64(8) provided that whenever the term *whipping* is used by any section of the code without specifying the number, it shall mean whipping not more than one hundred and not less than twenty-five lashes. Such broad discretion in sentencing is clearly based on the Shari'a power of *ta'zir*, which can hardly be justified in a modern system of criminal justice because of the unacceptable degree of uncertainty and potential for abuse.[81]

Shari'a principles of homicide were also superimposed on the preexisting law of homicide and its special defenses, creating additional ambiguities. For example, section 252 made the death penalty mandatory in what the code calls *qatl amd ghila* without defining what it means. Although this term is used by treatises on Islamic jurisprudence to indicate some forms of aggravated murder, they provide no precise definition for the offense. Again, curious results follow the use of Shari'a categories of homicide. For instance, the code admits consideration of provocation or consent of the deceased as partial defenses reducing what is otherwise murder into semimurder *(qatl shiph amd)*. This can hardly be consistent with Islamic religious mores.

The serious consequences of the ambiguity of Shari'a sources on the *hadd* of *haraba* or *qat al-tariq* are illustrated by the application of this *hadd* to a wide variety of offenses under the 1983 Penal Code. Besides applying the Shari'a punishments for this *hadd* to robbery and related offenses as defined by the previous code,[82] the 1983 code applies the same punishment to a variety of other offenses which may not necessarily involve either the taking of property by force or the use of violence against the state or any private person.[83] Presumably, the wide application of this *hadd* punishment is based on the assumption that such conduct constitutes "mischief or corruption" in the land. When we note that this *hadd* punishment, as stated in verse 5:33 of the Qur'an, is either death or crucifixion or amputation of one hand and the opposite foot (cross-amputation) or banishment, we can realize the extreme importance of restricting its application to the maximum possible degree.[84] Yet the ambiguity of the definition under Shari'a permits its application to a wide variety of offenses.

The problems of applying *hudud* to non-Muslims are clearly raised by the 1983 Penal Code. For one thing, Shari'a punishments for *hudud* of *sariqa* (theft), *qat al-tariq* (highway robbery), and *qadhf* (unproven accusation of *zina*, fornication) are applicable to all offenders, regardless of their religion or belief.[85] This raises questions of penological justification discussed earlier in this chapter. The basic issue here is why non-Muslims should be subjected to strict and harsh punishments derived from the religious beliefs of Muslims.

In what appears to be a response to this concern, and perhaps because of Shari'a's own special rules in relation to the *hadd* of *zina*, the punishment for this offense is made dependent on the religion of the offender. Following the statement of the Shari'a *hadd* punishment for *zina*, section 318 of the 1983 Penal Code provides that this punishment shall not be imposed on any person whose "heavenly religion" established a different punishment for this offense. In such a case, the offender shall receive the punishment established by his own heavenly religion. If there is no such punishment in the offender's religion, he shall be punished with not more than eighty lashes and fine or with imprisonment for more than one year.

This provision raises serious problems. Since the section does not define what it means by "heavenly religion," the question becomes, Which criteria are to be used in determining whether the offender has a heavenly religion? Is this question to be determined by the court, using its own (presumably Shari'a) criteria of what constitutes a heavenly religion, or is it to be decided by the offender's own belief that he has such a religion? Similar questions arise in relation to the punishment provided for *zina* by the offender's heavenly religion. Is this matter to be determined by the court applying its own (presumably Shari'a) sources on what that punishment is, or is it to be determined by religious authorities within the offender's heavenly religion?

Another problem arises when the code attempts to conceal Shari'a discrimination on grounds of religion in relation to the *hadd* of *qadhf*. According to the founding jurists, the *hadd* offense of *qadhf* does not arise unless the victim is a Muslim. Attributing *zina* to a non-Muslim without the necessary proof may be punished under the discretionary power of *ta'zir*, but not as a *hadd*.[86] The reasoning behind this rule of Shari'a is that non-Muslims lack the positive quality of *ihsan* (sanctity of moral character), which would be violated by *qadhf*, because that quality presupposes Islam.[87] This rationale is a serious affront to the dignity of all non-Muslims because it assumes that they are of lesser moral character simply because they are non-Muslims. The Penal Code makes no reference to the distinction between Muslims and non-Muslims in its definition of *qadhf* under section 433 but maintains it in punishment under section 434. This is hardly satisfactory because the element of religious discrimination is as offensive, and as unconstitutional, whether present in the definition or punishment of the offense.

Again, the code's unsuccessful attempt to evade one constitutional objection in relation to *ridda* (apostasy) gives rise to another constitutional objection. Though not expressly penalizing *ridda* under any of its provisions, section 458(3) of the Penal Code states that the absence of express provision in the code does not preclude the imposition of any *hadd* punishment provided for by Shari'a. Since *ridda* is the only possible *hadd* under Shari'a not expressly provided for in the code, it follows that this subsection must be intended to permit the enforcement of this *hadd* without mentioning it by name. This interpretation was in fact applied to the subsection by the Special Criminal Court of Appeal in confirming the death sentence for *ridda* on *Ustadh* Mahmoud Mohamed Taha in January 1985.[88] Such an approach violates the principle of legality in that it permits the imposition of criminal punishment, and the ultimate punishment at that, in the absence of express and definite penal legislation. Moreover, and however achieved, imposing a criminal punishment or other negative legal consequences on any person because he changed his religion or belief violates the fundamental right to freedom of religion or belief.

Constitutional objection to discrimination on grounds of religion and gender can also be raised against the Sudanese Evidence Act of 1983, which reflects such discrimination as dictated by Shari'a. For example, discrimination underlies the act's determination of testimonial competence following Shari'a principles which disqualify non-Muslims and women as witnesses in some cases. Although section 27 of the 1983 Evidence Act provides that any sane person who is knowledgeable of the facts at issue is a competent witness, several other specific and general provisions of the same act deny non-Muslims and women such competence. Sections 77 and 78 of the act, by enacting Shari'a rules of evidence in proof of *hudud* offenses, discriminate against non-Muslims and women in relation to testimonial competence. Furthermore, and to ensure complete compliance with the Shari'a rules that disqualify non-Muslims and women as witnesses in certain cases, section 81 of the act expressly states that no provision of the act may be interpreted in any way inconsistent with Shari'a. Thus testimonial competence under the act is determined in accordance with Shari'a, notwithstanding the otherwise neutral terms of section 27 of the act.[89]

These problems, which are raised by the recent Sudanese legislation purporting to enforce principles of Shari'a criminal law, will arise in any country that attempts to implement the criminal law of Shari'a without first addressing and redressing the issues highlighted in this chapter. It may be helpful to note the human and political dimensions of the Sudanese experience. Once again, it should be emphasized that the case of the Sudan may offer clear and concrete illustration of these human and political dimensions, but they are by no means peculiar to the Sudan.

Human and Political Dimensions

Shari'a criminal law was enforced in the Sudan at a time when the country was suffering from severe economic difficulties.[90] The vast majority of the population lives under conditions of extreme poverty and need. Under such conditions, it is not surprising that theft and other property crimes are the only way of life known to many persons. No serious effort was made to cater to the economic needs of such people. In a grotesque gesture at setting the scene for the enforcement of Shari'a punishments, President Numayry ordered the immediate release of some thirteen thousand convicted offenders from prisons throughout the Sudan in September 1983. To help those offenders, many of whom were habitual offenders and recidivists who spent the majority of their adult lives in prison, start a new life away from crime, each released prisoner was granted the equivalent of the "minimum wage" of one month. Therefore, it was not surprising that several of those released from the Central Prison in Khartoum were back in police custody within a few hours for having committed new crimes. Some of the first amputations of hands and feet for the newly enforced *hudud* of *sariqa*, theft, and *qat al-tariq*, robbery, were executed on recently released former offenders.[91]

Moreover, and although the majority of Sudanese are nominally Muslims, their normal behavior hardly conforms to the religious dictates of Islam. Many Muslim Sudanese used to drink intoxicating beverages without giving much thought to Shari'a's prohibition of the practice. In fact, many poor women maintain themselves and families by the private manufacture and sale of native beer and liquor in the main towns of the country, including Khartoum, the capital. No special effort was made to educate and assist those Muslim Sudanese who engaged in daily violations of Shari'a before imposing harsh criminal punishments for such conduct. Consequently, *hudud* punishments were inflicted in excessively high numbers.[92]

Many of those who suffered harsh Shari'a punishments were non-Muslim Sudanese who did not subscribe to the religious rationale of Islamic punishments.[93] It was not surprising, therefore, to find that some leaders of non-Muslim Sudanese voiced their objections to the imposition of Shari'a punishments in the country. Thus a statement signed by the Sudanese Catholic bishops and leaders of the Episcopalian church, the Sudanese Church of Christ, the Presbyterian church in the Sudan and the Sudan Council of Churches, said: "Moslems must live by the dictates of their religion. But they have no right to impose their convictions on others who have different beliefs." The Christian leaders objected "to the enforcement of Islamic Shari'a on all citizens, irrespective of their beliefs," and "to the move of declaring the Sudan an Islamic state when over a third of its citizens are non-Muslims." The statement added: "A policy that enforces uniformity without considering the fact of having a pluriform society does not enhance unity and peace. The road to unity and peace is through understanding, mutual respect and dialogue."[94]

In resentment and frustration, other non-Muslim Sudanese resorted to armed rebellion over the issue. This brings into view the political dimension of the policy. To understand this aspect, however, some reference must be made to the intricate problem of the southern Sudan.

There are many causes for the conflict between the predominantly Muslim and somewhat Arabized northern Sudan and the predominantly non-Muslim and more purely African southern Sudan.[95] Besides deep-rooted distrust and hostility between the two parts of the country, southern Sudanese feel a sense of political and economic grievance because they do not enjoy a proportionate share of political power and economic development. Moreover, the non-Muslim southern Sudanese feared the application of Shari'a by the Muslim north because they understood that it would adversely affect their fundamental rights as citizens. These and other reasons led to the first rebellion by southern elements of the Sudanese army on the eve of independence in August 1955. That rebellion soon evolved into full-scale civil war, which lasted about seventeen years before it was ended through a political settlement incorporated in what is known as the Addis Ababa Agreement of 1972, which gave the south regional autonomy and guarantees of fundamental rights under the 1973 Constitution.[96] As a result of that arrangement, the southern region enjoyed relative political stability and economic development until the early 1980s.

Several actions of the government of former President Numayry in the late 1970s and early 1980s were seen by southern Sudanese as evidence of bad faith and a desire to deprive them of the benefits they had achieved under the 1972 agreement. The fears of southern Sudanese were confirmed by the decision of former President Numayry on June 5, 1983, to divide the southern region into three separate regions, in violation of the Constitution of the Sudan and the Addis Ababa Agreement. Within a few months of that decision, in September 1983, former President Numayry imposed Shari'a throughout the country. That drastic decision fueled the new rebellion, which had already started in the south, and the country was once more thrown into wide-scale and extremely costly civil war.[97]

Although observers may differ in their assessment of the various social, economic, and political causes of the north-south conflict in the Sudan, all would agree that the imposition of Shari'a is a major, if not the primary, cause of the current phase of the civil war. In any case, the spectacle of amputations and other harsh punishments inflicted on non-Muslims, together with clear evidence of discrimination on grounds of religion, provide non-Muslim Sudanese with strong motivations for continuing the civil war.

Observers would also agree that the resumption of the civil war in the southern part of the country compounded the economic and political problems of the country and contributed to the downfall of former President Numayry. In its effort to achieve another political settlement of the conflict, the current government has repeatedly promised to repeal the 1983 laws. Yet it has so far failed to do so because of the dilemma that course of action presents to the political leadershp of the country. On one hand, the political constituencies of the major parties in the north demand the application of Shari'a, whether through maintaining the 1983 laws in force or replacing them with the so-called substitute Islamic laws.[98] On the other hand, in whatever form Shari'a is applied, constitutional and practical problems will arise. The only way out of this dilemma is to revise and reform Shari'a principles, whether in criminal law or other matters, to remove all constitutional and other problems associated with its enforcement in a modern nation-state.

TOWARD A HUMANE AND PRACTICAL ISLAMIC SYSTEM
OF CRIMINAL JUSTICE

Responsibility for the recent abuses in the application of Islamic criminal law in countries such as the Sudan no doubt lies partially with unscrupulous rulers who manipulated historical formulations of Shari'a to their own selfish political ends. Such manipulation was unfortunately supported by Islamic traditionalist and fundamentalist Muslims, who claimed, for their own reasons, that Shari'a criminal law is ready for immediate enforcement.[99] The phenomenon of premature and arbitrary application of Islamic criminal law can best be understood as a function of what may be called the politics of Islamization.

Principles of Western criminal law have replaced Shari'a criminal law in the vast majority of Muslim countries throughout the world. In many Muslim countries, there is a heated debate over the future of their legal system, especially its criminal law aspects, following two models. On one hand, secularist elements of the population insist on continuing to apply Western principles, subject to slight modifications to suit local conditions. Traditionalist and fundamentalist Muslims, on the other hand, demand the immediate and total application of Shari'a criminal law. Neither side, unfortunately, appears to be willing to consider the valid concerns of the other.

Differences over the nature and content of the criminal law are, of course, not peculiar to Muslim countries and must be resolved in the same intelligent and democratic method that should be followed in settling such disputes wherever they may arise. The intelligent and democratic method in the case of a Muslim country debating the application of Shari'a criminal law will have to take into account the religious nature of that law. This basic fact has a twofold implication for all Muslim countries that have a non-Muslim or a secularist Muslim minority. On one hand, religious Muslims take Shari'a criminal law to be valid and binding by virtue of its religious authority and irrespective of any penological justifications that may be cited in its support. On the other hand, and since the Islamic religious factor is irrelevant to non-Muslims and is not taken as an irresistible imperative by secularist Muslims, Shari'a criminal law will have to be justified to these segments of the population in terms acceptable to them.

It is therefore essential that each side be allowed complete freedom of expression and association to compete for public approval of its position before introducing drastic change in criminal legislation. This opportunity for free and orderly debate must remain available for continuous reform and readjustment of the criminal law to reflect the true consensus of the total population.

Although the fate of each proposed piece of criminal legislation is ultimately decided through the formal legislative process in accordance with democratic principles, it should be remembered that democracy does not mean the tyranny of the majority. In a constitutional state, all legislation, and particularly criminal legislation, must conform with constitutional guarantees of fundamental rights. For example, the principle of constitutional government explained in the previous chapter of this book requires that there must be no discrimination on grounds such as gender, religion, or belief. Any legislation that has such discriminatory content or effect would necessarily be unconstitutional. It should be beyond the power of the majority, however large it may be, to enact any legislation that discriminates on grounds such as gender or religion. If such legislation is enacted, it must be nullified as unconstitutional through the appropriate organ and procedure established for that purpose in the constitution of the particular state, be it a supreme court or other organ or procedure.

This is, in my view, the basic framework within which criminal legislation, whether derived from Islamic or other sources, must be enacted and enforced. But because this book is about Islamic law, some conclusions must be offered on the problematic aspects of that law highlighted in this chapter.

Most of my own proposed answers to the questions in each section of this chapter are implicit in the discussion. For example, the discretionary power of *ta'zir* must be vested in the regular legislative organ of the state and be exercised within the framework of criminal legislation outlined above. The same applies to questions of general principles of criminal responsibility, evidence, and procedure. Some of the problems raised by *hudud* and *jinayat* must be resolved in the same way. As to the application of *hudud* and *qisas* to non-Muslims, I would suggest that these exceptional punishments should not be enforced as the general law of the land without sufficient penological justification acceptable to the generality of the population. If religious Muslims wish to have these punishments enforced regardless of the religion of the offender or victim, they must convince non-Muslims and secularist Muslims of the social utility and penological justification of each punishment. In other words, the proposed legislation must be supported by all segments of the population, including non-Muslims and secularist Muslims, and not simply imposed by the will of the Muslim majority. Even then, I submit, these strict and harsh punishments must be confined to the absolute minimum number of cases and following a preparatory stage when economic, educational, and other general conditions justifying their application have been established.

Given current penological and sociological thinking, it may seem extremely unlikely that non-Muslims and secularist Muslims would ever accept *hudud* and *qisas* punishments. Nevertheless, obtaining the consent of these segments of the population to the application of these punishments is the only fair and practical approach. As has been clearly demonstrated by the recent experience of the Sudan, imposing Shari'a punishments on non-Muslim citizens against their will is a clear violation of their fundamental rights. It is the obligation of religious Muslims who favor the application of these punishments to find ways of convincing non-Muslims and secularist Muslims of the validity and utility of these punishments.

It has been suggested that the application of Shari'a punishments should be restricted to Muslims. But this approach may not be acceptable to the Muslim majority because it is contrary to Shari'a. Moreover, as explained earlier, linking the application of penal laws to religion raises serious practical difficulties in daily enforcement.

$\succ$ 6 $\prec$

Shari'a and Modern International Law

$\mathcal{T}$HIS CHAPTER focuses on certain conflicts and tensions between essential purposes and principles of modern international law and corresponding principles of historical Shari'a. In accord with the main objectives of this book, and the scheme adopted in the preceding chapters, this chapter will also end with a discussion of the prospects of achieving genuine and lasting reconciliation between Islamic law, on the one hand, and essential international law, on the other.

WHITHER INTERNATIONAL LAW?

It is important to distinguish clearly between the fundamental character and purposes of international law and the current manifestations of this system of law. The inadequacies and defects of current international law do not negate its essential character and purpose.[1] Although the following discussion does not accept every aspect of the status quo in international relations, it is premised on a realistic vision of what is possible to achieve in this field. It is my submission that it is not only possible to achieve compliance with essential international law but imperative to do so in the interest of justice and peace in the world.

I take the fundamental purpose and function of modern international law to be the regulation of the relationship between all the members of the international community of states in accordance with principles of equality and justice under the law to promote peaceful coexistence and enhance the security and well-being of states and their individual subjects.[2] States are the principal subjects of international law in that they are the primary entities capable of possessing international rights and duties and endowed with the capacity to take action on the international plane.

137

It would therefore seem to me that the ultimate test of legitimacy for international law should be the same as that for national law, namely, the ability to reconcile the interest of each individual (state) in achieving complete personal (national) freedom and the interest of the community in achieving total social justice. Several significant practical differences between the two types of law obviously follow from the difference in their sphere of operation, but that does not, in my view, negate the similarity of their fundamental purpose. In particular, the fact that international law deals with individual persons through the intermediacy of states does not exclude the interests of individual persons from its fundamental purpose.[3]

I would further suggest that the totality of the international legal system, as well as specific aspects thereof, should be assessed, modified, and developed according to the above test of legitimacy. This is the underlying premise behind the following remarks about modern international law and the identification of its most essential purposes and principles. It is also the underlying premise of the conception of human rights to be discussed in the next chapter.

How International Has Modern International Law Been?

Modern international law is usually traced to the practice of the European city-states, as developed in the emerging European nation-states since the seventeenth century. That practice, of course, was determined by such factors as expediency and self-interest, as well as ancient notions of reciprocity and binding force of agreements or treaties.[4]

As a system of law which was developed by the European states, modern international law came to reflect the perceptions and interests of those states.[5] According to European imperialist perception and self-interest, the native peoples of Africa, Asia, and the Americas did not qualify for membership in the "civilized" community of nations.[6] Consequently, these peoples had no say in the formulation of the main principles of what is sometimes called traditional international law. This state of affairs was obviously unsatisfactory because the binding force of the principles of international law presupposes participation of all nations in establishing those principles.[7]

With the drastic change in the realities of international relations, especially since the end of World War II, previously colonized and disfranchised peoples have achieved independent statehood, which enables them to make their contribution to the continuing revision and development of international law.[8] In other words, although traditional international law was not initially truly international, it is becoming increasingly more so and reflective of the perceptions and interests of all the nations of the world. The question therefore arises, What ought to be the philosophical underpinnings and practical direction for the future development of international law?

One possible approach to the study of international law is to concentrate on the realities of power relations and the actual practice of states.[9] These factors and their cultural and ideological underpinnings[10] are obviously extremely important in understanding the internal and external forces and processes of international relations, including the formulation and implementation of international law. The validity and utility of this approach would be enhanced by constantly keeping the moral imperatives of international relations and the consequent objectives of international law in sight. It is true that one should not confuse what the law is with what the law ought to be, but that does not mean that one should have no reference whatsoever to the "ought" proposition in any given case.

Although states have always been primarily concerned with their own national self-interest (as perceived, of course, by the political forces in control of the states) such perceptions of self-interest have tended to change over time. Without shedding their preoccupation with national self-interest, I maintain, the political forces in control of any given state are now more capable of having enlightened and long-sighted perceptions of that self-interest. This fact is sufficiently demonstrated by numerous developments in the content of modern international law, especially in restricting the use of force, conceding the right to self-determination, and protecting and promoting human rights.[11] Although much more needs to be done to give these developments their full significance and logical implications, their acceptance in principle is extremely important.

The clear conclusion is that international law is now more truly international than it used to be and that state practice, which is the primary force behind the formulations of principles of international law, is increasingly motivated by higher and more enlightened goals. To maintain this position is not to overlook problems with the theory and practice of current international law. In particular, one should not underestimate the dangers of the tendency of powerful states to be selective in their compliance with international law. Nevertheless, I would argue that it is imperative to promote the positive developments achieved so far and to be clear on what ought to be the future line of action. This would involve the identification of the fundamental purposes of international law and of those principles which are indispensable for this system of law to achieve its desired purposes.

Essential Purposes and Principles of International Law

The Charter of the United Nations may be the best source of what is taken by this study to be the essential purposes and principles of international law because it is a treaty which is legally binding on almost all the states of the world, including all modern Muslim states.[12] Article 1 of the charter states the purposes of the United Nations as follows:

> 1. To maintain international peace and security, and to that end: to take effective collective measures for the prevention and removal of threats to the peace, and for the suppression of acts of aggression or other breaches of the peace, and to bring about by peaceful means, and in conformity with the principles of justice and international law, adjustment or settlement of international disputes or situations which might lead to a breach of the peace;
> 2. To develop friendly relations among nations based on respect for the principle of equal rights and self-determination of peoples, and to take other appropriate measures to strengthen universal peace;
> 3. To achieve international co-operation in solving international problems of an economic, social, cultural, or humanitarian character, and in promoting and encouraging respect for human rights and for fundamental freedoms for all without distinction as to race, sex, language, or religion.

The principles specified by Article 2 of the charter as binding on the organization of the United Nations and its members include the following:

> • The Organization is based on the principle of the sovereign equality of all its Members.
> • All Members shall settle their international disputes by peaceful means in such a manner that international peace and security, and justice, are not endangered.
> • All Members shall refrain in their international relations from the threat or use of force against the territorial integrity or political independence of any state, or in any other manner inconsistent with the purposes of the United Nations.
> • The Organization shall ensure that states which are not Members of the United Nations shall act in accordance with these principles so far as may be necessary for the maintenance of international peace and security.
> • Nothing contained in this [United Nations] Charter shall authorize the United Nations to intervene in matters which are essentially within

the domestic jurisdiction of any state or shall require the Members to submit such matters to settlement under the present Charter; but this principle shall not prejudice the application of enforcement measures under Chapter VII [of the Charter, that is to say, action with respect to threats to the peace, breaches of the peace and acts of aggression].

The significance of various aspects of these purposes and principles will become apparent during the course of this chapter. Two main points may be noted at this stage. First, it is obvious that the primary concern of the charter is the maintenance of international peace and security. All member states are bound to observe this purpose and principle themselves and to ensure that non-member states comply with it. Moreover, the last-quoted principle, which precludes intervention "in matters which are *essentially* within the domestic jurisdiction of any state," expressly provides that it does not apply to any matter that threatens international peace and security. Thus, although the "domestic jurisdiction" limitation can hinder international action against violations of some human rights standards, this limitation has no application when the violation constitutes a threat to international peace and security.

Second, failure to comply with a legal obligation does not necessarily diminish the binding force of that obligation. It is true that enforcement is generally an integral part of the binding nature and authority of the law, but, at least with reference to certain vital and fundamental laws, failure of enforcement mechanisms suggests the need for stronger enforcement action and not the abandonment of the effort. Thus, in the same way that the failure of domestic authorities to enforce the law prohibiting murder does not make it lawful or justifiable to murder any person, I submit that the current failure of the mechanisms of international law to enforce the prohibition of the threat or use of force in international relations does not make such violation of the charter lawful or justifiable. In other words, problems with the enforcement of essential international law of peaceful coexistence are reasons for stronger resolve and more concerted efforts at enforcement of these vital principles and not reasons for their abandonment.

SHARI'A AND INTERNATIONAL LAW

Much emphasis has been placed throughout this book on the importance of understanding Shari'a in its specific historical context. This is particularly important in understanding those principles and rules of Shari'a relevant to what is known in current terminology as international law. International law, in its modern sense and connotations, was the result of very recent developments, primarily since the beginning of this century. Nevertheless, since some Muslims are now contemplating the application of Shari'a in the modern national and international contexts, we need to identify and understand the corresponding principles of Shari'a and their relevance to Muslim practice through the ages. Before doing so, however, it may be helpful to recall the realities of power and international relations not only at the time of the revelation of the Qur'an and utterance of Sunna by the Prophet but also at the time when Shari'a was being developed as a comprehensive legal system by the founding jurists.

The Historical Context of Shari'a

Islam was born in an extremely harsh and violent environment and received a very hostile and aggressively violent reaction from the tribes of seventh-century Arabia.[13] The first Muslims had to fight for survival until Islam prevailed throughout Arabia by the time of the death of the Prophet. The preexisting norms of intertribal relations were heavily, if not completely, dependent on the use or threat of violent force by the claimant of any right, even the right to exist.[14]

The use or threat of force was also the norm among the various entities or polities of the region, including the two powerful empires to the northeast and northwest of Arabia, the Sasanian and Byzantine empires.[15] Thus, when the first Muslim state was established in seventh-century Arabia, force was the basic method of conducting what is known today as international relations.[16] It was therefore inevitable that Islam should endorse the use of force in Muslim relations with non-Muslims. In doing so, however, Shari'a introduced new norms to control the reasons for going to war as well as its actual practice.[17]

Whereas warfare among the tribes of Arabia and among the political entities of the region had been motivated by such considerations as tribal honor, territorial rivalry, and economic greed,[18] Shari'a restricted the use of force in international relations to self-defense and the propagation of Islam. To Muslims, these were the only legitimate reasons for war. Moreover, Muslims were constrained by certain rules regulating the actual conduct of warfare. For example, before using force in propagating Islam, they were required to offer the other side an opportunity to embrace the faith without fighting. If it was necessary to fight, hostilities had to be restricted to enemy combatant soldiers and then only in the battlefield.

This historical context continued throughout the formative stages of Shari'a and for over a millennium thereafter. The relevant basic texts of the Qur'an and Sunna, as well as the elaborate rules and regulations derived from them by the founding jurists of the eighth and ninth centuries, must be seen as a direct consequence of the prevalence of the use of force in international relations at the time. Since the Islamic state was defined in terms of submission to Shari'a rule, Islamic use of force was supposed to be directed against all non-Muslims who refused to submit to Shari'a rule and prohibited against non-Muslims who did so submit.

Thus it is important to emphasize the exclusive and limited nature of what may be described as ancient and premodern systems of international law. Customary rules and practices regulating relationships between various political entities before the rise of modern international law "were not truly 'international', in the modern sense, for each was exclusive and failed to recognize the principles of legal equality and reciprocity which are essential to any system if it is to become worldwide." The relevant branch of Shari'a, known to the early Muslim jurists as *siyar*, was therefore consistent with the conception of international law of the time.[19]

To argue that Shari'a was fully justified in endorsing the use of force in international relations in that historical context, and that it did in fact restrict and regulate the use of force, is not to say that such use of force is still justified. Rather, since the use of force was justified by the historical context of violent intercommunal and international relations, it must cease to be so justified in the present context, in which peaceable coexistence has become a vital necessity for the survival of humanity. Besides the growing trend toward an enlightened view of human relations and in favor of peace,[20] modern means of nuclear warfare have made hostile international relations unthinkable. It is true that limited use and threat of force are still practiced in international relations. The question is whether this should continue to be the basis of international law. I think it cannot possibly be.

It must be emphasized, however, that for Muslims the historical context, as such, can neither be the source of Shari'a in the past nor its source in the future. According to Muslim belief, Islamic law in the past, present, and future must be based on the Qur'an and Sunna. I fully accept this position and only wish to suggest that the historical context is merely the framework for the *interpretation and application* of these basic sources of Islam. In other words, it is not suggested here that Islamic law should simply follow the developments in human history regardless of the provisions of the Qur'an and Sunna. What is suggested is that the Qur'an and

Sunna have been the source of Shariʻa as the Islamic response to the concrete realities of the past and must be the source of modern Shariʻa as the Islamic response to the concrete realities of today.

To highlight the conflict and tension between Shariʻa and modern international law, and to illustrate the implications of this conflict and tension, then finally to argue for reconciliation, it is necessary to state clearly and authoritatively the relevant principles and rules of Shariʻa.

Main Relevant Principles of Shariʻa

The following statement of principles of Shariʻa is restricted to the main areas in which Shariʻa appears to be in conflict and tension with essential international law, namely, antagonism toward and the use of force against non-Muslims and nonconforming Muslims.

Antagonism and Use of Force against Non-Muslims

In addition to the explicit sources of Shariʻa on the use of force against non-Muslims and renegade Muslims to be reviewed below, many verses of the Qurʼan which were revealed after migration to Medina in 622 A.D. emphasized the internal cohesion of the Muslim community and sought to distinguish it from other communities in hostile and antagonistic terms. During the Medina stage, the Qurʼan repeatedly instructed the Muslims to support each other and disassociate themselves from non-Muslims and warned against taking non-Muslims as friends or allies. Thus, verses 3:28, 4:144, 8:72–73, 9:23 and 71, and 60:1 prohibited the Muslims from taking unbelievers as *awliya* (friends, helpers, and supporters) and instructed them to look for friendly relations and mutual support among themselves. Similarly, verse 5:51 instructs the Muslims not to take Jews and Christians as *awliya*, as they are *awliya* for each other, and any Muslim who turns to them (for friendship) becomes one of them.

These verses and related Sunna provided the general context within which the sources dealing specifically with the use of force against non-Muslims were understood and applied by the early Muslims. As will be emphasized below in relation to the specific sources on the use of force against non-Muslims, all the above-cited verses were revealed during the Medina period and not the earlier Mecca period. These sources should now be seen as having provided the necessary psychological support for the survival and cohesion of a vulnerable community of Muslims in a hostile and violent social and physical environment.

The commonly used Islamic term for the use of force in international relations is *jihad.* The literal meaning of the word *jihad* is effort and exertion, which includes, but is not necessarily restricted to, effort and exertion in war.[21] Thus, on one hand, both the Qur'an and Sunna have used the term *jihad* in this wider sense of self-exertion, sometimes in ways that have nothing to do with the use of force. In numerous verses of the Qur'an, such as 2:18, 5:54, and 8:72, the term *jihad* and its derivatives are used to refer to self-exertion, whether in combat or peaceful efforts. Even as against the unbelievers, verse 25:52 instructs the Prophet and Muslims to use the Qur'an in *jihad* against the unbelievers. This obviously refers to using the force and arguments of the Qur'an, and not the force of arms, in *jihad.* In Sunna, there is the well-known statement of the Prophet which describes the use of force in battle as the minor *jihad* and self-exertion in peaceful and personal compliance with the dictates of Islam as the major or superior *jihad.* In another Sunna, the Prophet is reported to have said that the best form of *jihad* is to speak the truth in the face of an oppressive ruler.[22]

On the other hand, both the Qur'an and Sunna have used the term *qital* (fighting) and its derivatives to refer to the use of force in international relations.[23] In view of this linguistic ambiguity and the frequent misuse of the term *jihad* by Muslims and non-Muslims alike, it may be better to use the term *use of force* to refer to this aspect of Shari'a. This latter term is further recommended because it has become a term of art in international law, especially since its use by the Charter of the United Nations. As such, this term can be applied in cross-cultural analysis of the issues.

Much can be learned about the Shari'a's view of the legitimate use of force in international relations through a review of the relevant sources of Shari'a in chronological order. This may be possible in relation to the Qur'an because of the relatively greater general agreement over the site or place and hence at least the approximate date of the revelation of each verse. It is much harder, if not impossible, to attempt a chronological survey of the Sunna because there is very little agreement on its chronological sequence. Sunna can be helpful, however, in understanding the meaning of a given verse of the Qur'an and will be used for this purpose in the following survey.

The first verses of the Qur'an which clearly sanction the use of force by Muslims against non-Muslims were revealed in Medina, after the Prophet and his Companions migrated from Mecca in 622 A.D. According to Ibn Kathir's leading interpretation and commentary on the Qur'an, the first verses instructing Muslims to use force in *jihad/qital* against unbelievers were 2:190–93 and 22:39, which may be translated, respectively, as follows:[24]

Fight in the cause of God those who fight you, but do not transgress the limits [initiate attack or aggression], for God does not love the transgressors. And slay them wherever you catch them, and turn them out from where they have turned you out, for tumult and oppression are worse than slaughter; but fight them not at the Sacred Mosque [of Mecca] unless they [first] fight you there; but if they fight you [there], slay them, [because] that is the reward of the unbelievers. But if they cease, God is Most Forgiving, Most Merciful. And fight them until [so that] there is no more tumult or oppression, and there prevails faith in God; but if they cease, let there be no hostility except to those who practice oppression.

Permission [to fight back] is [hereby] given to those against whom war is made; and God is Most Powerful and Able to support them. [They are] those who have been wrongfully expelled from their homes [for no cause or reason] except that they say "God is our Lord"; if God did not check one set of people by means of another, there would surely have been destruction of temples [of worship] and property.

Verses 4:90 and 8:39 and 61 of the Qur'an are identified by Ibn Khathir as having been revealed in Medina, though he states no exact date for their revelation. The first-mentioned verse comes in the context of instructing Muslims to disassociate themselves from the hypocrites and to confront and slay them wherever they find them. "But if they [the hypocrites] withdraw from you without fighting you," says verse 4:90, "and send you [guarantees] of peace, then God gives you no license or permission [to fight them]." Verse 8:39 may be translated as saying "and fight [the unbelievers] until [so that] there is no tumult or oppression, and faith in God completely prevails everywhere; but if they cease [their oppression] God is most Capable [Knowledgeable] of what they do." Following verse 8:60, which instructs Muslims to prepare for war to deter the unbelievers, verse 8:61 states: "But if they [the unbelievers] incline towards peace, you shall also incline towards it [peace] and place your trust [confidence] in God, He is the one who Hears and Knows [everything]."

The whole of chapter 9 of the Qur'an, which is identified by Ibn Khathir as having been revealed in the ninth year of Hijra, that is, around 631 A.D., is generally accepted to have been among the last of Qur'anic revelation. The verses of this chapter, such as verses 5, 12, 13, 29, 36, 73, and 123, contain the most categorical sanction for the use of force against non-Muslims and are generally taken to have repealed all previous verses that prohibit or restrict the use of force.[25] In particular, verse 5 of this chapter is said to have repealed, abrogated for the purposes of Shari'a, over one hundred preceding verses of the Qur'an which instruct Muslims to use peaceful means and arguments to convince unbelievers to embrace Islam.[26] This verse appears in the context of instructing the Prophet to declare that he repudiates his previous pledges of nonaggression to unbelievers, subject to a four-month period of grace, or until the end of the time set by a specific treaty of peace which the other side has not violated. Then comes verse 9:5, which may be translated as follows: "But once the forbidden months [the period of grace] are over then fight and slay the unbelievers [polytheists] wherever you find them, and seize them, beleaguer them, and lie in wait for them in every stratagem [of war]; but if they repent, and establish regular prayers and pay *zaka* [Islamic alms and religious tax] then open the way for them; for God is Most Forgiving, Most Merciful."

The other verse of this chapter which should be quoted in full is verse 29 because it applies to the use of force against *ahl al-kitab* ("People of the Book," non-Muslims believers who have received heavenly revealed scriptures), mainly Jews and Christians. This verse may be translated as follows: "Fight those People of the Book who do not believe in God or the Last Day, nor hold as forbidden what has been forbidden by God and His Apostle [the Prophet of Islam], nor acknowledge the Religion of Truth [Islam] until they pay *jizya* with willing submission, and feel themselves subdued."

Several conclusions can be drawn from this survey of the Qur'an on the use of force by Muslims against non-Muslims. The first clear conclusion is that this is an exclusively Medanese phenomenon, that is, it relates to the Medina period after migration from Mecca. Conversely, the vast majority of the verses of the Qur'an enjoining freedom of choice in religious belief, which would have guaranteed freedom of belief and the consequent equality and nondiscrimination for non-Muslims as a matter of law if they were implemented in Shari'a, are of the Mecca period.[27] Before migration to Medina in 622 A.D., there was no authorization in the Qur'an for the use of force against non-Muslims.[28]

The second clear conclusion from the above survey of the relevant verses of the Qur'an is that there was a progression in Qur'anic sanction for the use of force by Muslims against non-Muslims, from the use of force in self-defense to the use of force in propagating Islam. But because chapter 9 of the Qur'an was among the last revelations, it was taken by many Muslim jurists to have repealed, or abrogated for the purposes of Shari'a, all previously revealed inconsistent verses of the Qur'an. The meaning and implications of this principle of *naskh* (abrogation) in relation to the prospects of meaningful reform of Shari'a have already been discussed in Chapters 2 and 3 of this book. In the last section of this chapter, I will discuss the specific application of the reform methodology

proposed in Chapter 3 to the question of use of force and related matters.
The third conclusion is that the use of force was not permitted except for self-defense and propagation of Islam. Some modern Muslim writers claim that Shari'a permitted the use of force only in self-defense.[29] This claim is unfounded because both the Qur'an and Sunna did in fact, by the end of the Prophet's life, sanction the use of force in propagating Islam as well as in self-defense. It is not plausible to argue that the early Muslims were acting in self-defense when they conquered and ruled the whole of Syria, Iraq, northern Africa, and southern Spain to the west and Persia and northern India to the east.[30] As is clearly illustrated by the last practice of the Prophet and that of his caliphs, as well as the history of the early expansion of Islam,[31] Shari'a sanctioned and regulated the use of force by Muslims against non-Muslims, not only in self-defense but also as a means of propagating Islam.

Thus we find numerous reports of the Prophet, and his caliphs after him, instructing Muslim armies to offer the non-Muslim side the chance to embrace Islam, and that if they did accept the offer, no force could be used against them. If the non-Muslim side rejected the Muslim invitation to embrace Islam, and happened to be People of the Book, they were offered the second option of concluding a compact of *dhimma* with the Muslims, whereby they would agree to pay *jizya* and submit to Muslim sovereignty in exchange for being secure in their persons and property and allowed to practice their religion and apply their personal laws. The Muslim armies were instructed by the Prophet and his caliphs that whenever the offer to embrace Islam was not accepted and the option to pay *jizya* was rejected by those qualified to receive such an offer,[32] the Muslim armies must fight them. For example, the following Sunna is reported by Muslim, one of the most authoritative records of Sunna:

> Whenever the Prophet appointed a commander over an army or detachment, he enjoined upon him to fear God regarding himself and regarding the treatment of the Muslims who accompanied him. Then he used to say:
> Fight with the name of God and in the path of God. Combat those who disbelieve in God. Fight yet do not cheat, do not break trust, do not mutilate, do not kill minors.
> If you encounter an enemy from among the non-Muslims, then offer them three alternatives. Whichever of these they may accept, agree to it and withhold yourself from them: So call them to embrace Islam. If they accept, then agree to it and withhold yourself from them. If, however, they refuse, then call them to pay the *jizya*. If they accept, then agree to it and withhold yourself from them. If they refuse, then seek help from God and fight them.[33]

It is remarkable that, although he quoted this and other similar Sunna, Muhammad Hamidullah still attempted to avoid recognizing the true nature of Shari'a in this respect and called the use of force in propagating Islam the "idealistic" cause of war under Shari'a.[34] Another contemporary Muslim author attempted to avoid admitting that Shari'a required Muslims to use force against People of the Book, such as Christians and Jews, if they refused to pay *jizya*.[35] As often reiterated throughout this book, it would be better to recognize this and other aspects of Shari'a in their true nature and explain them in their historical context.

A related point is the tendency of some modern Muslim writers to insist that although Shari'a sanctioned the use of force to extend the universal rule of Islam, force was not used to impose religion as such. In support of this strained argument, these authors cite verse 2:257 of the Qur'an, which provides that "there shall be no compulsion in religion."[36] This view cannot be reconciled with the clear meaning of the other subsequent Qur'an and Sunna quoted above. Since non-Muslims were given the choice between embracing Islam, becoming *dhimmis* and paying *jizya* if they qualified for that status, or fighting the Muslims, it cannot be said that there was no compulsion in religion. Verse 2:257 of the Qur'an was deemed by some of the founding jurists to have been one of the abrogated verses from the point of view of positive law in Shari'a.[37] Once again, it is only by recognizing this aspect of Shari'a in its true nature and explaining it in its historical context that we can proceed to construct the alternative principle for modern Islamic public law.

Regulation of Use of Force and Peace Treaties

Besides restricting the legitimate use of force by Muslims against non-Muslims to self-defense and propagation of Islam, Shari'a regulated the actual conduct of war.[38] First, the requirement of offering the other side the option of embracing Islam and accepting *dhimma* when appropriate constituted what is known in modern terminology as a formal declaration of war and fair warning as a necessary prerequisite to commencement of hostilities.[39] Furthermore, Shari'a regulated in detail the conduct of Muslim armies in combat. In his above-quoted Sunna, the Prophet instructed Muslim armies not to cheat, betray trust, mutilate, or kill minors. In other reports he broadened the prohibition of killing noncombatants to include women, monks, and others.[40] Abu Bakr and Umar, the first and second caliphs, who can safely be assumed to represent the accurate position of Shari'a, are often quoted as instructing Muslim armies not to embezzle, cheat, betray trust, mutilate, kill a minor or an old man or a woman, hew down a date palm or burn it, cut down a fruit tree, or slaughter a goat or cow or camel except for food. They are also quoted instructing Muslim armies not to interfere with people who have secluded themselves in convents.[41]

If Muslim armies were victorious, however, they were entitled to take enemy property as *ghana'im* (spoils of war) in accordance with prevailing practice.[42] This is clearly recognized by the Qur'an, which regulates the distribution of such booty.[43] The rules of Shari'a regarding the fate of the vanquished non-Muslims will be explained below.

In light of all these sources, it is not surprising to find, as documented by Khadduri and other writers in the field, that those leading founding jurists of Shari'a who addressed intercommunal and international relations spoke of a permanent state of war between *dar al-Islam*, the abode of Islam or territory under Muslim rule, and *dar al-harb*, the abode of war or territory falling outside Muslim control.[44] According to those founding jurists of Shari'a, Muslims might have to conclude peace treaties, *sulh* or *ahd*, suspending hostilities with non-Muslim polities if Muslim interests required that, but such treaties must be of a temporary nature, for not longer than ten years according to Shafi'i, and only to permit Muslims to resolve their internal differences or prepare for the next round of fighting with the non-Muslims.[45]

As indicated by the rules for making peace treaties and shown by many sources of Shari'a and historical experience, the theoretically permanent state of war between Muslims and non-Muslims did not necessarily mean violence or fighting.[46] Nevertheless, it is important to remember that the theory of Shari'a is that Islam and unbelief cannot exist together in this world. Thus Shari'a requires that, whether through active fighting or other means, *dar al-harb* must be brought within *dar al-Islam*.[47]

Moreover, since upholding Islam is considered by Shari'a to be a legitimate reason for the use of force, such force can be used even against Muslims whose conduct is deemed to be subversive of the Muslim community or detrimental to the interests of Islam.[48] Thus we find the standard treatises of Shari'a discussing both types of the use of force in the same context and language.[49] This approach is understandable in view of the religious nature of the state. Since apostates and rebels were regarded as internal enemies of the Muslim community, they were to be treated on the same basis as external enemies.[50] Such reasoning is, of course, no longer valid or tenable under modern principles, which would not sanction the use of force against these groups unless they use force themselves.[51] Furthermore, since Muslims are now organized in different separate nation-states, the use of force among Muslim states, as in the case of the Iran-Iraq war, is now an international conflict that should be governed by the relevant rules of international law.

Conflict and Tension with Essential International Law

As can be seen from contrasting the principles of essential international law of peaceful coexistence and the corresponding principles of Shari‘a, some definite and generally agreed principles of Shari‘a are in clear conflict with corresponding principles of international law. Even some of the less definite and less generally agreed principles and detailed rules of Shari‘a still create a certain degree of tension, which may have a significant impact on Muslim response to these international norms. In other words, even if there is no agreement among the major schools of Islamic jurisprudence on the particular principle or detailed rule of Shari‘a, the existence of some authority for the given principle or rule creates significant tension between Shari‘a and relevant norms of modern international law. It is important to note this tension because the objective of this chapter is to argue for the reconciliation of Islamic law with international norms by removing actual conflict as well as less explicit tension between Islamic law and essential international law.

A comparison of the above-stated principles of essential international law with Shari‘a principles of nonrecognition of and the use of force against non-Muslim states leads to the inescapable conclusion that there is substantial and serious conflict between these two legal systems. Shari‘a is in direct conflict with the Charter of the United Nations because, whereas that charter prohibits the use of force in international relations except in self-defense, Shari‘a sanctions the use of force to propagate Islam or to uphold its integrity in another Muslim country. Moreover, Shari‘a's underlying theme of a permanent state of war with, and nonrecognition of, non-Muslim states repudiates the entire basis of modern international law. Those founding jurists who addressed the question spoke of a permanent state of war between the Muslims and non-Muslims which may be temporarily suspended by a peace treaty, *sulh* or *ahd*, without implying full recognition and permanent peace, as required by contemporary international law. Thus the clear and categorical conclusion is that there are certain areas of very serious conflict and tension between Shari‘a and modern international law which have to be resolved in an authoritative and conclusive manner.

RELEVANCE OF SHARI‘A TO CONTEMPORARY MUSLIM PRACTICE

Human conduct, whether at the individual or collective levels, is the product of a wide variety of complex psychological, economic, political, and social factors and forces. Human relationships are dynamic in nature in the sense that the action of one person or group of persons is part of the reaction of the other person or group. Law, especially religious law, is an important component of the processes that motivate and direct human action. Thus, although it is not suggested that Muslim behavior has ever been exclusively determined by the precepts of Shari'a, it cannot be denied that what Shari'a has to say on any subject is taken into account by individual persons and official policy makers. Obviously, the weight given to a Shari'a position varies with the individual person or group of persons, and it has certainly fluctuated from one period in history to another.

As explained in the first chapter of this book, there is sufficient evidence to support the proposition that the role of Islam in public life is continuing to expand and that its dictates are likely to have an increasing influence on the way Muslims behave. Such influence will no doubt be affected, either positively or negatively, by a variety of other internal and external factors and forces.

Background in Recent History

Whatever role Shari'a principles may have played in Muslim conduct of international relations until the sixteenth century, new factors have come into play since then.[52] With the rise of European power and the decline of Muslim power, the most powerful Islamic state of the modern era, the Ottoman Empire, was forced to accept the principles of international law as formulated by European nations.[53] Other Muslim powers of the time, such as the Safavids in Iran and Moghals in India, followed suit.[54] To be recognized as a responsible sovereign state and to receive the benefits of recognition of its rights under international law, the Ottoman Empire had to concede equal status and guarantee full recognition of the rights of other states. By the time other modern Muslim states came into existence, mainly through the disintegration of the Ottoman Empire after the end of World War I, the criteria for admission into the community of nations were already established and had to be accepted by all states.

By the beginning of the twentieth century, the majority of Muslim peoples came to live either under direct European colonial rule or within indirect European control. As such, these peoples lacked direct representation in the development of international law and relations throughout the first half of this century. Nevertheless, they eventually benefited from the development of international law and institutions, especially the rigorous program of decolonization endorsed and promoted under the Charter of the United Nations since 1945.

Now that previously colonized Muslim peoples have achieved political independence, they have to deal with other nations of the world within the basic framework of modern international law. Certain aspects of current international law and the power relationships it reinforces need to be revised and adjusted, but such revision and adjustment will not favor Shari'a's conception of international law and relations. Muslim states must concede full recognition of, and accept permanent peace with, non-Muslim states in the interest of securing their own sovereignty and political independence. All modern Muslims must accept and work within the framework of essential international law and not the corresponding principles of Shari'a.

Nevertheless, Shari'a is very much present in the hearts and minds of Muslims throughout the world. Even where it is not the formal legal system, Shari'a has a powerful influence on Muslim attitudes and policies in most Muslim countries. Shari'a notions are relevant to vital contemporary issues and are likely to have far-reaching consequences with serious international implications.

The Iran-Iraq War[55]

We are not concerned here with the very complex historical, economic, social, and political causes behind the Iran-Iraq war.[56] Of concern to the subject at hand is the application of Shari'a principles to the conflict. In assessing the war in terms of relevant Shari'a principles, we are not taking the use of Shari'a arguments by either side at face value.[57] Rather, we are interested in the objective Shari'a view of the conflict and its implications for international law and relations. Nevertheless, the use of Shari'a arguments by both sides is significant in that it demonstrates the belief of the leaders of both countries that such arguments carry weight with their respective populations. However cynical and manipulative the leaders may be in their use of Shari'a arguments in justifying their positions, it is important to realize that Shari'a principles do lend themselves to such manipulation.

If it is true, as claimed by Iran, that Iraq started the war in 1979 by attacking Iranian territory, Iran would have the right under Shari'a to use force in self-defense. But once Iraqi forces have been driven out of Iranian territory, as was achieved several years ago, the right to use force in self-defense ends. Although Iran would still have the right to seek reparations against Iraq for the attack and the damage caused to Iranian interests, this right should be pursued, at least initially, through negotiations and arbitration and not by continuing to use force against Iraq. Nevertheless, Iran can continue to use force under a completely different Shari'a argument, the alleged right to intervene to save the Muslim people of Iraq from tyrannical and oppressive secular rule and establishing an Islamic state in that country. Is there basis for this argument under Shari'a?

It seems that such an argument can be supported under Shari'a. Several verses of the Qur'an and examples of early Muslim practice can be interpreted as creating a right, if not an obligation, for Muslims to use force to establish genuine and just Islamic government. Given the framework within which the jurists interpreted the Qur'an, the various verses enjoining the Muslims to strive for justice and the cause of God and to combat injustice and evil, such as 3:110, 9:71 and 22:41, can be interpreted in this manner. For example, verse 4:75, often quoted by Khomeini and other Iranian leaders, may be translated in the following general terms: "Why do you [believers] not fight in the cause of God and the oppressed among men, women and children who call upon God to rescue them and raise someone in their support and help." As we shall see, there are Sunna reports which seem to require direct action, whenever possible, in removing injustice.

It is true that these sources can and should, in my view, *now* be interpreted in ways that are consistent with the rule of law, both domestic and international, and that struggle and fighting against injustice and evil should be done by means other than force. But this does not change the fact that these sources have been interpreted in the past as supporting direct violent action against what is perceived to be injustice and evil. As was explained in Chapter 4 of this book, Shari'a permits such use of force within the Muslim community itself. Thus the position attributed to Iran brings out the conflict between the old notion of pan-Islamic unity of the *Umma*, nation of Islam, and the modern notion of separate sovereignty for the population of each nation-state as constituted within given geopolitical boundaries.[58]

In the past, the Iran-Iraq war may have been classified as an internal or civil war within the *Umma* of Islam. But since the consensus of modern Muslim peoples has accepted the reality of separate nation-states,[59] the use of force by one Muslim state against another is a matter of international and not domestic concern. Nevertheless, it is interesting to note the implications of verse 49:9 of the Qur'an, which provides for intervention by other Muslims when two groups of Muslims are engaged in fighting. This verse may be translated as follows: "If two parties of the believers [Muslims] fall to fighting, then make peace between them. But if one of them transgresses beyond bounds against the other, then you all shall fight against the one that transgresses until it complies with the command of God. Once it complies, then make peace between them with justice and be fair [just]; for God loves those who are fair [just]."

There is an unavoidable element of ambiguity in the Shari'a principle based on this verse, as illustrated by its application to the Iran-Iraq war. According to the verse, if the efforts of the total Muslim community to mediate peace between the two warring Muslim parties fail, then all Muslims must fight the transgressor until it complies with the command of God. The question will then arise, Who is the transgressor and what is the command of God with which it must comply?

On one hand, Iran could claim that Iraq is the transgressor not only in initiating the attack but also in being a secular state that does not implement Shari'a in its system of government. According to this point of view, Iran would demand that all other Muslims join it in fighting Iraq until an Islamic state is established in Iraq. This may well be the rationale of the often-quoted demand of Iran that the Ba'thist government of President Sadam Hessian must be overthrown as a condition of ending the war.

On the other hand, Iraq could claim that Iran is the transgressor not only in perpetrating historical wrongs against Iraq but also in continuing its current attack despite Iraq's repeated declarations of its willingness to end the war and reach a negotiated settlement. In response to Iranian charges against the nature of the political regime and its ideological orientation, Iraq could claim that this is a domestic matter for the Iraqi people to decide without intervention by external forces, even if they are fellow Muslims.

Both aspects of Shari'a, its authorization of the use of force to establish an Islamic state and its provision for intervention between Muslim groups at war with each other, have very serious implications for modern international relations. Since Muslims may reasonably differ on what constitutes a proper Islamic state, does the first-mentioned aspect of Shari'a give any Muslim state a license to intervene, by force if necessary, in the internal affairs of another whenever the first state deems the second not to be in conformity with the dictates of Shari'a? Moreover, since the conditions for intervention under the second-mentioned aspect can be controversial, does this mean that other Muslims, or other Muslim states, may intervene against whichever side they deem to be at fault? How can international peace be maintained if Muslim states can use force against each other in this way?

It would seem necessarily to follow that the rule of international law must prevail in international relations, whether among Muslim states or between Muslim and non-Muslim states.[60] As will be suggested in the last section of this chapter, the relevant verses of the Qur'an and other sources of Shari'a must be interpreted in this light.

International Terrorism

It is often said that it is difficult to agree on a general definition for that form of politically motivated violence commonly known as terrorism because each situation has to be seen in its own specific context, including factors such as the causes of the underlying conflict and the options available to the parties in seeking to achieve their objectives.[61] Which factors are relevant and in what relationship would seem to depend on the purpose of the definition, that is, whether one is trying to understand the phenomenon from a political, sociological, or psychological point of view.[62] For our purposes here, terrorism is defined as the use of clandestine violence against noncombatants for political ends.[63] As such, terrorism can be perpetrated by official as well as private persons. When either the planning, preparation, and/or execution of such acts of violence is done in more than one country, terrorism becomes the object of international concern.

Although the use of clandestine violence against noncombatants contravenes Shari'a rules on the conduct of legitimate use of force, some texts of Qur'an and Sunna and some precedents in Islamic history may be taken as sanctioning direct action to remedy injustice and redress grievances. Some of the relevant verses have already been quoted. A Sunna reported in the most authoritative compilations of Sunna, which seems to support this interpretation, has been translated as follows: "The Prophet is reported to have said: Whoever from among you [Muslims] sees an indecency [injustice], he must change it by his hand; if he cannot, he must do so by his tongue; if he cannot, he must do so by his heart [through disapproval, etc.] but this last [method] would testify to the extreme weakness of Faith."[64] An enlightened interpretation of these sources, including the above-quoted Sunna, would indicate that they do not necessarily sanction direct violent action. I would suggest that these sources should now be interpreted as indicating nonviolent action, which is consistent with the rule of law. Nevertheless, it has to be admitted that these sources are open to and have been interpreted in the past as sanctioning direct violent action.

This is a clear example of what has been described as tension between the general orientation of Shari'a and essential international law. Qur'an and Sunna sources, first received and understood in a totally different political and sociological context, lend themselves to being used as justification of clandestine violent action under radically transformed circumstances.

The potential for such abuse of Islamic sources out of their proper historical context can be defeated only through the following principle of interpretation. The existence of Qur'anic and Sunna sources in support of direct and violent action and the historical use of these sources to justify such action in early Islamic history are beyond dispute. It must therefore be established, as a fundamental principle of construction, that although the interpretation given to those sources, and the authority they were deemed to provide for direct violent action in the past, may have been justified in a previous historical context, such interpretation is no longer valid, and such authority is no longer acceptable as sufficient. Given the previous weakness of the rule of law in the domestic context and its almost total absence in international relations, it was natural for the founding jurists to interpret those sources as sanctioning self-help and direct violent action. Such an interpretation is no longer viable because of the much stronger rule of law in both the domestic and international spheres. In any case, since self-help and direct violent action can only mean disaster and the collapse of civilized national and international society today, the previous interpretation must be excluded as a matter of policy.

Muslims may feel threatened by the encroachment of secularism and materialism on their world and may have serious concerns over "un-Islamic" cultural and intellectual influences. But as long as these threats and influences are nonviolent, Muslims are entitled to respond only in nonviolent ways. They should seek to reinforce Islamic moral values within their societies and respond to the cultural and intellectual threat to their faith and lifestyle in peaceful and nonoppressive ways. I believe that it is in the best interest of Muslims to respond to the challenge culturally and intellectually rather than seek to oppress and intimidate their "enemies." It is wrong and counterproductive for a major world religion like Islam to rely on oppression and intimidation of dissent and unorthodoxy to maintain the adherence of its followers.

RECONCILIATION AND POSITIVE CONTRIBUTION

The reform methodology that seems to offer the best prospects of achieving the complete reconciliation of Islamic law with essential international law is the one that was explained in Chapter 3. Fortunately, the preexisting theory and reality of Islamic international relations already include some elements that can be used as foundations for the reconciliation of Islamic law and modern international law. First, in spite of the theoretical antagonism and constant state of war between Muslims and non-Muslims, Muslims have experienced peaceful coexistence with non-Muslims in the past. Second, there is very strong support for the sanctity of treaties between Muslims and non-Muslims. This is emphasized by both the Qur'an and Sunna and supported by ancient Muslim practice. Third, we have the acceptance of established methods of peaceful international intercourse and settlement of disputes through diplomacy and arbitration.[65] All of these and possibly other positive elements of the Islamic tradition can now be used in the construction of a comprehensive theory of modern Islamic law which is fully consistent with essential international law.

The only way to achieve the necessary degree of reform is to substitute as bases of Islamic law those clear and definite verses of the Qur'an and related Sunna that sanction the use of force in propagating Islam among non-Muslims and in upholding it among renegade Muslims with texts of the Qur'an and Sunna that enjoin the use of peaceful means in achieving those objectives. In accordance with the fundamental premise that both the Qur'an and Sunna must be understood in their historical context, the proposed reform would replace those elements of Shari'a based on the Qur'an of Medina and related Sunna, and on the practice of that stage, with modern Islamic law based on the Qur'an of Mecca and related Sunna.

All the verses of the Qur'an and related Sunna that sanction the use of force in propagating Islam among Muslims and in upholding it among renegade Muslims were revealed and uttered by the Prophet during the Medina stage. In accordance with the principle of *naskh*, abrogation or repeal, the founding jurists have held that these subsequent texts of Medina and the practice of the first Islamic state that was based on them must have legally abrogated or repealed all previous texts and practices that were inconsistent with what was perceived to be the final message of the Prophet in Medina. In this way, the earlier Meccan texts and practices were seen as a transitional stage, dictated by tactical considerations, namely, the small numbers and the relative weakness of Muslims during that stage. With the massive conversion of Arabs to Islam and the establishment of the Islamic state in Medina, it was perceived that the Muslims became strong enough to propagate their faith by force and subjugate all the enemies of the Islamic state, whether within or outside the Muslim community.

Given the historical context in which the founding jurists undertook interpretation of the sources of Islam and construction of Shari'a as a comprehensive legal system, that understanding and application of the principle of *naskh* was both logical and necessary. Islam would probably not have survived if the Muslims were denied the use of force in propagating the faith and maintaining the cohesion and stability of the community. It was impracticable to maintain a nonviolent society at a time when violent force *was* the law. But as has often been reiterated in this study, the context within which the sources of Islam were interpreted and applied initially has changed drastically, thereby making it necessary to modify the law derived from those sources. For that reason, it is now both logical and necessary to reverse the process of *naskh*.

I believe that it would be easily appreciated by all Muslims today that the quality of faith in Islam achieved through peaceful and completely voluntary conversion is far superior to that achieved through the use or threat of use of force. Moreover, the quality of the Muslim community, which is held together by genuine legitimacy and justice, is far superior to that of a community held together by repression of dissent and unorthodoxy. This would make the earlier texts of Mecca superior in content to those of Medina. Consequently, it was the Medina model of intercommunal and international relations which was transitional and tactical and not that of Mecca.

Once accepted in principle, this interpretation would achieve a large degree of reconciliation of Islamic law with essential international law because it would repudiate the religious legitimacy of using force in propagating Islam or upholding it among Muslims. To follow the principle of reciprocity, cited in previous chapters and further developed in Chapter 7, modern Muslim states must concede to all states, whether Islamic or not, the same degree of self-determination and national sovereignty they would claim for themselves.

This approach will not work unless the Muslims can see and appreciate the drastic change in historical context. The principles of essential international law must be upheld and respected by all other major cultural traditions and political ideologies if the Muslims are to be convinced of the need to abandon those elements of Shari'a which are inconsistent with modern international law. In that way, non-Muslims would be entitled to demand reciprocal respect for international law from the Muslims. The process is dynamic in that, whereas compliance by all participants is likely to generate greater compliance and further positive developments, serious failure to comply by some of the major participants is likely to lead to noncompliance and frustration of the effort by other participants.

For example, the clear inconsistency and flagrant disregard of international law by a major power like the United States of America is bound to have negative consequences for the credibility of the rule of law in international relations. When the rest of the world witnessed the United States invading the small island of Grenada, it might reasonably conclude that international law is merely a tool used by the powerful against the weak rather than a credible force for maintaining the rule of law in international relations.[66] A similar conclusion may be drawn from the United States's refusal to comply with the decision of the International Court of Justice in the case of *Nicaragua* v. *United States*.[67]

Nevertheless, it would be completely irresponsible, in my view, to argue that these negative developments suggest that we should abandon efforts to establish the rule of law in international relations. On the contrary, I believe that these developments should strengthen our resolve to enforce the rule of law against whoever violates or threatens to violate it in international relations. To maintain otherwise is to surrender to total chaos, if not the annihilation of humankind through nuclear war.

$$\gg 7 \ll$$

Shari'a and Basic Human Rights Concerns

$\mathcal{S}$OME OF THE ISSUES discussed in Chapters 4 and 5 in relation to constitutionalism and criminal justice can be seen as issues of human rights in the domestic context of the modern nation-state. In that context, however, they are commonly known as fundamental constitutional rights. As used in this chapter, the term *human rights* refers to those rights recognized by and promoted through international law and institutions. Thus, although fundamental constitutional rights and international human rights are both concerned with the same type of claim or entitlement, the former deals with these claims and/or entitlements in the context of a domestic legal system while the latter deals with them in the context of the international legal system.

In accordance with the fundamental purpose of this book—to enable Muslims to exercise their right to self-determination without violating the rights of others to the same—this chapter will attempt to identify areas of conflict between Shari'a and universal standards of human rights and seek a reconciliation and positive relationship between the two systems. The hypothesis of this chapter, like that of the preceding chapters, is that if they implement historical Shari'a, Muslims cannot exercise their right to self-determination without violating the rights of others. It is possible, however, to achieve a balance within the framework of Islam as a whole by developing appropriate principles of modern Islamic public law.

Stating the objectives of the chapter in this way raises the initial question of the relevance of so-called universal human rights to Shari'a, or for that matter to Islam itself. Why should universal human rights be a criterion for judging Shari'a and an objective of modern Islamic public law?

161

UNIVERSALITY OF HUMAN RIGHTS

Article 1.3 of the Charter of the United Nations, quoted in Chapter 6 above, imposes on all members of the United Nations the obligation to cooperate in promoting and encouraging respect for human rights and fundamental freedoms for all without distinction as to race, sex (gender), language, or religion. But the charter did not define the terms *human rights* and *fundamental freedoms*. That task was undertaken by the United Nations in a series of declarations, conventions, and covenants drafted and adopted since 1948.[1] The U.N. human rights documents and regional documents of Europe, the Americas, and Africa[2] all have the same premise – that there shall be universal standards of human rights which must be observed by all countries of the world, or countries of the region in the case of regional documents.

There is some debate as to the genuine universality of some of these standards,[3] and there are some serious problems of enforcement. This does not mean, however, that there are no universal and binding standards or that enforcement efforts should be abandoned. The position adopted here is that there are certain universal standards of human rights which are binding under international law and that every effort should be made to enforce them in practice. Thus the principle of respect for and protection of human rights has been described as *jus cogens*, that is, such a fundamental principle of international law that states may not repudiate by their agreement.[4] This would, of course, be true of respect for and protection of human rights in principle. It is easier to give examples of human rights of this stature, such as the prohibition of genocide and slavery, than to define the concept in a categorical fashion. Nevertheless, such a definition, or at least a criterion by which human rights may be identified, will be attempted below.

The main difficulty with working to establish universal standards across cultural, and particularly religious, boundaries is that each tradition has its own internal frame of reference because each tradition derives the validity of its precepts and norms from its own sources. If a cultural, especially religious, tradition relates to other traditions at all, it is likely to do so in a negative and perhaps even hostile way. To claim the loyalty and conformity of its members, a cultural or religious tradition would normally assert its own superiority over other traditions.[5]

Nevertheless, there is a common normative principle shared by all the major cultural traditions which, if construed in an enlightened manner, is capable of sustaining universal standards of human rights. That is the principle that one should treat other people as he or she wishes to be treated by them. This golden rule, referred to earlier as the principle of reciprocity, is shared by all the major religious traditions of the world. Moreover, the moral and logical force of this simple proposition can easily be appreciated by all human beings of whatever cultural tradition or philosophical persuasion.

It is not easy to place oneself in the exact position of another person, especially if that other person is of a different gender or religious belief.[6] The purpose of the principle of reciprocity, as applied to the present argument, is that one should try to achieve the closest possible approximation to placing oneself in the position of the other person. Assuming that one is in the exact position of the other person in all material respects, including gender and religious belief or other convictions, what basic human rights would one demand?

It should be emphasized that reciprocity is mutual so that when one identifies with another person, one would ascribe equivalent reciprocity to the belief system of the other person. Thus, when person X accepts the status or belief of person Y for the purposes of conceding Y's right to the same treatment which X would demand for himself, X would assume that Y accepts the same principle of reciprocity toward X by conceding to X the same rights he would demand for himself. In other words, X should not be entitled to deny Y's rights on the grounds that Y is unlikely to afford X the same rights because Y's belief system does not impose that obligation upon Y. If Y's belief system in fact fails to accord X the same rights, the answer would be for X to insist on reciprocity from Y rather than abdicate his obligation to afford Y the same rights he would claim for himself.

The problem with using the principle of reciprocity in this context is the tendency of cultural, and particularly religious, traditions to restrict the application of the principle to other members of its cultural or religious tradition, if not to a certain group within the given tradition.[7] The historical conception of the principle of reciprocity under Shari'a did not apply to women and non-Muslims to the same extent that it applied to Muslim men.[8] In other words, by granting women and non-Muslims a lower status and sanctioning discriminatory treatment against them, Shari'a denies women and non-Muslims the same degree of honor and human dignity it guarantees to Muslim men.

This general problem will have to be addressed within each cultural tradition. In the case of Islam, for example, one must be able to establish a technique for reinterpreting the basic sources, the Qur'an and Sunna, in a way that would enable us to remove the basis of discrimination against women and non-Muslims. The technique I find most promising has already been explained in Chapter 3 and applied to questions of constitutionalism, criminal justice, and international relations. In the remainder of this chapter, I hope to explain the inadequacy of Shari'a as a basis for human rights in the Muslim context and propose an alternative Islamic foundation for universal human rights.

Without going into the details of arguments that may be too closely identified with a particular cultural tradition,[9] one can make the following basic transcultural justification for universal standards of human rights. The criteria I would adopt for identifying universal human rights is that they are rights to which human beings are entitled by virtue of being human. In other words, universal standards of human rights are, by definition, appreciated by a wide variety of cultural traditions because they pertain to the inherent dignity and well-being of every human being, regardless of race, gender, language, or religion.[10] It follows that the practical test by which these rights should be identified is whether the right in question is claimed by the particular cultural tradition for its own members. Applying the principle of reciprocity among all human beings rather than just among the members of a particular group, I would argue that universal human rights are those which a cultural tradition would claim for its own members and must therefore concede to members of other traditions if it is to expect reciprocal treatment from those others.

In content and substance, I submit that universal human rights are based on the two primary forces that motivate all human behavior, the will to live and the will to be free.[11] Through the will to live, human beings have always striven to secure their food, shelter, health, and all other means for the preservation of life. Moreover, people have always striven to improve the quality of their lives through the development and manipulation of available physical resources and through political struggle to achieve the fair and equitable distribution of wealth and power among the members of the particular community. At one level, the will to be free overlaps with the will to live, in that it is the will to be free from physical constraints and to be secure in food, shelter, health, and other necessities of a good life. At another level, the will to be free exceeds the will to live in that it is the driving force behind the pursuit of spiritual, moral, and artistic well-being and excellence.

The right to seek the satisfaction of the legitimate claims of these two forces is granted by every cultural tradition to its own members and must therefore, in accordance with the principle of reciprocity, be granted to the members of other traditions. This is, in my view, the basis of the universality of certain minimum human rights. By applying this simple criterion, we can identify those rights, claims, and entitlements that ought to be protected as human rights even if they are not identified as such by any formal document.

Relevant Standards of Human Rights

Our primary concern here is to establish cross-cultural foundations for the universality of human rights. Consequently, other major and important issues, such as the relationship between strategic goals and tactical means, the question of hierarchy and trade-offs between different sets of rights, and the legitimacy of permitting derogations from certain obligations in times of emergency are not discussed in this book.

Being consistent with its own historical context, Shari'a restricted the application of the principle of reciprocity in relation to women and non-Muslims. As frequently suggested throughout this book, the inadequacy of the public law of Shari'a can only be understood and supplemented through a consideration of the impact of the historical context within which Shari'a was constructed by the founding jurists of the eighth and ninth centuries out of the original sources of Islam. In that historical context, it was natural for the Muslim jurists to restrict the "other person" in the reciprocity rule to other Muslim men. This is a common feature of all historical cultural traditions and is also reflected in attitudes and policies of modern nation-states. It is for this aspect of the historical interpretation of the principle of reciprocity that I have said earlier that this principle can sustain universal human rights "if it is construed in an enlightened manner." An enlightened construction would extend the "other person" to all human beings, regardless of gender, religion, race, or language.

If such an enlightened construction is to be effective in changing Muslim attitudes and policies, two conditions must be satisfied. First, the proposed broad construction of the other person has to be valid and credible from the Islamic point of view. This can be done only through Islamic arguments that repudiate the historical restrictive construction and support the alternative broader construction. Second, other cultural and religious traditions must undertake a similar process of enlightened construction. It seems to me that the historical restriction of the other person to male members of one's own culture was unavoidable when other cultural traditions practiced similar exclusion of women and nonmembers of the particular culture. It would therefore seem to follow that we need to overcome historical hostility and resentment through concurrent action, each working within his or her own cultural tradition toward the same goal.

In the following outline of the relevant universal human rights, it is useful to quote international custom and treaties that recognize these rights because they establish norms that are binding on Muslim states under international law. In quoting these documents, however, it is not suggested that the given rights are accepted as universal simply because they are recognized as such by the documents. Rather, the rights are recognized by the documents because they *are* universal human rights, that is, rights to which every human being is entitled by virtue of being human.

Slavery is one of the most serious impediments on both the will to live and the will to be free. Although it has been practiced by every major human civilization throughout history, slavery, in the sense of institutionalized and legal ownership of human beings as chattel, has finally come to be universally condemned and outlawed by both domestic and international law.[12] More effort is needed to eradicate all shades and forms of economic exploitation and degradation reminiscent of slavery. In the present context, however, we are concerned with slavery as a legal institution.

The abolition of slavery may well be the first example of the acceptance of an international human right as a limitation on domestic jurisdiction.[13] In other words, the antislavery movement established a precedent for recognizing the principle that the violation of a universal human right by one country is the legitimate concern of other countries.[14] As a result of this movement, a series of international agreements was concluded, culminating in one of the most widely ratified conventions condemning and prohibiting slavery under international law.[15] Moreover, several major international treaties have since reiterated the prohibition of slavery and required signatory states to outlaw and eliminate its practice in their domestic jurisdictions.[16]

Another early example of international cooperation in the field of human rights is the movement to eliminate the persecution of and discrimination against religious minorities.[17] Besides the moral abhorrence of such practices, persecution and discrimination on grounds of religion were perceived to be among the major causes of international conflict and war.[18] Consequently, a number of international treaties declared such persecution and discrimination a violation of human rights.[19]

A third area of emerging universal human rights, as defined above, is the prohibition of discrimination on grounds of gender. Although this right did not receive international attention as early as the other two rights, it has now come to be recognized as a universal human right under a variety of international conventions.[20]

The principle of nondiscrimination does not preclude all differential treatment on grounds such as race, gender, or religion. In this respect, I would agree with the proposition that one has to judge the nature of differential treatment in light of its purpose. "If the purpose or effect is to nullify or impair the enjoyment of human rights on an equal footing, the practice is discriminatory."[21] In this way, one would accept action that has the purpose or effect of enhancing rather than impairing the enjoyment of human rights on an equal footing.[22] It is not necessary to go into these issues in detail in this context. What is being affirmed here is that discrimination on grounds such as gender and religion violates human rights.

PROBLEMS OF IMPLEMENTATION AND ENFORCEMENT

It would be misleading to leave the preceding discussion and definition of universal human rights without reference to their status under current international law or without an assessment of the realistic prospects of their implementation and enforcement in practice. The belief that there are certain universal standards of human rights which ought to prevail in practice will have to be translated into concrete policy and action in everyday life.

As a matter of strict international law, however, states can only be bound by their own agreement as expressed in treaties or through customary international law. Consequently, a modern Muslim state would be bound to respect and uphold a certain human right only if it had agreed to do so by becoming a party to an international agreement which created that obligation or if the obligation to respect and uphold the particular right could be shown to be part of customary international law.[23] A treaty obligation prohibiting slavery and discrimination on grounds of gender or religion can be demonstrated with respect to a number of modern Muslim states.[24] Moreover, slavery, and possibly discrimination on grounds of religion, are prohibited by customary international law, thereby creating a legal obligation on all countries of the world to prevent these practices within their own domestic jurisdictions.

Although evidence in support of a customary international law right against gender discrimination is mounting, it may be too early to maintain that such a right has already been established.[25] For the time being, therefore, it seems that we have to rely on international agreements as a source of a legal obligation on states parties to the particular agreements to respect and uphold a human right against gender discrimination.

The existence of legal obligations under international law is not sufficient by itself to ensure compliance. Adequate mechanisms and resources may be necessary for the enforcement or implementation of the obligation. Conversely, states may be influenced by political and other factors into greater compliance with human rights standards without having a legal obligation to do so. In fact, I would place greater reliance on the influence of general education and enlightenment of public opinion in improving compliance with universal human rights standards than I would on legal obligations under international law. Nevertheless, the value of establishing legal obligations under international law should not be underestimated, if only as existing norms to which appeal may be made in domestic struggles and as the basis for international cooperation in the field.

Reference has already been made to the conflict between traditional notions of national sovereignty and efforts to enforce international standards, including efforts to ensure compliance with universal standards of human rights.[26] In the present context, it must be emphasized that national sovereignty is in itself a manifestation of the collective human right to self-determination as established under customary international law and recognized by the U.N. Charter and various international human rights instruments. This principle is most authoritatively defined by the Declaration on Principles of International Law Concerning Friendly Relations and Co-operation among States in Accordance with the Charter of the United Nations, adopted by the U.N. General Assembly without a vote on October 24, 1970.[27] In that declaration, the principle of equal rights and self-determination of peoples is defined as follows: "By virtue of the principle of equal rights and self-determination of peoples enshrined in the Charter of the United Nations, all peoples have the right freely to determine, without external interference, their political status and to pursue their economic and cultural development, and every State has the duty to respect this right in accordance with the provisions of the Charter." The tenor of this and other principles of international law affirmed in this declaration by the consensus of all members of the United Nations is one of concern for the rights of peoples to assert their self-identity and the right to seek to realize justice and peace for themselves without interference by other states. As such, the right to self-determination cannot include the violation of the basic human rights of the subjects of a particular state. In fact, the principle of equal rights and self-determination of the Declaration on Principles of International Law Concerning Friendly Relations and Co-operation proceeds to specify that "every State has the duty to promote through joint and separate action universal respect for and observance of human rights and fundamental freedoms in accordance with the Charter [of the United Nations]."[28]

The primary apprehension in relation to the right to self-determination is the fear of both old and newly independent states, especially in Africa and Asia, that this right may give impetus to secessionist movements by ethnic, religious, or linguistic minorities.[29] Thus, although this right is now universally acknowledged for peoples under colonial or foreign domination, it is often resisted within the context of a given nation-state. This vast and highly complex dimension of the subject is not within the scope of the present study.[30] My position in this respect is that even if, and to the extent that, the right to self-determination does not necessarily mean a right to separate independent statehood for a people distinguished by religion or culture from the main or dominant segments of the population, it does require granting the full range of civil, political, economic, social, and cultural human rights associated with this fundamental principle.

Thus, I would submit that, far from having to challenge the legitimate domain of self-determination and national sovereignty to establish the right of other states and international organizations to act in support of universal human rights, the obligation to respect human rights is an integral part of the right to self-determination and a perfectly justified limitation on national sovereignty. The right to self-determination is the right of a state to assert and realize the human rights of all its population, without distinction on grounds of race, gender, language, or religion, and not the right of a state to negate, deny, or otherwise frustrate the human rights of its subjects.

It is not surprising that governments that are guilty of human rights violations attempt to conceal their misconduct behind claims of national sovereignty and security or protest against interference in matters of domestic jurisdiction. What is important in this regard, however, is that the international community cannot afford to let such governments manipulate the valid and indispensable principles of self-determination and national sovereignty in ways that defeat the other equally valid and indispensable principles of universal human rights.[31] Given previous experience with Nazi Germany and current experience within the Republic of South Africa, for example, it must be established once and for all that no state is free to violate the universal human rights of its subjects under the guise of national sovereignty and domestic jurisdiction.

To maintain that a state's violation of the human rights of its own nationals is a matter of international concern does not mean that other states may intervene by force to remedy the situation. National sovereignty must be respected because it is the manifestation of the right of the people of that state to self-determination. What is suggested here is that mechanisms should be developed to enable the international community to ensure that every state respects the human rights of its own nationals. As correctly stated by Richard Falk, "the renunciation of intervention does not substitute a policy of nonintervention; it involves the development of some form of *collective intervention*."[32] Otherwise, we would be left with one of two unsatisfactory consequences: either tolerate a state's violation of the human rights of its own nationals or permit other states to practice so-called humanitarian intervention. Although this principle has been asserted in the past with some justification, there is an obvious potential for abuse because humanitarian intervention can be used as a pretext for the violation of the national sovereignty of other states in furtherance of antihumanitarian objectives.[33]

SHARI'A AND HUMAN RIGHTS

In Chapter 6 it was argued that the historical context within which Shari'a was constructed and applied by the early Muslims explained and justified its sanction of Muslim antagonism toward non-Muslims and its countenance of the use of force against them. By the same token, Shari'a's position on what is known in modern terminology as human rights was also justified by the historical context. During the formative stages of Shari'a (and for the next millennium at least) there was no conception of universal human rights anywhere in the world. Slavery was an established and lawful institution in many parts of the world throughout this period. Until the nineteenth century, moreover, it was normal throughout the world to determine a person's status and rights by his religion. Similarly, up to the twentieth century, women were not normally recognized as persons capable of exercising legal rights and capacities comparable to those enjoyed by men. Full citizenship and its benefits were to be restricted to the men of certain ethnic or racial groups within a particular polity in the same way that status and its benefits were restricted by Shari'a to Muslim men. The most that Shari'a could do, and did in fact do, in that historical context was to modify and lighten the harsh consequences of slavery and discrimination on grounds of religion or gender.[34]

Once again, to argue that Shari'a's restrictive view of human rights was justified by the historical context and that it was an improvement on the preexisting situation is not to say that this view is still justified. On the contrary, my position is that since Shari'a's view of human rights was justified by the historical context, it ceases to be so justified in the present drastically different context. By the same token that Shari'a as a practical legal system could not have disregarded the conception of human rights prevailing at the time it purported to apply in the seventh century, modern Islamic law cannot disregard the present conception of human rights if it is to be applied today.

In an early short piece, Khadduri said: "Human rights in Islam, as prescribed by the divine law [Shari'a] are the privilege only of persons of full legal capacity. A person with full legal capacity is a living human being of mature age, free, and of Moslem faith. It follows, accordingly,

that non-Moslems and slaves who lived in the Islamic state were only partially protected by law or had no legal capacity at all."[35] While accepting
this statement as a substantially accurate presentation of the position under
Shari'a,[36] I would add the following qualification with respect to the status of Muslim women: although it is true that they have full legal capacity
under Shari'a in relation to civil and commercial law matters, in the sense
that they have the requisite legal personality to hold and dispose of property and otherwise acquire or lose civil liabilities in their own independent
right, Muslim women do not enjoy human rights on an equal footing with
Muslim men under Shari'a. Moreover, in accepting Khadduri's statement
of the position under Shari'a, I would also reiterate my often-stated position that this aspect of Shari'a is not the final word of Islam on the subject. As I shall argue at the end of this chapter, an alternative formulation
of Islamic public law which would eliminate these limitations on human
rights is both desirable and possible.

    When we consider writings by contemporary Muslim scholars, we
find that most of the published expositions of human rights in Islam are
not helpful because they overlook the problems of slavery and discrimination against women and non-Muslims.[37]

    One of the better discussions of human rights in Islam, which
shows sensitivity to gender discrimination, is that by Riffat Hassan entitled "On Human Rights and the Qur'anic Perspectives."[38] The problem
with this article is that it is selective in its choice of the Qur'anic perspectives. In overlooking some relevant verses of the Qur'an, the author fails
to confront those Qur'anic perspectives which are not consistent with her
vision of the Qur'anic perspectives on human rights. As will be suggested
at the end of this chapter, the only effective approach to achieve *sufficient*
reform of Shari'a in relation to universal human rights is to cite sources
in the Qur'an and Sunna which are inconsistent with universal human rights
and explain them in historical context, while citing those sources which
are supportive of human rights as the basis of the legally applicable principles and rules of Islamic law today.

    In contrast to the generally evasive approach of the majority of
Muslim writers on human rights issues, a few other Muslim writers have
adopted a more honest and candid approach. A good example of this approach is Sultanhussein Tabandeh's *Muslim Commentary on the Universal Declaration of Human Rights*. This short book has the merit of clearly
indicating the inconsistencies between Shari'a and the 1948 Universal Declaration of Human Rights in relation to the status of women and non-
Muslims.[39] Tabandeh notes these inconsistencies to argue that Muslims are
not bound by the Universal Declaration of Human Rights in these respects,
whereas I am suggesting that it is Shari'a which should be revised, from

an Islamic point of view, to provide for these universal human rights. I welcome the clear statement of the inconsistencies between Shari'a and universal human rights as part of my argument for Islamic law reform. It should be recalled, however, that the proposed reform must maintain its Islamic legitimacy if it is to be effective in changing Muslim attitudes and policies on these issues.

For our purposes here, we need not go into an exhaustive statement of all human rights because there are no fundamental problems with Shari'a except for slavery and discrimination on grounds of gender and religion. It is more to the point to focus on those human rights standards which are violated by Shari'a, the prohibition of slavery and discrimination on grounds of gender and religion.

Slavery

It is obvious that Shari'a did not introduce slavery, which was the norm throughout the world at the time. Shari'a recognized slavery as an institution but sought to restrict the sources of acquisition of slaves, to improve their condition, and to encourage their emancipation through a variety of religious and civil methods.[40] Nevertheless, slavery is lawful under Shari'a to the present day.[41] It is unlikely today that institutionalized slavery will be formally sanctioned in any Muslim country.[42] If the right conditions under which slaves may be acquired should arise today and someone was made a slave under those conditions, Shari'a would protect the "rights" of both the master and the slave in the same way it did thirteen centuries ago. In this respect, one would appreciate the candid and honest statement of the situation under Shari'a by Tabandeh, who noted the absence of any possibility of finding confirmation of the legality of the enslavement of any person today, and then proceeded to say:

> Nonetheless, should the legal condition for the enslavement of any-
> one be proven (because he had been taken prisoner fighting against
> Islam with a view to its extirpation and persisted in invincible ignorance
> in his sacrilegious and infidel convictions, or because there did exist
> legal proof that all his ancestors without exception had been slaves
> descended from a person taken prisoner conducting a warfare of such
> invincible ignorance) Islam would be bound to recognize such slavery
> as legal, even though recommending the freeing of the person and if
> possible his conversion, in this modern age.[43]

In accepting this as an accurate statement of Shari'a, I am not accepting this aspect of Shari'a as the final and conclusive law of Islam. In this light, it would be lawful, from Shari'a's point of view, if slavery is reestablished in a modern Islamic state. As I have argued in Chapter 3 of this book, however, there is the possibility of replacing these dated and archaic aspects of Shari'a with modern and humane principles of Islamic law. Such an enlightened construction would prohibit slavery as a matter of *Islamic* law. Thus it is Shari'a and not Islam that "would be bound to recognize such slavery" under Tabandeh's statement.

To make an Islamic argument for the prohibition of slavery, we first need to know the circumstances under which slavery is permitted by Shari'a and its rules regarding the treatment and emancipation of slaves.

There is no verse in the Qur'an which directly sanctions the enslavement of any person, but many verses do so by implication when, for example, the Qur'an speaks of a Muslim's right to cohabit with his slave concubine, which clearly presupposes the existence of such slave women. The same can be said of Sunna on the subject.[44] The only way a person who is born free may be brought into slavery under Shari'a is through military defeat in a war sanctioned by Shari'a.[45] According to the founding jurists, subjecting the vanquished unbelievers to slavery is one of the options open to Muslims under Shari'a. Thus the Shafi'i school allowed the imam four options in dealing with prisoners of war: immediate execution, enslavement, or release with or without ransom. The Maliki school restricted the options to execution, enslavement, or release with ransom, and the Hanafi school reduced them further to either execution or enslavement.[46]

Once a person is brought into slavery through military conquest or is born to slave parents, he or she remains a slave until emancipated. While a slave, he or she may be employed in whatever manner deemed fit by his or her master but must be treated with kindness and compassion as required by Shari'a.[47] That does not preclude the sale of slaves in principle, but it may place some limitations on the conditions under which the sale is concluded, such as a requirement not to separate a mother and child when they are sold as slaves.[48]

Shari'a encouraged the emancipation of slaves through a variety of methods. The emancipation of slaves is designated by verses 9:60 and 2:177 of the Qur'an as one of the prescribed items of expenditure of the official treasury or private charity. Moreover, the emancipation of a slave is prescribed by some verses of the Qur'an, such as verses 4:92 and 58:3, as religious penance and atonement for some sins, and recommended by others, such as verses 2:177 and 90:11–13, as a most meritorious act. Verse 24:33 of the Qur'an encourages a Muslim to grant the wish of a slave who wants to contract with the master for emancipation in exchange for the payment of a certain sum of money or performance of certain services.

Given the entrenched position of slavery throughout the world at the time, Islam had no choice but to recognize the institution of slavery in that historical context and do its best to improve the conditions under which slaves were to endure their unfortunate status. It can also be argued that Islam was aiming at the elimination of slavery by restricting its incidence and encouraging its termination. But since there was no internal mechanism by which slavery was to be rendered unlawful by Shari'a, it continued to be lawful under that system of law up to the present day.

Riffat Hassan quoted with approval the argument made by G. A. Parwez to the effect that since the Qur'an restricted the source of slavery to prisoners of war, and then prescribed in verse 47:4 that prisoners of war were to be set free either for ransom or as a favor, it follows that "the door for future slavery was thus closed by the Qur'an forever. Whatever happened in subsequent history was the responsibility of the Muslims and not of the Qur'an."[49] Similarly, it is sometimes argued by modern Muslims that verse 47:4 of the Qur'an prohibits the enslavement of captives after a war with Muslims. The relevant part of this verse may be translated as follows: "When you meet the unbelievers [in battle], smite at their necks [kill them]. Once you have thoroughly subdued them, then [hold] and bind [them]. Thereafter [practice] either generosity [by freeing them without compensation] or [for] ransom, until war is terminated."

These arguments are, in my view, examples of selective citation of Shari'a sources leading to serious distortion and confusion. When we consider that both the Qur'an and Sunna did recognize and regulate slavery in a number of ways, that the Prophet himself and leading Companions had slaves, and that all the founding jurists of Shari'a took the existence of slavery for granted and elaborated rules for its regulation, we cannot dismiss the matter as the alleged failure of generations of Muslims to implement the intention of the Qur'an to abolish slavery. Despite the apparent limitation by verse 47:4 of the options open to Muslims over their captives, it is a historical fact that Muslim armies, during and after the Prophet's time, have continued to exercise the option to enslave their captives. Moreover, it should be emphasized that the founding jurists of Shari'a did not perceive this verse as excluding the option of enslavement of captives.[50] This verse may now be used in an argument for prohibiting enslavement as a matter of Islamic law, but this possible construction of the verse should not be confused with the position under Shari'a as it has been established by early Muslim practice and authoritatively stated by the founding jurists.

I believe that the early Muslims were correct in interpreting the Qur'an and Sunna as recognizing the institution of slavery *in the histori-*

cal context of early Islam. In the current historical context and with a new principle of interpretation such as the one proposed in the present study, the basic premise of the argument by modern Muslims against slavery may now be used to abolish slavery under Islamic law in an authoritative manner. Although those arguments cannot be accepted to alter the legal and historical fact that Shari'a recognized slavery, and continues to do so to the present day, they provide a very significant indication of the eagerness of modern Muslims to abolish slavery in Islamic law. Modern Muslims should welcome the evolutionary approach proposed by *Ustadh* Mahmoud Mohamed Taha. As applied to slavery, for example, that principle would conclude that though Shari'a implemented the transitional legislative intent to permit slavery, subject to certain limitations and safeguards, modern Islamic law should now implement the fundamental Islamic legislative intent to prohibit slavery forever.

When slavery was eventually abolished in modern Muslim states, in some cases as late as the 1960s and after, that result was achieved through secular law and not Shari'a.[51] Given the formal abolition of slavery in all Muslim countries, some may argue that it is no longer an issue. I disagree and believe that slavery is a fundamental human rights issue for Muslims until it is abolished in Islamic law.

In my view, it is utterly abhorrent and morally indefensible for Shari'a to continue to sanction slavery today, regardless of the prospects of its practice. Moreover, the fact that slavery is permissible under Shari'a does have serious practical consequences not only in perpetuating negative social attitudes toward former slaves and segments of the population that used to be a source of slaves but also in legitimizing forms of secret practices akin to slavery. In the Sudan, for example, images of slavery under Shari'a and Islamic literature continue to support negative stereotypes of Sudanese from the southern and western parts of the country, which were sources of slaves until the late nineteenth century. Moreover, recent news reports indicate that Muslim tribesmen of southwestern Sudan feel justified in capturing non-Muslims from southern Sudan and keeping them in secret slavery.

Discrimination on Grounds of Gender and Religion

A similar analysis applies to discrimination against women and non-Muslims under Shari'a. Both types of discrimination were the norm at the time.[52] While accepting such discrimination in principle, Shari'a restricted its incidence and reduced its scope.[53] Nevertheless, when viewed in modern perspective, principles of Shari'a sanctioning serious and unacceptable discrimination on grounds of gender and religion are, in my view, untenable today.

According to Shari'a, non-Muslims may live within a Muslim state either under the status of *dhimma* for non-Muslim subjects or the status of *aman* (pledge of security or safe-conduct) for non-Muslim aliens.[54] Various examples of discrimination under the public law of Shari'a on grounds of religion were given in the chapters on constitutionalism and criminal justice. As explained earlier, personal and private law matters for non-Muslims within an Islamic state were left to their own personal law and communal arrangements for administration. Should the matter involve a Muslim, Shari'a would apply.

Discriminatory Shari'a rules of personal and private law include the following:

• A Muslim man may marry a Christian or Jewish woman, but a Christian or Jewish man may not marry a Muslim woman.[55] Both Muslim men and women are precluded from marrying an unbeliever, that is, one who does not believe in one of the heavenly revealed scriptures.[56]

• Difference in religion is a total bar to inheritance. Thus a Muslim may neither inherit from nor leave inheritance to a non-Muslim.[57]

Examples of discrimination on grounds of gender in family and private law include the following:[58]

• A Muslim man may be married to up to four wives at the same time but a Muslim woman can only be married to one man at a time.[59]

• A Muslim man may divorce his wife, or any of his wives, by unilateral repudiation, *talaq*, without having to give any reasons or justify his action to any person or authority. In contrast, a Muslim woman can obtain divorce only by consent of the husband or by judicial decree for limited specific grounds such as the husband's inability or unwillingness to provide for his wife.[60]

• In inheritance, a Muslim woman receives less than the share of a Muslim man when both have equal degree of relationship to the deceased person.[61]

We are not concerned here with the historical justification of these instances of discrimination on grounds of religion or gender. Reasonable people may differ in their view of the historical sufficiency of any justifications that may be offered for any particular instance of discrimination. For example, it may be argued that economic and social conditions of seventh-century Arabia did not justify some or all of the discriminatory rules cited above. It is my submission, however, that regardless of differences over the historical sufficiency of justifications, these instances of discrimination against women and non-Muslims under Shari'a are no longer justified.

It should be emphasized here that such unacceptable discrimination exists despite the modern reforms of personal law in several Muslim countries. As explained in Chapter 3, these efforts cannot achieve the desired degree of reform because of the internal limitations of reform within the framework of historical Shari'a. Moreover, the limited benefits achieved through these modern reforms are constantly challenged and threatened by more fundamental principles of Shari'a which remain intact in the jurisprudence and legal practice of the countries that introduced those reforms.

In light of the preceding discussion, the following conclusions seem justified. First, in continuing to recognize slavery as a lawful institution, even if only in theory, Shari'a is in complete violation of a most fundamental and universal human right. It is very significant that slavery was abolished in the Muslim world through secular law and not Shari'a and that Shari'a does not object to the reinstitution of slavery under its own conditions regarding the source of slaves and conditions for their treatment. Although the vast majority of contemporary Muslims abhor slavery, it remains part of their religious law.

Second, discrimination on grounds of religion and gender under Shari'a also violates established universal human rights. Discrimination on grounds of religion has been found to be one of the major causes of international conflict and war because other countries that sympathize with the persecuted non-Muslim minority are likely to be prompted into acting in support of the victims of religious discrimination, thereby creating a situation of international conflict and possibly war. More important, it is my submission that discrimination on grounds of either gender or religion is morally repugnant and politically untenable today.

These are, in my view, the most serious points of conflict and tension between Shari'a and universal human rights as defined in the present study. Before proceeding to an application of the method of reconciliation adopted in this book, it may be helpful to highlight the relevance of this conflict and tension. Is it of purely historical interest or is it relevant to the current policy and practice of Muslim states?

CURRENT MUSLIM AMBIVALENCE ON HUMAN RIGHTS

The basic inconsistency between a historical, religiously determined conception of individual and collective rights under Shari'a and a contemporary universalistic conception of human rights is clearly reflected in the ambivalence of modern Muslim states on the issue. The policies of these countries are influenced, whether consciously or unconsciously, by inherently contradictory forces. On one hand, there is the pull of historical religious traditions which sanction discrimination on grounds of religion and gender. On the other hand, there is the push of modernist domestic and international forces in favor of human rights and against discrimination on grounds of religion or gender. This ambivalence is reflected, in my view, in the subscription by some Muslim countries to international human rights documents which they are unable to uphold within their national jurisdictions because of the role of Shari'a in the domestic legal systems of those countries.

It is difficult to provide detailed and conclusive documentation of human rights violations in many countries, especially in the Muslim world, because of the lack of verifiable records.[62] Moreover, it is much more difficult to link those violations, to the extent that they are documented, to the influence of Shari'a.[63] Nevertheless, the ambivalence of Muslim countries in the field of human rights can be illustrated by comparing the content of the international human rights documents to which a particular Muslim country has subscribed and the Shari'a rules being enforced in that country as a matter of domestic law. A clear example can be found by contrasting Egypt's international obligation to eliminate discrimination on grounds of gender with rules of Shari'a personal law that apply to Muslims in Egypt.[64]

Article 1 of the 1979 International Convention on the Elimination of All Forms of Discrimination against Women, to which Egypt is a party, defines discrimination against women as "any distinction, exclusion or restriction made on the basis of sex which has the effect or purpose of impairing or nullifying the recognition, enjoyment or exercise by women, irrespective of their marital status, on a basis of equality of men and women, of human rights and fundamental freedoms in the political, economic, social, cultural, civil or any other field." Articles 3 to 16 of the convention implement this definition through very specific and precise provisions for the elimination of discrimination against women in the fields of political and public life, education, employment, health care, and others.

In ratifying this convention, Egypt entered reservations on Articles 9, 16, and 29. Although the reservations on Articles 9 and 29, dealing with nationality of children and submission to arbitration under the convention, may be based on national policy not necessarily related to Shari'a, the one on Article 16 is expressly related to Shari'a. Whereas the article requires complete equality between men and women in all matters relating to marriage and family relations during the marriage and upon its dissolu-

tion, Egypt's reservation states that its obligations "must be without prejudice to the Islamic Shari'a provisions." In this way, it can be said that Egypt
is aware of the conflict between the international obligation established
by that article and its own Shari'a personal law for Muslims. As long as
this is the only aspect of Egyptian law based on Shari'a which is inconsistent with Egypt's obligation under this convention and other international
human rights instruments, it can be said that Egypt is honest in its position and serious in its intention to honor its international human rights
obligations. That is not enough. Egypt and all other Muslim countries
should bring every aspect of their law, including personal law for Muslims, into complete conformity with human rights standards.

Given the various ways in which Shari'a discriminates against
women and non-Muslims and the powerful influence of Shari'a on private
as well as official Muslim behavior throughout the world, however, it is
reasonable to conclude that more serious consequences of Muslim ambivalence on human rights are unavoidable. Moreover, this ambivalence is likely
to increase in scope and degree if the current trend toward greater Islamization of public life in Muslim countries should continue.

The relevance of Shari'a to contemporary Muslim practice raises
the basic issue of how to reconcile Shari'a with universal standards of human rights. As in the case of similar issues raised in our discussion of questions of constitutionalism, criminal justice, and international law, reconciliation can be achieved only through the drastic reform of Shari'a. It
now remains to be seen how the reform technique explained earlier operates in achieving the desired reconciliation between Islamic law and universal human rights from within the Islamic tradition.

UNIVERSAL HUMAN RIGHTS IN ISLAM

Once again, and in culmination of the basic argument of this book, we
come to the same conclusion. Unless the basis of modern Islamic law is
shifted away from those texts of the Qur'an and Sunna of the Medina stage,
which constituted the foundations of the construction of Shari'a, there is
no way of avoiding drastic and serious violation of universal standards
of human rights. There is no way to abolish slavery as a legal institution
and no way to eliminate all forms and shades of discrimination against
women and non-Muslims as long as we remain bound by the framework
of Shari'a. As stated in Chapter 3 and explained in relation to constitutionalism, criminal justice, and international law, the traditional techniques
of reform within the framework of Shari'a are inadequate for achieving

the *necessary* degree of reform. To achieve that degree of reform, we must be able to set aside clear and definite texts of the Qur'an and Sunna of the Medina stage as having served their transitional purpose and implement those texts of the Meccan stage which were previously inappropriate for practical application but are now the only way to proceed.

A similar approach is proposed for achieving the reconciliation of Islamic law with the full range of universal human rights identified through the criteria indicated earlier in this chapter. The key to the success of this part of the effort is to convince Muslims that the other person with whom they must identify and accept as their equal in human dignity and rights includes all other human beings, regardless of gender and religion. This would require an explanation of why the verses of antagonism which instructed Muslims to be *awliya*, friends and supporters, of each other and disassociate themselves from all non-Muslims, should not apply today. It would also require showing that verse 4:34 of the Qur'an, which establishes general male guardianship over women, and other verses which establish specific instances of discrimination against women, should not be implemented today.

In accordance with the logic of the evolutionary principle proposed by *Ustadh* Mahmoud Mohamed Taha, the texts of the Qur'an emphasizing exclusive Muslim solidarity were revealed during the Medina stage to provide the emerging Muslim community with psychological support in the face of the violent adversity of non-Muslims. In contrast to these verses, the fundamental and eternal message of Islam, as revealed in the Qur'an of the Mecca period, preached the solidarity of all humanity. In view of the vital need for peaceful coexistence in today's global human society, Muslims should emphasize the eternal message of universal solidarity of the Qur'an of the Mecca period rather than the exclusive Muslim solidarity of the transitional Medina message. Otherwise, Muslims would only provoke counter exclusive solidarity by non-Muslims, thereby repudiating the prospects for peaceful coexistence and cooperation in promoting and protecting universal human rights.

The application of *Ustadh* Mahmoud's evolutionary principle to male *qawama*, guardianship, over women has already been explained. Male guardianship over women has been rationalized by verse 4:34 as following from the economic and security dependence of women on men. Because such dependence is no longer necessarily true, argued *Ustadh* Mahmoud, male guardianship over women should be terminated. Both men and women should now be equally free and equally responsible before the law, which guarantees economic opportunity and security for all members of the community.

The application of this evolutionary principle of interpretation to specific instances of discrimination against women and non-Muslims can be illustrated by the rule of Shari'a prohibiting marriage between a Muslim woman and a non-Muslim man. This rule is based on the combined operation of the guardianship of the man, in this case the husband, over his wife, and that of a Muslim over a non-Muslim. Since a non-Muslim husband may not be the guardian of his Muslim wife, Shari'a prohibits such a marriage. If either form of guardianship, of a husband over his wife or of a Muslim over a non-Muslim, is repudiated, there would be no justification for prohibiting marriage between a Muslim woman and a non-Muslim man. The evolutionary principle of *Ustadh* Mahmoud would repudiate both types of guardianship.

The evolutionary principle will also repudiate another possible rationale of the prohibition of marriage between a Muslim woman and a non-Muslim man, namely the assumption that a wife is more susceptible to influence by her husband than vice versa. In other words, it appears to be assumed that if such a marriage is permitted, it is more likely that the non-Muslim husband will draw his Muslim wife away from Islam than that she will draw him to Islam. This rationale is, of course, part of the wider sociological phenomenon, namely, the lack of confidence in a woman's integrity and good judgment. Educational and other efforts are needed to repudiate this sociological phenomenon in all its manifestations. Besides its immediate practical impact, legal reform can also be an effective tool of education and leadership. This task can be begun by removing, through the application of the evolutionary principle of *Ustadh* Mahmoud, all aspects of the law which discriminate against women, thereby encouraging and sustaining a positive view of women.

Conclusion

SALMAN RUSHDIE, an Indian-born Muslim novelist who became a British citizen, published in Britain a novel entitled *Satanic Verses* in September 1988. In various parts of the novel, and especially in a dream sequence therein, irreverent references are made to the Prophet of Islam, his wives, and leading Companions. Although made in metaphorical fictitious form, the associations and negative connotations are obvious.

Within a few months, thousands of Muslims were demonstrating in various parts of the Muslim world, burning copies of the book, and demanding that it be banned not only in their own countries but throughout the world. Some of the demonstrators called for the death of Rushdie. In mid-February 1989, Imam Khomeini of Iran issued a declaration in which he called on Muslims to kill Rushdie and any person associated with the publication and sale of the book. When Rushdie issued a statement a few days later expressing his regrets for any affront and anguish his book may have caused Muslims, Khomeini responded by saying that Rushdie's apology would not be accepted and that he should be killed even if he repented and recanted his insults to Islam and the Muslims. These events were widely reported in the media all over the world.

In the following remarks, I am assuming, for the sake of argument, that Rushdie's book is extremely offensive to Muslims. I am also assuming that freedom of expression is not absolute. It is conceivable that a published work, whether claiming to be a work of fiction or scholarship, can cause such harm to some identifiable private or public interest as to justify the banning or restriction of its circulation. Although I believe that it should be extremely difficult to make a convincing case for banning a work, I am assuming that it is not impossible to do so. Moreover, I am also assuming that Rushdie's book warrants examination with a view to its possible banning by the appropriate authorities.

Assuming all this, I find it extremely disturbing that thousands

182

of Muslims in many parts of the world are demanding not only the banning of the book but also the murder of the author. What is even more disturbing is that a head of a Muslim country, Imam Khomeini of Iran, has called on Muslims to seek out and murder a citizen of another country, and a non-Muslim country at that, without the benefit of trial and a chance to defend himself. Khomeini does not speak for all the Shi'a Muslims of the world, let alone the Sunni Muslims, who are by far the vast majority of Muslims today. Nevertheless, since the vast majority of Muslims have failed to condemn Khomeini's action, they are to be taken as acquiescing to it.

Even though Shari'a rules of procedure are extremely underdeveloped, many Muslims would argue that sufficient authority can be found to support the conclusion that Khomeini's action is totally wrong and invalid in Shari'a for at least three reasons. First, assuming that Khomeini is the undisputed ruler of an Islamic state *(dar al-Islam)*, his jurisdiction under Shari'a does not extend to a non-Islamic state *(dar al-harb)*. In modern terms, Shari'a does not give the ruler of an Islamic state the power to punish the citizen of a non-Islamic state. Second, even if Khomeini were to have jurisdiction over Rushdie on the absurd ground that the ruler of an Islamic state has universal jurisdiction over Muslims anywhere in the world, Shari'a requires that a person be charged with an offense and allowed a chance to defend himself before he may be punished. Third, repentance and recantation of heretic views is always a complete defense against a charge of apostasy *(ridda)*, which is presumably the offense Rushdie is supposed to have committed.

All of these objections to Khomeini's action are procedural and formal in nature. That thousands of Muslims in many parts of the Muslim world have demanded the death of Rushdie can only mean that they continue to perceive this to be the appropriate penalty for apostasy. In other words, Muslims are saying that if Rushdie is subject to the jurisdiction of an Islamic state, was duly charged and tried, and refused to recant his views, he should be put to death. This is the prevailing view of Shari'a, which is not disputed by the vast majority of Muslims, who are demanding the application of Shari'a today as the public law of Muslim countries. Even those Muslims who argue that the death penalty is not required by Shari'a for peaceable nonviolent apostasy would still have to concede the variety of other negative legal consequences to the apostate noted earlier, including the possibility of a discretionary punishment *(ta'zir)* short of death.

Although I know this to be the position under Shari'a, I am unable *as a Muslim* to accept the law of apostasy as part of the law of Islam today. If the prevailing view of apostasy remains valid today, a Muslim could be put to death for expressing views in a given Muslim country which are deemed by the dominant view in that country to be tantamount to apostasy. For example, from some Sunni perspectives, the views of many Shi'a Muslims amount to apostasy; and from some Shi'a perspectives, the views of many Sunni Muslims amount to apostasy. If the Shari'a law of apostasy is to be applied today, it would be conceivable for some Shi'a Muslims to be sentenced to death in a Sunni country and vice versa.

Furthermore, it is conceivable for a Muslim within the Sunni tradition, for example, to be put to death for apostasy by the authorities even though many contemporary Muslims regard that person to be an exemplary Muslim. Numerous examples can be cited from Muslim history of leading *Sufi* (Muslim mystic) men who were killed for apostasy despite their large following among Muslims at the time. Other examples can be cited of currently respected scholars, such as Ibn Taymiyya, who could have been put to death under the pretext of the Shari'a law of apostasy if their opponents were in control of the machinery of the state at the time. Many modern Muslim intellectuals, such as Ali Abd al-Raziq, have been denounced and threatened with death for expressing profound scholarly views. *Ustadh* Mahmoud Mohamed Taha was executed for apostasy in the Sudan in January 1985 for his views on Islamic reform.

These instances would suggest to me that toleration of unorthodoxy and dissent is vital for the spiritual and intellectual benefit of Islam itself. The Shari'a law of apostasy can easily be abused and has been abused in the past to suppress political opposition and inhibit spiritual and intellectual growth. This aspect of Shari'a is fundamentally inconsistent with the numerous provisions of the Qur'an and Sunna which enjoin freedom of religion and expression.

Another aspect of the historical experience of Muslims brought into focus by the Rushdie affair is the tradition of direct violent action and self-help, which goes back to the earliest times of Islam. Examples can be cited of the Prophet instructing Muslims to kill someone on sight or to correct an injustice by direct action. Unless these instances are identified and explained in their specific historical contexts or other special circumstances, they will continue to be used to undermine the rule of law and motivate terrorist action.

The Rushdie affair has attracted much attention because of its international, especially Western, dimension. Although I am fully aware of the realities of international power politics, I still believe that this affair is useful in publicizing the drastic incompatibility between Shari'a and modern standards of international relations and human rights. Some of those who rushed to defend Rushdie no doubt had their ulterior motives; some may have acted out of spite for Islam and Muslims. As a Muslim, however, I have to concede that it was Muslim actions that gave occasion for such reactions. More important, I am concerned with the views of men and women of goodwill and sensitivity and wish to emphasize the value of this affair in illustrating the need for Islamic reform.

Although many contemporary Muslims would privately object to Shari'a's suppression of freedom of belief and expression, very few are willing to express their objections publicly for fear of being branded as apostates themselves — guilt by association. Other Muslims would find it difficult to admit their objections, even to themselves, for fear of losing their faith in the process. As long as the public law of Shari'a continues to be regarded as the only valid view of the law of Islam, most Muslims would find it extremely difficult to object to any of its principles and rules or to resist their practical implementation, however repugnant and inappropriate they may find them to be.

The public law of Shari'a has not been applied for many generations in most parts of the Muslim world. Moreover, the nature and style of classical treatises on Shari'a make them generally inaccessible even to the highly educated contemporary Muslim. As a result of these and other factors, the vast majority of Muslims today are unaware of the full implications of the modern application of the public law of Shari'a. If contemporary Muslims can clearly envisage the ways in which the application of Shari'a would affect their daily lives, and if they were given a free choice in opposing the application of Shari'a without the threat of prosecution for apostasy or the fear of losing their faith in Islam, I believe that most of them would strongly oppose the application of Shari'a today.

The fundamental objective of this book is to start a process of drastic reform of Islamic law that would enable Muslims to seek to achieve their right to self-determination in terms of an Islamic identity (whether Sunni, Shi'i, or variations thereof), including the application of Islamic law, without violating the rights of others to self-determination. To this end, the book explains the negative consequences of the modern application of Shari'a to demonstrate that it is *not* the appropriate vehicle for Islamic self-determination in the present context. An *Islamic* alternative to Shari'a is provided as the appropriate framework for Muslims to exercise their right to self-determination while fully respecting the rights of others, whether within their own countries or in other lands.

Reference has already been made to the difficulties facing Muslims who would otherwise criticize Shari'a and oppose its application today. To help these Muslims overcome their inhibitions, I have shown that Shari'a was in fact *constructed* by Muslim jurists over the first three centuries of Islam. Although derived from the fundamental divine sources of Islam, the Qur'an and Sunna, Shari'a is not divine because it is the product of *human interpretation* of those sources. Moreover, this process of construction through human interpretation took place within a specific historical context which is drastically different from our own. It should therefore be possible for contemporary Muslims to undertake a similar process of interpretation and application of the Qur'an and Sunna in the present historical context to develop an alternative public law of Islam which is appropriate for implementation today.

In addition to explaining and documenting the validity of this premise, I have suggested that the reform methodology developed by the late Sudanese Muslim reformer *Ustadh* Mahmoud Mohamed Taha appears to be the most appropriate means for constructing the modern public law of Islam out of the Qur'an and Sunna as interpreted in the present historical context. Whether this particular methodology is accepted or rejected by contemporary Muslims, the need for drastic reform of the public law of Shari'a is beyond dispute.

Optimism is a necessity of life, especially for a Muslim today. As a Muslim optimist, I believe in the power of ideas, when expounded in the right way at the right time, to inspire significant social and political change. I also believe in the progressive force of life and the ability of people to struggle for and achieve a quality of life compatible with their human dignity and well-being. It would be irresponsible wishful thinking on my part, however, to overlook the power of reactionary forces or to underestimate the difficulties facing the struggle for human dignity and well-being.

I am painfully aware that the vast majority of the Muslim peoples throughout the world live at a superficial level of both Islam and modern civilization. Although they claim adherence to Islam and exhibit apparent commitment to its ritualistic formalities, most contemporary Muslims fail to appreciate and live up to its moral and spiritual essence. Moreover, although they have grown accustomed to enjoying the benefits of modern technology and claim adherence to modern institutions, the majority of Muslim peoples have little appreciation of the values and ways of thinking that underlie and sustain that technology and those institutions. Many distinguished modern Muslim scholars have lamented this state of affairs in the Muslim world, but as long as it persists, the voices of fanaticism will find receptive ears and the forces of regression will have eager followers.

It may therefore appear presumptuous to expect a book that is written in English and is likely to be banned in some Muslim countries to have any significant impact in the Muslim world. Despite the oppressive nature of most political regimes and the conservative orientation of many societies in the Muslim world, however, I believe that the ideas expressed here will reach the hearts and minds of many Muslims. For one thing, most of these ideas already exist, perhaps in somewhat rudimentary and reticent form, in the hearts and minds of many Muslims, especially the younger generations, who are the more active agents of social change. It is my hope and expectation that this book will act as a catalyst for change in the Muslim world by presenting these ideas in a systematic and comprehensive fashion and providing them with an Islamic rationale. Moreover, the cultural interdependence of the modern world is making it increasingly difficult to exclude ideas and diminish their impact.

Contemporary Muslims are not the only audience for this book. Although issues of Islamic law reform and social and political change in the Muslim world are primarily the business of the peoples of Muslim countries, these matters are the legitimate concern of all humankind because of their impact on the human rights and fundamental freedoms of human beings. Conversely, the peoples of Muslim countries should be concerned with similar matters in non-Muslim lands. Humanity can no longer disclaim responsibility for the fate of human beings in any part of the world. This is the glorious achievement of the modern international human rights movement. All the peoples of the world are hereby invited to assist Muslims in their predicament and to accept the assistance of Muslims to non-Muslims in their predicaments. It should be emphasized, however, that these efforts of mutual assistance must be undertaken with due sensitivity and goodwill if they are to be most effective.

It is my conviction as a Muslim that the public law of Shari'a does not represent the law of Islam which contemporary Muslims are supposed to implement in fulfillment of their religious obligation. I also strongly believe that the application of the public law of Shari'a today will be counterproductive and detrimental to Muslims and to Islam itself. I hope that this book, with the help and guidance of God, will contribute in bringing all Muslims to a clear realization of these facts and in enabling them to develop and implement the appropriate public law of Islam for today.

My trust in God leads me to believe that current efforts to implement the public law of Shari'a will fail because they are harmful to the best interests of Islam and the Muslims. These efforts will fail because the public law of Shari'a is fundamentally inconsistent with the realities of modern life. This is my firm conviction as a Muslim. My only concern is to avoid the human suffering which is likely to be caused by this doomed endeavor. May this book, by the grace of God, contribute to minimizing that suffering.

NOTES
SELECTED BIBLIOGRAPHY
INDEX

NOTES

FOREWORD

1. Carolyn Fluehr-Lobban, *Islamic Law and Society in the Sudan* (London: Frank Cass, 1987), p. 110.

2. Mahmoud Mohamed Taha, *The Second Message of Islam*, translated with an Introduction by Abdullahi Ahmed An-Na'im (Syracuse: Syracuse University Press, 1987).

3. An-Na'im, "Introduction," ibid., p. 28.

4. See, for example, his articles in the English-language magazine published in Khartoum, *Sudanow*, in November 1977 and November 1979. An American scholar working in Khartoum at the time described An-Na'im as "one of the movement's young and highly articulate spokesmen" (Paul J. Magnarella, "The Republican Brothers: A Reformist Movement in the Sudan," *Muslim World* 72 [January 1982]: 15).

5. An account of the detention and trial is given by An-Na'im in his "Introduction" to *The Second Message*, pp. 10–19.

6. See, for example, his recent writings: "Religious Minorities under Islamic Law and the Limits of Cultural Relativism," *Human Rights Quarterly* 9 (1987); "Islamic Law, International Relations and Human Rights: Challenge and Response," *Cornell International Law Journal* 20 (1987); "The Rights of Women and International Law in the Muslim Context," *Whittier Law Review* 9 (1987).

7. An-Na'im, "Introduction," *Second Message*, p. 28.

1. PUBLIC LAW IN THE MUSLIM WORLD

1. On the history and development of the principle of self-determination see Michla Pomerance, *Self-Determination in Law and Practice* (The Hague: Martinus Nijhoff, 1982). For further and specialized material on the subject see the extensive bibliography, ibid., pp. 130–38.

2. Besides the sources cited in the following notes, recent scholarly works on this subject include Mohammad Ayoob, ed., *The Politics of Islamic Reassertion* (New York: St. Martin's Press, 1981); Ali E. Hillal Desouki, ed., *Islamic Resurgence in the Arab World* (New York: Praeger, 1982); James P. Piscatori, ed., *Islam in the Political Process* (Cambridge: Cambridge University Press, 1983).

3. Daniel Pipes, for example, defined Islamic fundamentalism as "a rejection of compromise and an attempt to implement the sacred law [Shari'a] in its entirety" (*In the Path of God: Islam and Political Power* [New York: Basic Books, 1983], p. 64).

4. See generally, George Marsden, *Fundamentalism and American Culture* (New York: Oxford University Press, 1982); James Barr, *Fundamentalism*, 2d ed. (London: SCM Press, 1982); and Marla J. Selvidge, ed., *Fundamentalism Today: What Makes It So Attractive?* (Elgin, Ill.: Brethren Press, 1984).

5. Some of the writers on the Christian phenomenon appear willing to extend the term to Muslims. See Marsden, *Fundamentalism*, pp. 227-28; and Barr, *Fundamentalism*, p. 7. Some contemporary Muslim writers object to the application of this term to Islamic resurgence. See, for example, Khurshid Ahmad, "The Nature of the Islamic Resurgence," in John L. Esposito, ed., *Voices of Resurgent Islam* (New York: Oxford University Press, 1983), pp. 225-26.

6. For example, and with reference to the Arab-Muslim world, it was concluded at the end of a study which analyzed 246 articles selected from Arab periodicals published between 1945 and 1970 that "Islam is an element of the basic substratum of Arab-Muslim identity. Of this there is no doubt. What is not clear is the form that Islam will take finally in contemporary Arab society. It is not easy to imagine a contemporary society in which Islamic institutions of another age continue to play a vital role as some proponents of an 'Islamic society' seem to champion, nor is a new identity without a prominent Islamic element very likely" (John J. Donohue, "Islam and the Search for Identity in the Arab World," in Esposito, ed., *Voices of Resurgent Islam*, p. 59).

7. Michael C. Hudson, "Islam and Political Development," in John L. Esposito, ed., *Islam and Development: Religion and Sociopolitical Change* (Syracuse: Syracuse University Press, 1980), p. 5.

8. Bernard Lewis, "The Return of Islam," in Michael Curtis, ed., *Religion and Politics in the Middle East* (Boulder, Colo.: Westview Press, 1981), p. 11.

9. Ibid. See also John L. Esposito, "Introduction: Islam and Muslim Politics," in Esposito, ed., *Voices of Resurgent Islam*, pp. 3-5; and Pipes, *In the Path of God*, pp. 4ff.

10. Lewis, "The Return of Islam," p. 12. See also Pipes, *In the Path of God*, pp. 15-16.

11. For brief surveys of such movements since the eighteenth century see Lewis, "The Return of Islam," pp. 12ff.; and Esposito, "Introduction," pp. 5-11. For more extensive surveys see John O. Voll, *Islam: Continuity and Change in the Modern World* (Boulder, Colo.: Westview Press, 1982), chap. 3; and John L. Esposito, *Islam and Politics*, 2d rev. ed. (Syracuse: Syracuse University Press, 1987), chap. 2.

12. John O. Voll, "Renewal and Reform in Islamic History: *Tajdid* and *Islah*," in Esposito, ed., *Voices of Resurgent Islam*, p. 32. See also Ira M. Lapidus, *Contemporary Islamic Movements in Historical Perspectives* (Berkeley: Institute of International Studies, University of California, 1983).

13. Esposito, *Islam and Politics*, p. 39.

14. R. Hrair Dekmejian, "The Anatomy of Islamic Revival: Legitimacy Crisis, Ethnic Conflict, and the Search for Islamic Alternatives," in Curtis, ed., *Religion and Politics in the Middle East*, p. 33.

15. Secularism has been defined as the process whereby religious thinking, practice, and institutions lose social significance and become increasingly restricted to the domain of private faith. See Ernest Krausz, "Religion and Secularization: A Matter of Definitions," *Social Compass* 18 (1971-72): 212.

16. Dekmejian, "The Anatomy of Islamic Revival," p. 39. For a similar analysis, see Esposito, "Introduction," pp. 11-13.

17. W. C. Smith, *Islam in Modern History* (Princeton: Princeton University Press, 1957), p. 47.

18. Ahmad, "The Nature of the Islamic Resurgence," pp. 218-19, 228.

19. It is not suggested here that all Muslims have always responded from an exclusively Islamic point of view. As shown by John Voll and others, modern Muslims have reacted to their predicament in a variety of ways. See, for example, Voll, *Islam*, chaps. 4 and 7; and Anouar Abdel Malek, ed., *Contemporary Arab Political Thought*, trans. Michael Pallis, (London: Zed Press, 1983).

20. Joseph Schacht, "Islamic Law in Contemporary States," *American Journal of Comparative Law* 8 (1959): 139 and n. 14.

21. Except for a small book by Abu Yusuf (d. 798), entitled *Kitab al-Kharaj*, none of the founding jurists addressed constitutional questions as such. Somewhat specialized treatment of these issues started with al-Baqillani (d. 1012), al-Baghdadi (d. 1037), and al-Mawardi (d. 1058), followed by al-Ghazzali (d. 1111); Ibn Jama'a (d. 1333); Ibn Taymiyya (d. 1328), and Ibn Khaldun (d. 1406). For brief surveys and discussions of the views of these scholars see Erwin I. J. Rosenthal, *Political Thought in Medieval Islam* (Cambridge: Cambridge University Press, 1958), pp. 27-61; and Kemal A. Faruki, *The Evolution of Islamic Constitutional Theory and Practice from 610 to 1926* (Karachi, Decca: National Publishing House, 1971), pp. 43-52, 56-66.

22. As pointed out by Khalid M. Ishaque, in "Al-Ahkam Al-Sultaniya: Laws of Government in Islam," *Islamic Studies* 4 (1965): 275-76, the lack of specialized treatment of constitutional law issues was also true of medieval European political thought as illustrated by works such as R. M. MacIver, *The Modern State* (Oxford: Oxford University Press, 1928); and Bernard Bosanquet, *The Philosophical Theory of the State* (New York: Macmillan, 1899).

23. H. A. R. Gibb, "Constitutional Organization," in Majid Khadduri and Herbert Liebesny, eds., *Law in the Middle East* (Washington, D.C.: Middle East Institute, 1955), p. 19. This sad conclusion is confirmed by the often quoted statement of al-Ghazzali emphasizing the duty of the Muslim population to obey whoever is in power, however evil-doing and barbarous he may be (ibid., pp. 19-20). The need for law and order, at almost any cost, was carried to extremes by later scholars such as ibn Jama'a (ibid., p. 23). See also, H. A. R. Gibb, *Studies on the Civilization of Islam*, ed. Standford J. Shaw and William R. Polk (Princeton: Princeton University Press, 1982), pp. 141-54.

24. See, for example, his book *Minhaj al-Sunna*, 2:86.

25. The tendency to write for an ideal situation, with little regard for the realities of Muslim life at the time, is a common criticism of medieval Muslim writers. G. E. von Grunebaum, for example, said that al-Mawardi in *al-Ahkam al-Sulataniyya* recognized and deplored the shortcomings of his period but took no note of them for his system (*Islam: Essays in the Nature and Growth of a Cultural Tradition* [London: Routledge & Kegan Paul, 1955], p. 68). See also Malcolm H. Kerr, *Islamic Reform: The Political and Legal Theories of Muhammad Abduh and Rashid Rida* (Berkeley and Los Angeles: University of California Press, 1966), p. 220.

26. In fact, there may have been some Islamic influence in the development of the European public law. See, for example, Marcel A. Boisard, "On the Probable Influence of Islam on Western Public and International Law," *International Journal of Middle East Studies* 11 (July 1980): 429.

27. James Norman D. Anderson, *Law Reform in the Muslim World* (London: University of London, Athlone Press, 1976), pp. 1–2, 33.

28. Herbert Liebesny, *The Law of the Near and Middle East* (Albany: State University of New York Press, 1975), p. 56. See also Noel Coulson, *A History of Islamic Law* (Edinburgh: Edinburgh University Press, 1964), p. 161.

29. These reforms will be discussed in Chapter 3.

30. The practical displacement of Shari'a by secular law may have been the norm in the actual practice of Muslims for many centuries (David Bonderman, "Modernization and Changing Perceptions of Islamic Law," *Harvard Law Review* 81 [1968]: 1175).

31. Anderson, *Law Reform in the Muslim World,* p. 36.

32. Even Muslim countries that were not formally colonized, such as Saudi Arabia, have attempted to adopt some of the power structures and legal concepts of the modern nation-state. See, for example, Bryant W. Seaman, "Islamic Law and Modern Government: Saudi Arabia Supplements the *Shari'a* to Regulate Development," *Columbia Journal of Transnational Law* 18, no. 3 (1980): 413.

33. For an excellent analysis of the experience of the United States in this light see Kenneth L. Karst, "Paths to Belonging: The Constitution and Cultural Identity," *North Carolina Law Review* 64, no. 2 (1986): 303.

34. See, for example, Daniel Crecedlius, "The Course of Secularization in Modern Egypt," and Mangol Bayat, "Islam in Pahlavi and Post-Pahlavi Iran: A Cultural Revolution," both in Esposito, ed., *Islam and Development,* pp. 49–70 and 87–106.

2. ON THE SOURCES AND DEVELOPMENT OF SHARI'A

1. S. G. Vesey-Fitzgerald, "Nature and Sources of the Shari'a," in Khadduri and Liebesny, eds., *Law in the Middle East,* p. 85. For analysis of the development of the concept of Shari'a see Fazlur Rahman, *Islam* (Chicago: University of Chicago Press, 1979), pp. 101–9.

2. This offense and its recent enforcement in the Sudan are discussed in Chapter 5.

3. Detailed accounts and analysis of the two phases of Mecca and Medina may be found in Montgomery Watt, *Muhammad at Mecca* and *Muhammad at Medina* (Oxford: Oxford University Press, 1953 and 1958, respectively). An English translation of an authoritative biography by an early Muslim secular, ibn Hisham, has been prepared by Alfred Guillaume and published as *The Life of Muhammad* (Oxford: Oxford University Press, 1958). See also Muhammad Husayn Haykal, *The Life of Muhammad,* trans. Isma'il al-Faruqi (Indianapolis: American Trust Publications, 1976).

4. See Haykal, *Life of Muhammad,* chaps. 19 and 20.

5. The paramount and continuing significance of that early contest and its settlement will be discussed in Chapter 4.

6. Although Umayyad rule extended throughout Muslim domains, Abbasid rule was challenged by some elements of the Umayyads, who succeeded in establishing their own state in Muslim Spain in 756. Other groups also established regional states, such as that of the Fatimid of Egypt between 910 and 1171. Nevertheless, the Abbasids held the main and generally acknowledged caliphate until the middle of the thirteenth century. See generally, P. M. Holt, Ann K. S. Lambton, and Bernard Lewis, eds., *The Cambridge History of Islam* (Cambridge: Cambridge University Press, 1970), vol. 1, chaps. 3 and 4.

7. For a survey of these and other related factors and processes see Marshall G. S. Hodgson, *The Venture of Islam* (Chicago: University of Chicago Press, 1974), vol. 1, bk. 1, chaps. 1-3; Holt, Lambton, and Lewis, eds., *The Cambridge History of Islam*, pp. 58-63; and Ira M. Lapidus, *A History of Islamic Societies* (Cambridge: Cambridge University Press, 1988), chaps. 3 and 4.

8. Vesey-Fitzgerald, "Nature and Sources of the Shari'a," pp. 91-92; Majid Khadduri, "Nature and Sources of Islamic Law," *George Washington Law Review* 22 (1953): 3-6; and Herbert J. Liebesny, "Comparative Legal History: Its Role in the Analysis of Islamic and Modern Near Eastern Legal Institutions," *American Journal of Comparative Law* 20 (1972): 38. See generally, H. A. R. Gibb, *The Arab Conquests in Central Asia* (London: Royal Asiatic Society, 1923).

9. 40 Hijri/660 A.D. Whenever two dates are given, the first will be of the Islamic Hijri calendar and the second will be A.D.

10. Rahman, *Islam*, p. 79. See also Coulson, *History of Islamic Law*, pp. 23-27.

11. Ignaz Goldziher, *Introduction to Islamic Theology and Law*, trans. Andras Hamori and Ruth Hamori (Princeton: Princeton University Press, 1981), p. 37; Joseph Schacht, *An Introduction to Islamic Law* (Oxford: Clarendon Press, 1964), p. 23; and Coulson, *History of Islamic Law*, p. 27.

12. Goldziher, *Introduction to Islamic Theology and Law*, p. 45; Schacht, *Introduction to Islamic Law*, p. 49; and Rahman, *Islam*, p. 93.

13. The dichotomy between the theory of Shari'a and actual Abbasid practice is noted by all the authors cited in the preceding note.

14. The minority of Muslims belong to Shi'a schools. The establishment of both groups of schools is briefly outlined below.

15. Companions, with a capital "C," is used in this book to refer to the first generation of Muslims, commonly known as *sahaba*, Companions of the Prophet.

16. Schacht, *Introduction to Islamic Law*, p. 18; and Coulson, *History of Islamic Law*, p. 65.

17. Here I am adopting the position of Coulson, in qualifying that of Schacht. See Coulson, *History of Islamic Law*, p. 65. Cf. Schacht, *Introduction to Islamic Law*, p. 18, where he states that many rules of Islamic law were based on the Qur'an from the very beginning but makes no mention of the Sunna of the Prophet.

The Qur'an authorized legislation by the Prophet, Qur'an 7:157, and repeatedly emphasized the duty of Muslims to obey the Prophet. See, for example, the Qur'an 3:32 and 132; 4:59, 65, and 80; and 59:7.

18. The Sunna of the Prophet and traditions of his Companions were not recorded during the first century of Islam. Al-Azami attempted to demonstrate that specific opinions and rulings were recorded from the earliest times, yet all the sources he could cite were recorded in the second century of Islam. See Muhammad Al-Azami, *On Schacht's Origins of Muhammadan Jurisprudence* (New York: Wiley, 1985), pp. 20ff.

19. This is the sense in which I would accept Schacht's statement that "during the greater part of the first century [of Islam], Islamic law, *in the technical meaning of the term*, did not as yet exist" (*Introduction to Islamic Law*, p. 19; emphasis added).

20. Ahmad Hasan, *The Early Development of Islamic Jurisprudence* (Islamabad: Islamic Research Institute, 1970), pp. 20-21, lists the names and dates of death of the leading members of this early generation of jurists. The group also includes the governors/judges appointed by the Prophet, the caliphs of Medina, and the Umayyads. For references to Mus-

lim primary sources on the appointment and work of the earliest governors/judges see Al-Azami, *On Schacht's Origins of Muhammadan Jurisprudence*, pp. 21–22.

This group is referred to here as governors/judges to indicate that their appointments were not to exclusively judicial functions, as they also performed executive functions at the same time. Notions of separation of powers and independence of the judiciary were not developed, if at all known or appreciated, in the theory and practice of Shari'a.

21. Abu Abdallah Muhammad Ibn Idris al-Shafi'i, *al-Umm* (Cairo: Maktabat al-Kuliyat al-Azhariyah, 1961), 3:246–57. See also Coulson, *History of Islamic Law*, pp. 30–33.

22. Rahman, *Islam*, pp. 81–83.

23. Coulson, *History of Islamic Law*, p. 37.

24. Students such as Shaybani, the leading student of Abu-Hanifa, and Ibn al-Qasim, the leading student of Malik, may be the real founders of their schools. Nevertheless, the schools were named after the nominal founder. See Coulson, *History of Islamic Law*, pp. 51–52.

25. Beside the Awaz'i school, the other now extinct Sunni schools were founded by Da'ud ibn Khalaf of the Zahiri school (d. 269/882) and Tabari (d. 310/922) (Mahmassani, *Falsafat Al-Tashri Fi Al-Islam*, English trans., F. Ziadah [Leiden: E. J. Brill, 1961], pp. 33–35.

26. Schacht, *Introduction to Islamic Law*, pp. 45–48, 58ff.; *Islamic Jurisprudence, Shafi'i's Risala*, trans. Majid Khadduri (Baltimore: Johns Hopkins Press, 1961), pp. 40–84; Hasan, *Early Development of Islamic Jurisprudence*, chap. 8; Coulson, *History of Islamic Law*, chap. 4; and George Makdisi, "The Juridical Theology of Shafi'i: Origins and Significance of Usul Al-Fiqh," *Studia Islamica* 59 (1984): 5–47.

27. The work of this and other "reformers" or "renewers" of Shari'a will be discussed in Chapter 3.

28. Hasan, *Early Development of Islamic Jurisprudence*, p. 40.

29. It is somewhat misleading to think of the Qur'an as the Bible of Muslims. According to Muslim belief, every word and letter of the Qur'an is direct revelation. According to this belief, to doubt the direct and totally divine nature of any part of the text of the Qur'an is to cease to be a Muslim.

30. This is my belief as a Muslim. Some Western scholars have disputed this and attempted to show that what we have today as the Qur'an is in fact one version of the original text. See John Burton, *The Collection of the Qur'an* (Cambridge: Cambridge University Press, 1977), esp. chap. 8.

31. Coulson, *History of Islamic Law*, p. 11.

This is not to suggest, of course, that the Prophet had no role as a political legislator. Such a role was contemplated by the Qur'an and reflected in the Prophet's own practice. See, for example, verse 7:157 of the Qur'an, which authorized the Prophet to legislate; and verses 3:32 and 132, 4:59, 65, and 80, and 59:7, which emphasize the duty of Muslims to obey the Prophet. Rather, the point is that the primary role of the Prophet was not that of political legislator.

32. Coulson, *History of Islamic Law*, p. 11. See also Rahman, *Islam*, pp. 33–37.

33. Coulson, *History of Islamic Law*, p. 12.

34. Vesey-Fitzgerald, "Nature and Sources of the Shari'a," p. 87. See also Coulson, *History of Islamic Law*, p. 17.

35. Vesey-Fitzgerald, "Nature and Sources of the Shari'a," p. 87; Liebesny, *The Law of the Near and Middle East*, p. 12; Rahman, *Islam*, p. 69; and Coulson, *History of Islamic Law*, p. 12.

36. Vesey-Fitzgerald, "Nature and Sources of the Shari'a," pp. 87–88, cites some examples of the use of nonlegal verses to support rules of commercial law.

37. Joseph Schacht, *The Origins of Muhammadan Jurisprudence* (Oxford: Oxford University Press, 1959), p. 224. See also Coulson, *History of Islamic Law*, p. 64; and Hasan, *Early Development of Islamic Jurisprudence*, pp. 46–47.

38. The abrogation or repeal of some verses and "enactment" of others was not done, of course, by a formal legislature, but the results were the same as formal repeal and enactment in the modern sense of these terms.

39. This proposition, and related matters such as the criteria for selection of the verses to be abrogated or enacted and the mechanism or procedure for achieving the change in legal efficacy, will be discussed in Chapter 3.

40. Fazlur Rahman, "Concepts of *Sunnah, Ijtihad* and *Ijma'* in the Early Period," *Islamic Studies* 1 (1962): 6.

41. Rahman, *Islam*, p. 44.

42. Ignaz Goldziher, *Muhammedanische Studien,* as translated and quoted in Liebesny, *The Law of the Near and Middle East,* p. 13.

43. Schacht expressed this position at length in *Origins of Muhammadan Jurisprudence* and reiterated it in *Introduction to Islamic Law,* pp. 28ff. Cf. Coulson, *History of Islamic Law,* pp. 64–70.

For the other point of view see Rahman, "Concepts of *Sunnah, Ijtihad* and *Ijma'* in the Early Period," and *Islam,* chap. 3.

44. Rahman, *Islam,* pp. 53–58; and Hasan, *Early Development of Islamic Jurisprudence,* chap. 5.

45. This can be illustrated not only from the usage of early Muslims but also from the usage of the Prophet himself when he speaks of reward for any Muslim who establishes a good *sunna* and punishment for any Muslim who establishes a bad *sunna.* See Al-Azami, *On Schacht's Origins of Muhammadan Jurisprudence,* pp. 31ff.

To distinguish the Sunna of the Prophet as a formal source of Shari'a from the *sunna* of leading early Muslims and communities that may have persuasive but not formal authority, the former is written here with a capital "S" while the latter is italicized, indicating that reference is being made to the Arabic term for tradition rather than the formal and technical second source of Shari'a.

46. Rahman, *Islam,* p. 58.

47. Ibid., p. 59.

48. Vesey-Fitzgerald, "Nature and Sources of the Shari'a," p. 93. See also Coulson, *History of Islamic Law,* p. 42, for a similar analysis of this phenomenon.

49. Rahman, *Islam,* pp. 63–65; Schacht, *Origins of Muhammadan Jurisprudence,* pp. 3–4. The six recognized scholars of Sunna are al-Bukhari (d. 256/870), Muslim (d. 261/875), Abu Da'ud (d. 275/888), Tirmidhi (d. 279/892), Nasa'i (d. 303/916), and Ibn Maja (d. 273/886).

50. See, for example, Ibn Khaldun, *The Muqaddimah: An Introduction to History,* 2:448–60, as translated and quoted in Liebesny, *The Law of the Near and Middle East,* pp. 15–16; Schacht, *Origins of Muhammadan Jurisprudence,* pp. 36–39. For more extensive treatment see James Robson, ed. and trans., *An Introduction to the Science of Tradition by al-Hakim an-Naysaburi* (London, 1953).

51. Vesey-Fitzgerald, "Nature and Sources of the Shari'a," p. 94. Coulson made the same point even more strongly in *History of Islamic Law,* p. 63.

Cf. Shafi'i, as translated in Schacht, *Origins of Muhammadan Jurisprudence*, pp. 37–38, suggests that the usual criterion of the truthfulness of the transmitter may be disregarded "when he relates what cannot possibly be the case, or what is contradicted by better-authenticated information."

52. Rahman, *Islam*, pp. 60–61, 70; Schacht, *Origins of Muhammadan Jurisprudence*, pp. 94–95.

53. Khadduri, "Nature and Sources of Islamic Law," p. 14.

54. Ignaz Goldziher, *Vorlesungen uber den Islam*, pp. 52–53, as translated and quoted in Liebesny, *The Law of the Near and Middle East*, p. 17.

55. Hasan, *Early Development of Islamic Jurisprudence*, chap. 7; Ahmad Hasan, "The Classical Definition of 'Ijma': The Nature of Consensus," *Islamic Studies* 14 (1975): 261–70; and Schacht, *Origins of Muhammadan Jurisprudence*, pp. 82–94.

56. Khadduri, "Nature and Sources of Islamic Law," p. 16.

57. Rahman, *Islam*, p. 71.

58. Schacht, *Origins of Muhammadan Jurisprudence*, pp. 98–99; Coulson, *History of Islamic Law*, p. 60.

59. Vesey-Fitzgerald, "Nature and Sources of the Shari'a," p. 101.

60. R. Paret, "Istihsan and Istislah," in *Encyclopedia of Islam (Supplement)* (Leiden: E. J. Brill, 1938), p. 102.

61. Ibid., pp. 102–4.

62. Vesey-Fitzgerald, "Nature and Sources of the Shari'a," p. 101.

63. Ibid., p. 102; Coulson, *History of Islamic Law*, p. 92.

64. Paret, "Istihsan and Istislah," p. 104. I will return to these positions and their implications for modern reform in the next chapter.

65. Verses 2:173, 5:3, and 16:115 of the Qur'an. See also verse 16:106 for the general license to show disbelief in Islam under coercion so long as one remains faithful at heart.

66. Vesey-Fitzgerald, "Nature and Sources of the Shari'a," pp. 109–10.

67. The best-known Sunna in support of *ijtihad* is the record of the conversation between the Prophet and Ma'adh ibn Jabal, when the latter was appointed governor/judge to Yemen. According to this Sunna, the Prophet asked Ma'adh about the sources he would look to in governing his province and adjudicating among his subjects. Ma'adh replied that he would look to the Qur'an first, and if it was silent on the subject, he would look to the Sunna of the Prophet. If he found no applicable Sunna, Ma'adh said he would exercise his best personal opinion or judgment, "*ajtahidu ra'yy wa la alu.*" The Prophet is reported to have approved this ranking of Shari'a sources.

For a full translation of this Sunna see Duncan B. MacDonald, *Development of Muslim Theology, Jurisprudence and Constitutional Theory* (Lahore: Premier Book House, 1972), p. 86. See also Vesey-Fitzgerald, "Nature and Sources of the Shari'a," p. 93; and Khadduri, Nature and Sources of Islamic Law," p. 11, n. 10.

68. Differences in the *ijtihad* of jurists in the interpretation of the Qur'an and Sunna, since the earliest times, account for the differences in their conclusions on whether a given text is relevant and what it means in relation to the facts (Shafi'i, *al-Umm*, 7:245).

69. Coulson, *History of Islamic Law*, pp. 80–81; and Schacht, *Introduction to Islamic Law*, pp. 69ff.

Some contemporary writers have argued against this commonly held belief. See, for example, Wael B. Hallaq, "Was the Gate of Ijtihad Closed?" *International Journal of Middle East Studies* 16 (1984): 3.

70. These scholars and their impact are discussed in such works as C. C. Adams, *Islam and Modernism in Egypt* (London: 1953); H. A. R. Gibb, *Modern Trends in Islam* (Chicago: University of Chicago Press, 1947); and Malcolm H. Kerr, *Islamic Reform: The Political and Legal Theories of Muhammad Abduh and Rashid Rida* (Berkeley and Los Angeles: University of California Press, 1966). Efforts at reform through *ijtihad* whether in its historical conception or in a modified form, are discussed in Chapter 3 of this book.

71. Coulson, *History of Islamic Law*, p. 60.

72. Several examples of Umar's *ijtihad* are discussed in Muhammad Bultajiy, *Manhaj Umar ibn al-Khatab fi al-Tashri* (Cairo: Dar al-Fikr al-Arabi, 1970). Bultajiy explains each of these instances in order to conclude that Umar did not contravene the Qur'an and Sunna. What is significant for our purposes here is that Umar's action illustrates that it is possible to exercise *ijtihad* in matters governed by clear and definite texts of the Qur'an and Sunna.

73. Ibid., pp. 180, 132-35; Abu Yusuf, *Kitab al-Kharaj* (Cairo: Al-Matba'ah al-Salafiyah, 1962-63/1302 Hijri), pp. 13-15.

74. Fazlur Rahman, *Islamic Methodology in History* (Karachi: Central Institute of Islamic Research, 1965), pp. 180-81; Hasan, *Early Development of Islamic Jurisprudence*, pp. 120-21.

75. Such as the Mu'tazila and Kharijites. See Schacht, *Origins of Muhammadan Jurisprudence*, pp. 40-44, 128, 258-59, 260-61.

76. Coulson said in *A History of Islamic Law*, p. 106, that because each of these three groups has its own distinct legal system, it is not meaningful to speak of Shi'a law as such. This is true for specific purposes or with reference to particular legal issues. Our main concern here, however, is to assess the potential of the perspectives of these Shi'a subsects as they relate to reforming the public law of Shari'a.

77. For a theological account of these subsects see Montgomery Watt, *Islamic Philosophy and Theology* (Edinburgh: Edinburgh University Press, 1962), pp. 20-26, 50-56, 99-104.

78. Mahmassani, *Falsafat Al-Tashri Fi Al-Islam*, p. 38.

79. A. A. A. Fyzee, "Shi'i Legal Theories," in Khadduri and Liebesny, eds., *Law in the Middle East*, p. 115.

80. Ibid.; Khadduri, "Nature and Sources of Islamic Law," p. 22.

81. Fyzee, "Shi'i Legal Theories," p. 115.

82. Ibid., pp. 120-21. On the imamate of the Twelvers Shi'a in particular, of special interest to this book because they are in power in Iran and have been attempting to implement their beliefs for several years, see Joseph Eliash, "The Ithna 'ashari Shi'i Juristic Theory of Political and Legal Authority," *Studia Islamica* 29 (1969): 2-30.

83. Eliash, "The Ithna 'ashari Shi'i Juristic Theory of Political and Legal Authority," p. 29 at n. 1. Cf. W. St. Clair Tisdall, "Shi'ah Additions to the Koran," *Moslem World* 3 (1913): 227-41.

84. Coulson, *History of Islamic Law*, p. 105.

85. Fyzee, "Shi'i Legal Theories," p. 123; Khadduri, "Nature and Sources of Islamic Law," p. 23.

86. Eliash, "Ithna 'ashari Juristic Theory," p. 27. See also Coulson, *History of Islamic Law*, pp. 106-8.

87. Khadduri, "Nature and Sources of Islamic Law," p. 22.

88. Contrast, for example, Schacht, *Origins of Muhammadan Jurisprudence,* p. 260, with Coulson, *History of Islamic Law,* p. 105.

89. Coulson, *History of Islamic Law,* p. 108.

90. Ibid., p. 120.

91. Vesey-Fitzgerald, "Nature and Sources of the Shari'a," p. 91.

92. Schacht, *Origins of Muhammadan Jurisprudence,* p. 84.

93. Coulson, *History of Islamic Law,* p. 121.

94. Even countries that claim a theoretical commitment to Shari'a today, such as Saudi Arabia, do in fact engage in secular legislation and practice. See Samir Shamma, "Law and Lawyers in Saudi Arabia," *International and Comparative Law Quarterly* 14 (1965): 1034; and Seaman, "Islamic Law and Modern Government," pp. 424ff.

95. Schacht, *Introduction to Islamic Law,* p. 76.

96. Coulson, *History of Islamic Law,* p. 120.

97. Ibid., pp. 82–84. Individual jurists preferred different variations of these basic general categories. See Hasan, *Early Development of Islamic Jurisprudence,* pp. 34–39; and Rahman, *Islam,* pp. 83–84.

98. Kemal A. Faruki, *Islamic Jurisprudence,* rev. ed. (Karachi: Pakistan Publishing House, 1975), pp. 166–94; and Coulson, *History of Islamic Law,* pp. 47–51.

99. Schacht, *Introduction to Islamic Law,* p. 68, n. 1.

100. Coulson, *History of Islamic Law,* pp. 87–88, 197–201; Schacht, *Introduction to Islamic Law,* p. 106; Vesey-Fitzgerald, "Nature and Sources of the Shari'a," p. 110.

101. Liebesny, *Law in the Near and Middle East,* chaps. 3–5. See also his article "Impact of Western Law in the Countries of the Near East," *George Washington Law Review* 22 (1953): 1, 126.

3. TOWARD AN ADEQUATE REFORM METHODOLOGY

1. The Arabic word *Ustadh* means revered teacher. This title is popularly used in the Sudan in relation to the late Mahmoud Mohamed Taha.

2. For example, Fazlur Rahman speaks of Ibn Taymiyya in glowing terms in many parts of his book *Islam,* describing him as a rare, bright, and bold spirit (p. 79); celebrated doctor and theologian (p. 83); and describing his work as monumental and of lasting import (p. 123).

Al-Mawdudi said that Ibn Taymiyya "was not simply bold in rejecting stagnant *taqlid* [blind following of the tradition], but he was also, even more, an example in the practice of *ijtihad*" (quoted by Voll in "Renewal and Reform in Islamic History," p. 38).

3. Ibn Taymiyya was involved in controversy on a variety of theological, jurisprudential, and political issues which attracted the hostility of many opponents and led to his imprisonment. See Rahman, *Islam,* pp. 94, 111–15, 147–49, 162; Omar A. Farrukh, *Ibn Taimiyya on Public and Private Law in Islam or Public Policy in Islamic Jurisprudence* (Beirut: Khayats, 1966), pp. 4–7; and Ann K. S. Lambton, *State and Government in Medieval Islam* (Oxford: Oxford University Press, 1981), pp. 144–51. We are not concerned here with those aspects of his work.

4. Five years before his birth, Baghdad (the capital of the caliphate at the time) was sacked by the Mongolian invaders, the final act in the disintegration of the by then nominally unified Islamic state. The Crusaders were still occupying parts of Ibn Taymiyya's home

province, Syria. See Farrukh, *Ibn Taimiyya on Public and Private Law in Islam*, p. 3; and Lambton, *State and Government in Medieval Islam*, pp. 143–44.

5. Rahman, *Islam*, pp. 79, 111.

6. Muhammad Mubarak, ed. (Beirut, 1966). This book was translated by Omar Farrukh as *Ibn Taimiyya on Public and Private Law in Islam*.

7. Lambton, *State and Government in Medieval Islam*, pp. 144–45, 147; Farrukh, *Ibn Taimiyya on Public and Private Law in Islam*, pp. 187–88.

8. Rahman, *Islam*, p. 237.

9. Joseph Schacht, "Islamic Law in Contemporary States," *American Journal of Comparative Law* 8 (1959): 147.

10. Lambton, *State and Government in Medieval Islam*, pp. 147–48.

11. Ibid., pp. 148–49.

12. Ibid., p. 149.

13. Rahman, *Islam*, pp. 196–206; and Esposito, *Islam and Politics*, pp. 33–36. Ibn Taymiyya's ideas are very influential in present-day Saudi Arabia. They have also been adopted and developed by "Muslim Brothers" in many parts of the Muslim world.

14. Ishtiaq Ahmed, *The Concept of an Islamic State: An Analysis of the Ideological Controversy in Pakistan* (New York: St. Martin's Press, 1987).

15. Ishtiaq Ahmed used this term for the traditional *Ulama* and extremist individual proponents of Shari'a.

16. According to Ahmed's scheme of classification, these positions are subdivided into two groups, those who advocate the sacred state excluding human will and those who advocate the sacred state including human will. See ibid., pp. 31–36.

The other three positions analyzed by Ahmed, those of Zafar, Usman, and Munir, are subdivided by him as those who advocate a secular state while admitting divine will and those who advocate a secular state excluding divine will. See ibid., pp. 36–38.

17. Ibid., pp. 178–79. Ahmed discusses and cites the sources from his subjects in various parts of the book. Since we are concerned with these positions in the present context only as illustrations of current thinking, reference is made here and in the following to pages in Ahmed's chapter 9, in which he undertakes a systematic analysis and summary of all the above-mentioned positions.

18. Ibid., pp. 179–81.

19. Ibid., pp. 187–89.

20. Ibid., pp. 183–84.

21. I cannot elaborate on the nature and development of this and other "Islamic" movements in the Sudan or the role of Islam in Sudanese politics. Some idea of these aspects can be gained from Esposito, *Islam and Politics*, Epilogue to 2d ed., rev., pp. 281–91; John Esposito, "Sudan's Islamic Experiment," *Muslim World* 76 (1986): 181; Khalid Duran, "The Centrifugal Forces of Religion in Sudanese Politics," *Orient* 26 (1985): 572.

22. A rare but well-known example is the confrontation by Reverend Philip Abbas Qabush, a Christian leader in the Sudan, who forced Turabi to admit, after an unsuccessful effort to evade the issue, that a non-Muslim citizen of an Islamic state is disqualified by Shari'a from holding the office of head of state. For a record of this revealing confrontation see Abdullahi An-Na'im, "The Elusive Islamic Constitution: The Sudanese Experience," *Orient* 26 (1985): 329.

23. This is the basic theme of his public lectures in the Sudan. See, for example,

the one published in Rashid al-Ghnnushy and Hassan al-Turabi, *Al-Haraka al-Islamiya wa al-Tahdith* (Beirut: Dar al-Jiyl, 1980), p. 45.

24. Published in Esposito, *Voices of Resurgent Islam*, p. 241.

25. Ibid., p. 243; emphasis added.

26. Other examples of unsubstantiated, bold assertions can be found throughout the essay. For example, at ibid., p. 247, Turabi states that "the Islamic government was not a totally alien institution superimposed upon society. To the extent that it was — in the sense that it was not legitimate — *the jurists saw to it that it should be relatively powerless. . . .* Furthermore, *the individual was largely free because the lawmaking and financial powers were so limited; so there was not any intolerable oppression"* (emphasis added). Neither evidence nor explanation of historical facts in support of these assertions was offered.

27. Ibid., pp. 242–43, 246–49.

28. Ibid., p. 244; emphasis added.

29. As we shall see in the next chapter, these are some of the pertinent issues over which Shari'a is at variance with modern constitutionalism.

30. Ibid., p. 250.

31. Ibid.

32. Kerr, *Islamic Reform*, p. 1.

33. Albert Hourani, *Arabic Thought in the Liberal Age, 1798–1939* (Cambridge: Cambridge University Press, 1983), pp. 144–45. The reference to later developments in the direction of complete secularism is to chapter 7 of Hourani's book. The other group of Abduh's students developed into the *Salafiya* movement of Rashid Rida and other proponents of a strict Shari'a state.

The same observation is made by other commentators such as Sylvia G. Haim, *Arab Nationalism: An Anthology* (Berkeley and Los Angeles: University of California Press, 1964), p. 18; and Majid Khadduri, *Political Trends in the Arab World* (Baltimore: Johns Hopkins Press, 1970), pp. 64–65.

34. (Islam and the foundations of government). The edition used here is that published by Dar Maktabat al-Haya, Beirut, 1966. Excerpts of this book as translated into English from a French translation can be found in John J. Donohue and John L. Esposito, eds., *Islam in Transition: Muslim Perspectives* (New York: Oxford University Press, 1982), pp. 29–37. See Hourani, *Arabic Thought in the Liberal Age*, pp. 183–88, for a summary of Ali Abd al-Raziq's views; and pp. 188–91 for the violently critical and negative reaction to his thesis by the religious establishment and Islamic activists.

35. Abd al-Raziq, *Al-Islam wa Usul al-Hukm*, pp. 39ff. On pages 82–83, he concludes that the caliphate as historically defined by Muslim jurists (and outlined on pages 12–18 of his book) is not only unnecessary but is in fact a catastrophe for Islam and the Muslims and a source of evil and corruption, as clearly demonstrated by Muslim history.

36. Ibid., pp. 122ff. On pages 171–72, he concludes that a close examination of what was provided by Islam and applied by the Prophet had very little to do with political government and the regulations of civil administration. According to him, all Islamic regulations in matters of faith, social dealings, and ethics and penal measures are purely religious and designed for the religious benefit and interest of people without purporting to regulate their temporal life in this world.

37. Ibid., pp. 181–82.

38. Rahman, *Islam*, p. 229.

39. It is important to emphasize that the secularist modernists "are everywhere

an elite, imposing their reforms through their control of the power structure. As a result, the mass of Muslims, who at least knew the principles of shari'a, understand its successor temporal law in only the most elementary sense" (Bonderman, "Modernization and Changing Perceptions of Islamic Law," p. 1190).

40. For example, every effort has been made to secularize Iran since the 1920s. Yet Iran now presents the proponents of Shari'a with their most spectacular success. It is also significant that thoroughly secularized Muslim countries such as Turkey and Tunisia have recently faced mounting demands for Islamization. On the current debate over the application of Shari'a in Egypt, for example, see Donohue and Esposito, eds., Islam in Transition, pp. 239–50.

41. The following summary is based on Anderson, Law Reform in the Muslim World, pp. 43–82. Many authors have explained and discussed these reforms and quoted the relevant legislation. See, for example, Liebesny, The Law of the Near and Middle East, chaps. 3 and 4; Bonderman, "Modernization and Changing Perceptions of Islamic Law," pp. 1177–89; Fazlur Rahman, "Islamic Modernism: Its Scope, Methods and Alternatives," International Journal of Middle Eastern Studies 1 (1970): 324ff.; and John Esposito, "Perspectives on Islamic Law Reform: The Case of Pakistan," New York University Journal of International Law and Politics 13 (Fall 1980): 220–35.

42. For an example of this practice see A. A. A. Fyzee, Outlines of Muhammadan Law, 3d ed. (Oxford: Oxford University Press, 1964), pp. 104ff.

43. Quoted in Esposito, "Perspectives on Islamic Law Reform," p. 237.

44. Voll, "Renewal and Reform in Islamic History," pp. 35, 37.

45. Ibid., p. 40.

46. Ibid., p. 41.

47. The other modes that, according to Voll, have engaged in conscious cultural syntheses are the preservationist mode of a conservative religious establishment and that of rulers who employed the methods of accommodation and toleration. See ibid., p. 41.

48. Ibid.

49. This is how Voll described the reformer-renewer attitude, ibid., p. 42.

50. Ibid., pp. 42–43.

51. See, for example, Muhammad Nuwayhi, "A Revolution in Religious Thought," in Donohue and Esposito, eds., Islam in Transition, pp. 160–68.

52. This is, of course, true of all fundamental and especially religious and constitutional texts and has exercised thinkers and reformers through the ages. See, for example, Terence Ball, "Deadly Hermeneutics; Or, SINN and the Social Scientist," in Terence Ball, ed., Idioms of Inquiry (Albany: State University of New York Press, 1987), pp. 97–102.

53. These aspects of Shari'a are explained in detail in subsequent chapters.

54. Although the jurists of Shari'a relied on the Prophet's conduct in selecting which verses were to be enacted and which were to be repealed or abrogated, there were no explicit instructions by the Prophet on the matter.

55. These problems will be explained in detail in subsequent chapters.

56. Esposito, "Perspectives on Islamic Law Reform," pp. 240–44. Esposito expressed similar views in his earlier article "Muslim Family Law Reform: Towards an Islamic Methodology," Islamic Studies 15 (Spring 1976): 19.

57. See, for example, Faruki, Islamic Jurisprudence, pp. 18–19; Fyzee, Outlines of Muhammadan Law, pp. 14–17.

58. Esposito, "Perspectives on Islamic Law Reform," p. 241, citing Mahamasani's *Falsafat al-Tashri fi al-Islam* (trans. F. J. Ziadeh, 1961) and Isma'il al-Faruqi's "Towards a Methodology of Qur'anic Exegesis," *Islamic Studies* 1 (1962): 35.

59. Esposito, "Perspectives on Islamic Law Reform," pp. 241-42.

60. See R. Paret, "Istihsan and Istislah," pp. 104-5.

61. See, for example, Fazlur Rahman, "Towards Reformulating the Methodology of Islamic Law," *New York University Journal of International Law and Politics* 12 (Fall 1979): 219.

62. Esposito, "Perspectives on Islamic Law Reform," pp. 243-44, citing Iqbal's *The Reconstruction of Religious Thought in Islam*, pp. 173-74, and Faruki's *Islamic Jurisprudence*, pp. 86-87.

63. Ibid., p. 244. As noted by von Grunebaum, *ijma* under Shari'a operates only retrospectively and is therefore of extremely limited utility for future reform. Quoted in Liebesny, *The Law of the Near and Middle East*, pp. 17-18. I believe, however, that the basic principle and rationale of *ijma* can be seen as consistent with the modern legislative process, provided the reform methodology explained below is accepted.

64. Rahman, *Islam*, p. 214.

65. *Ustadh* Mahmoud was executed on January 18, 1985, for his opposition to what he believed to be an arbitrary and distorted application of Shari'a in the Sudan by former President Ja'far Numayry. It is very significant for the purposes of this book that the main charge for which *Ustadh* Mahmoud was executed was *ridda* (apostasy) because his views were deemed by the authorities to be heretical. There were, however, political circumstances which encouraged Numayry to confirm and execute the death penalty in this case. For a detailed discussion and critique of the trial and execution of *Ustadh* Mahmoud see Abdullahi A. An-Na'im, "The Islamic Law of Apostasy and Its Modern Applicability: A Case from the Sudan," *Religion* 16 (1986): 197.

66. All the writings of *Ustadh* Mahmoud were published in Arabic; my English translation of his main book, *The Second Message of Islam*, however, was published by Syracuse University Press in 1987. An earlier translation of the same book into Norwegian was prepared by Einar Berg and published by Oslo University Press in 1984. The following brief summary is based on my close knowledge of both the oral and written teachings of *Ustadh* Mahmoud.

67. This progression of Qur'anic sanction for the use of force against non-Muslims is explained fully in Chapter 6, below.

68. Abdulla Muhammad Al-Qurtubi, *Al-Jami li Ahkam al-Qur'an*, (Beirut: Dar al-Kitab al-Arabi, n.d.), 5:169.

69. The relevant verses and their commonly accepted interpretation under Shari'a will be explained in Chapter 6.

70. Taha, *Second Message of Islam*, p. 125.

71. It is important to note that there is no implication here of the Prophet having withheld, or failed to deliver, any part of the revelation. The point being made by *Ustadh* Mahmoud is that although the Prophet delivered the whole text of the Qur'an, he explained and applied that part which was most appropriate for immediate implementation.

72. Erwin I. J. Rosenthal, *Islam in the Modern National State* (Cambridge: Cambridge University Press, 1965), p. 49.

73. See, for example, Mustafa Zaid, *Al-Naskh fi al-Qur'an al-Karim*, 2 vols. (Cairo: Dar al-Fikr al-Arabi, 1963); Hasan, *Early Development of Islamic Jurisprudence*, chap. 4;

Burton, *The Collection of the Qur'an,* chaps. 3 and 4; K. I. Semaan, "AL-Nasikh wa Al-Mansukh: Abrogation and Its Application in Islam," *Islamic Quarterly* 5 (April-July 1959): 11-29.

74. Hasan, *Early Development of Islamic Jurisprudence,* p. 60; and Burton, *The Collection of the Qur'an,* pp. 46-67.

75. Burton, *The Collection of the Qur'an,* pp. 49ff.; Coulson, *History of Islamic Law,* pp. 58-59. Semaan, in "Al-Naskh wa Al-Mansukh," pp. 13-29, offered a translation of portions of Shafi'i's *Al-Risalah,* which are relevant to these issues.

76. As Ahmad Hasan correctly stated: "How and when the idea of the abrogation of certain Qur'anic verses emerged in the early history of Islam is not easy to establish. It seems, however, most probable that when the commentators and jurists could not reconcile certain apparently contradictory verses, they propounded this theory" (*Early Development of Islamic Jurisprudence,* p. 63).

77. See the sources cited and discussed in Chapter 6.

78. Hasan, *Early Development of Islamic Jurisprudence,* pp. 67.

79. See, for example, Muhammad Abduh, *Tafsir al-Manar* (Cairo: Dar al-Manar, 1367 Hijri), 2:138ff.

80. Such as Sayyid Ahmad Khan in *Tafsir al-Qur'an* (Lahore, n.d.), pp. 137-40; and Hasan, *Early Development of Islamic Jurisprudence,* pp. 70-79.

81. The word *ayah* used in this verse and in verse 16:101, also quoted by the jurists in support of their conception of *naskh,* can mean either a verse of the Qur'an or a sign, token or mark. Some authors have argued that the word in this context refers to pre-Islamic revelations in order to conclude that abrogation here applied to the law revealed to the previous prophets rather than to parts of the Qur'an. For this argument see Hasan, *Early Development of Islamic Jurisprudence,* pp. 70-71.

82. In some styles of recitation *(tilawa)* of the Qur'an the Arabic word translated here as "postpone" is written as *nunsiha,* which means to cause to be forgotten. In other styles of recitation, the word is written *nunsi'ha,* as quoted by *Ustadh* Mahmoud, which means to postpone. *Ustadh* Mahmoud's quotation and meaning are accepted by earliest and strongest authority in Islam. Ibn Khathir reported in his commentary on this verse that Ibn Abbas, one of the earliest and most authoritative Muslim jurists, said that he had heard Umar, the second caliph and leading Companion of the Prophet, read the verse in this manner and give it the meaning of postponement.

83. Taha, *Second Message of Islam,* pp. 40-41. By primary verse he meant those of the Mecca stage, while a subsidiary verse is one of the Medina stage.

84. Rahman, *Islam,* pp. 216-17.

85. Khadduri, *Political Trends in the Arab World,* pp. 64-65; Aharon Layish, "The Contribution of the Modernists to the Secularization of Islamic Law," *Middle Eastern Studies* 14 (October 1978): 263.

86. Rahman, *Islam,* p. 221.

87. It is interesting that although *Ustadh* Mahmoud graduated in civil engineering from the Gordon Memorial College (now the University of Khartoum) in 1936, he did not suffer from this inferiority complex in relation to the "specialists" of Shari'a. On the contrary, he believed that they were the biggest obstacle to genuine Islamic reform.

For biographical information on *Ustadh* Mahmoud, see the Translator's Introduction to Taha, *Second Message of Islam.*

88. Rahman, *Islam,* p. 230. See also Rahman, "Islamic Modernism," pp. 319, 324-26.

89. Rahman, *Islam*, p. 229.

90. Ibid., p. 231, citing Sayed Ameer Ali's *The Spirit of Islam* as the clearest example of this line of thinking.

91. Ibid.

92. Hasan, *Early Development of Islamic Jurisprudence*, pp. 78-79; emphasis added.

93. Professor Fazlur Rahman has passed away since the following comments on his work were first written. I have great respect for Fazlur Rahman's profound contribution to Islamic scholarship and was looking forward to his reading my comments and responding to them in due course. Now that he is no longer with us, I feel that it would have been his wish for these comments to be made.

94. Rahman, *Islam*, p. 232. He made the same point in his article "Islamic Modernism," p. 331.

95. Rahman, "Islamic Modernism," p. 329.

96. Ibid.

97. Ibid., p. 331. He drew on his own experience in Pakistan, hinted at in the same context, in support of his conclusion that Muslims are not ready for the "honest, true and practical" approach.

98. Rahman, *Islam*, p. 253.

99. Fazlur Rahman, *Islam and Modernity: Transformation of an Intellectual Tradition* (Chicago: University of Chicago Press, 1982).

100. Rahman, *Islam*, p. 251.

4. SHARI'A AND MODERN CONSTITUTIONALISM

1. Herbert J. Spiro, "The True Constitution," in C. P. Magrath, ed., *Constitutionalism and Politics: Conflict and Consensus* (Glencoe, Ill.: Scott, Foresman, 1968), pp. 4-12; and Ben O. Nwabueze, *Constitutionalism in the Emergent States* (Rutherford, N.J.: Fairleigh Dickinson University Press, 1973), pp. 2-3.

2. Henry C. Black, *Black's Law Dictionary*, 5th ed. (St. Paul: West Publishing, 1979), p. 282.

3. G. A. Forrest, "Constitution and Constitutional Law," in *Encyclopedia Britannica*, vol. 6 (1967), p. 398.

4. Lord Bolingbroke, as quoted in C. H. McIlwain, *Constitutionalism Ancient and Modern* (Ithaca: Cornell University Press, 1947), p. 3; emphasis added.

5. See generally, Piscatori, *Islam in a World of Nation-States*, esp. chaps. 2 and 3.

6. One of the basic rationales of this principle of equality, together with other aspects of constitutionalism, is the universal rule that one should treat others as he or she wishes to be treated by them. Further explanation of this rule and other rationales of the requirement of equality will be offered below.

7. K. C. Wheare, *Modern Constitutions* (London: Oxford University Press, 1966), p. 139.

8. McIlwain, *Constitutionalism Ancient and Modern*, pp. 37-38.

9. Nwabueze, *Constitutionalism in the Emergent States*, pp. 10-11.

10. It may be true that the term *constitution* was not used to denote the fundamental legal framework of the state before the seventeenth century, as tentatively suggested in McIlwain, *Constitutionalism Ancient and Modern*, p. 24. McIlwain traced forms of early constitutionalism expressed by the Greek as *politeia* and by the Latins as *constitutio*, and their interrelations in history (pp. 26ff.).

Regardless of the term used to describe the phenomenon, I would suggest that the substance of minimal constitutionalism can be seen in all large-scale political communities throughout history.

11. Even if we accept the view, expressed by McIlwain in *Constitutionalism Ancient and Modern*, pages 62ff., that popular sovereignty has Roman origins, the fact remains that the citizens who were entitled to exercise such sovereignty did not include all citizens, according to the definition adopted in the present study.

12. The most direct authority for this fundamental moral principle in Islam can be found in Sunna. The Prophet is reported to have said that one should treat other people in the same way he or she would like them to treat him or her. Another formulation of the same principle is the maxim *"kama tadinu tudan,"* you shall be treated as you treat others.

The universality and validity of this fundamental moral principle in other religious traditions is clearly demonstrated in David R. Williams, *World Religions and the Hope for Peace* (Boston: Beacon Press, 1951), pp. 180ff.

13. Cf. Nwabueze, *Constitutionalism in the Emergent States*, p. 2, where he says that "a colonial administration, operated in the interest of the rulers and the class interests they represent, is not necessarily non-constitutional. The crucial test is whether the government is limited by pre-determined rules."

I would respectfully disagree because government in the interest of the rulers cannot be in the interest of the ruled unless they are the same people. As explained above, it is not merely limitation by predetermined rules but also the nature and purpose of those rules and the processes by which they are made and implemented that give us valid criteria for judging the conformity of a system of government to constitutionalism.

14. On the acceptance of the principle of constitutionalism by African states, see ibid., chap. 2. In relation to Asia, see Lawrence W. Beer, ed., *Constitutionalism in Asia* (Berkeley and Los Angeles: University of California Press, 1979), pp. 8-9. Of particular interest from the perspective of the present book are chapters 2, 5, and 7, on Bangladesh, Indonesia, and Malaysia, respectively. As clearly shown in these chapters, these three predominantly Muslim Asian countries have opted for the principle of constitutionalism out of their own free will and continued to do so for several decades after independence.

15. Beer, "Constitutionalism in Asia and the United States," in Beer, ed., *Constitutionalism in Asia*, pp. 1-19.

16. A brief summary of the main historical events that have a special significance for constitutional issues was given in Chapter 2 of this book. For more detailed accounts from a wide variety of primary sources see Faruki, *Evolution of Islamic Constitutional Theory and Practice from 610 to 1926*, pp. 16-36; and Mohamed S. El-Awa, *On the Political System of the Islamic State* (Indianapolis: American Trust Publications, 1980), pp. 26-62.

17. Majid Khadduri in "The Nature of the Islamic State," *Islamic Culture* 21 (1947): 327-31, disussed both terms and preferred to describe the Islamic state under Shari'a as a nomocracy.

18. The Qur'an, 33:40, specifically stipulates that Muhammad is the final prophet and that the Qur'an is the conclusion of divine revelation.

19. T. W. Arnold, *The Caliphate* (New York: Barnes and Noble, 1966), pp. 29-30.

Besides using the same title, *Umar,* the second caliph, started the use of the other title, *Amir al-Mu'minin* (Commander of the Believers) (ibid., pp. 31-32). On the third title, imam, and its implications in Sunni and Shi'i traditions see ibid., pp. 33ff.

20. As indicated in Chapter 2, some Shi'a believe that the imam is more than an ordinary political ruler because he succeeds the Prophet in at least some of the attributes of prophethood. For Sunni Muslims, the assumption that the conduct of the affairs of the Muslim state by the first four caliphs is closest to the Prophet's own example is based on those men's long and close association with the Prophet, without any implication of divine authority on their part.

21. For an account of the selection and appointment of the first four Caliphs see Arnold, *The Caliphate,* pp. 19-22; and Faruki, *Evolution of Islamic Constitutional Theory and Practice,* pp. 16-19.

22. Mu'awya, the founder of the Umayyad dynasty, established the hereditary principle in 676 (four years before his death) by securing *by'a* for his son Yazid and having him confirmed as the next caliph during Mu'awya's own lifetime. This precedent was subsequently followed throughout the Umayyad and Abbasid dynasties. See Arnold, *The Caliphate,* pp. 22ff.

23. Ibid., p. 30; and Majid Khadduri, *War and Peace in the Law of Islam,* (Baltimore: Johns Hopkins Press, 1970), p. 12.

24. Khalid M. Ishaque, "Al-Ahkam Al-Sultaniya: Laws of Government in Islam," *Islamic Studies* 4 (1965): 288, 293.

25. In his well-known speech upon assuming the office of caliph, Abu Bakr emphasized his accountability to the Muslim community and made obedience to him conditional upon his conformity with the law of God in administering the affairs of the state. For the text of this speech see Ibn Qutaybah, *Al-Imama wa al-Siyasa* (Cairo: Mustafa al-Babi, 1957), p. 16.

Although this early and authoritative precedent may offer possibilities for the political and legal accountability of the government to the general population, it has not been developed as such under Shari'a. One problem that must be resolved if we wish to develop political and legal accountability out of Abu Bakr's statement is that it does not explain how the caliph's conformity with the law of God may be determined. Another question is how to hold the caliph accountable and to whom. As we shall see later, the caliph's constituency was never the totality of even the male Muslim population, let alone women and non-Muslims.

26. Gibb, "Constitutional Organization," p. 14.

27. Arnold, *The Caliphate,* pp. 45-46, 70-76.

28. It is reported that Abu Bakr objected to being addressed as *Khalifat Allah,* vicegerent of God, a title also mentioned by the poet Hassan ibn Thabit in an elegy to Uthman, the third caliph, upon his murder in 656. Some scholars protested that God can neither die nor be absent so as to have a vicegerent. Nevertheless, in the absence of human accountability, the caliph was, in effect, the vicegerent of God. By the Abbasid era, the caliph was openly described as such. See Arnold, *The Caliphate,* pp. 51-52; and Abu Yusuf, *Kitab al-Kharaj,* p. 6.

29. Abdur Rahim, *The Principles of Muhammadan Jurisprudence* (rpt. Westport, Conn.: Hyperion Press, 1981), p. 383; N. J. Coulson, "The State and the Individual in Islamic Law," *International and Comparative Law Quarterly* 6 (1957): 57; Rosenthal, *Political Thought in Medieval Islam,* pp. 22-23; Mohammad Mehdi, "Constitutionalism Western and Middle Eastern," Manuscript, (San Francisco, 1960), pp. 145-46; and Ishaque, "Al-Ahkam Al-Sultaniya," pp. 291, 293-95.

30. See, for example, Gibb, "Constitutional Organization," p. 3.

31. Faruki, *Evolution of Islamic Constitutional Theory and Practice*, p. 4.

32. Coulson, "The State and the Individual in Islamic Law," p. 55.

33. See, for example, Muhammad Rashid Rida, *Tafsir al-Manar* (Cairo: Dar Al-Manar, 1947/1376 Hijri), 4:45; Abd al-Qadir Auda, *Al-Islam wa Awda'una al-Siyasiya* (Beirut: Mu'assasat al-Risalah, 1980?), pp. 120–61; and El-Awa, *On the Political System of the Islamic State*, pp. 86–97.

34. Al-Tusi, *Tafsir al-Tibyan* (Al-Najaf: Maktabat al-Amin, n.d.), 3:32; al-Qasmiy, *Tafsir al-Qasmiy* (Cairo: Eisa al-Babi al-Halabi, 1957), 4:1020–22; Abd al-Hamid Mutwalli, *Mabadi Nizam al-Hukm fi al-Islam*, p. 245ff.; and Mehdi, "Constitutionalism: Western and Middle Eastern," p. 121. Cf. Fazlur Rahman, "A Recent Controversy over the Interpretation of *Shura*," *History of Religion* (1981): 291, where the author criticized a version of Mutwalli's thesis published in a treatise entitled *Mabadi al-Shura fi al-Islam* (1972).

35. To explain why the Prophet did not always consult his Companions and follow their advice, one author argued that consultation by the Prophet was confined to matters on which there was no revelation (El-Awa, *On the Political System of the Islamic State*, p. 89). Yet El-Awa's explanation (p. 94) of the Prophet's rejection of Umar's advice on the occasion of *al-hudybiya* is clearly strained and inconsistent with the facts. There is no evidence to support the view that the matter was the subject of direct revelation as distinguished from the Prophet's personal judgment.

36. Al-Tabari, *Jami al-Bayan an Ta'wiyl ayy al-Qur'an*, 2d ed. (Cairo: Mustafa al-Baki, 1954), 25:37; Al-Tusi, *Tafsir al-Tibyan*, 9:168; *Tafsir al-Qasmiy*, 14:5248.

37. El-Awa, *On the Political System of the Islamic State*, pp. 95–96, argued that in these major cases the Companions, after their initial disagreement with the Caliph, did come around to accepting his position so that, in the end, *shura* resulted in the caliph convincing his subjects of his point of view. Assuming that historical sources confirm that the dissenting Companions expressed agreement with the caliph, it cannot be said with certainty whether they changed their minds or simply resigned themselves to the will of the caliph rather than come out in open revolt against his authority.

38. As stated by Coulson in "The State and the Individual in Islamic Law," p. 57: "This failure [of Shari'a] to translate into actuality the ideal of the rule of law results from the absence, in Islamic legal theory and practice, of what must be, ultimately, the only real guarantee of individual liberty in any system, namely a powerful and independent judiciary." Cf. Ishaque, "Al-Ahkam Al-Sultaniya," p. 296, who emphasizes the importance of the political risk to the ruler who disregards Shari'a. But given the diversity of opinions among the jurists and the vagueness of the broad discretion allowed to the ruler under Shari'a, a caliph, or his modern equivalent, has much room for manipulation and repression without having to come out openly against Shari'a.

39. See, for example, Sharough Akhavi, "Iran: Implementation of an Islamic State," in John L. Esposito, ed., *Islam in Asia: Religion, Politics and Society* (New York: Oxford University Press, 1987), pp. 32–40.

40. This Arabic term is written in Farsi as *vilayat-i-faqih* (ibid., p. 32).

41. Thus the preamble to the 1979 Constitution provides under the subtitle "The Mandate to the Just Clergy" that "the constitution lays the groundwork for the realization of the leadership of a member of the eminent clergy who is recognized by the people as their leader . . . in order to guarantee that various organizations do not deviate from their real Islamic duties" (as translated in Albert P. Blaustein and Gisbert H. Flanz, eds., *Constitutions of the Countries of the World* (Dobbs Ferry, N.Y.: Oceana Publications, 1980), p. 9. Another

translation of this constitution can be found in *Middle East Journal* 34 [1980]: 184–204). This principle is embodied in Article 5 of the Constitution. Reference to clergy in the singular appears to be reference to Imam Khomeini, who is mentioned in the Constitution by name several times. A Council of Experts was established to appoint Khomeini's successor(s). See Akhavi, "Iran," p. 33.

42. Francis W. Coker, "Sovereignty," in Edwin R. A. Seligman, ed., *Encyclopaedia of the Social Sciences* (New York: Macmillan, 1930), 14:265; and Bernard Crick, "Sovereignty," in Sills, ed., *International Encyclopedia of the Social Sciences*, p. 77.

43. Black, *Black's Law Dictionary*, p. 1252; emphasis added.

44. See Crick, "Sovereignty"; and Coker, "Sovereignty," for brief historical surveys of this debate.

45. Crick, "Sovereignty," p. 81.

46. This is one of the main themes of the Qur'an as demonstrated by countless verses. See, for example, the Qur'an, 2:110 and 3:26–27. H. A. R. Gibb, *Mohammadanism* (New York: Mentor Books, 1955), p. 39; and Mehdi, "Constitutionalism Western and Middle Eastern," pp. 113–14.

47. As stated by Khadduri, in *War and Peace in the Law of Islam*, p. 10, "only possession of sovereignty resided with Allah [God], while its exercise was delegated to Muhammad who, as vicegerent of Allah, was instructed to rule with Justice. Allah, accordingly, was the Titular head of the State and its source of authority; Muhammad was its head of Government."

48. The masculine pronoun is used advisedly with reference to the ruler throughout this exposition of Shari'a because the ruler under Shari'a has to be a man.

49. This notion is either implicit or explicit in the writings of modern Muslim authors such as Muhammad B. al-Muti'i, *Haqiqat al-Islam wa Usul al-Hukm* (Cairo: Maktabat al-Nahda al-Haditha, 1344 Hijri); Auda, *Al-Islam wa Awda'una al-Siyasiya*; and Taj al-Din al-Nabhani, *Al-Dawla al-Islamiya* (Damascus: Al-Manar Press, 1952).

Auda, for example, said that the power of the caliph or imam, i.e., government, is and always will be derived exclusively from his (its) position as representative of the community which instated him (it) and has the right to check and prevent him (it, the government) from stepping outside the limits of his (its) representative role. He also described the relationship between the caliph, government, and community in terms of *aqd niyaba*, compact of representation, whereby the community entrusts the caliph to govern, and the latter accepts, in accordance with God's commandments. If the caliph violated the terms of the compact, the community should be able to depose him and instate another in his place (*Al-Islam wa Awda'una al-Siyasiya*, pp. 81–82).

See also al-Nabhani, *Al-Dawla al-Islamiya*, pp. 29, 38–39, where a similar notion is emphasized.

50. Khadduri, *Political Trends in the Arab World*, pp. 28, 47.

51. Carl Brinkmann, "Citizenship," in Seligman, ed., *Encyclopaedia of the Social Sciences*, 3:471.

52. Majid Khadduri, "The Juridical Theory of the Islamic State," *Muslim World* 41 (1951): 185.

53. Khadduri, *War and Peace in the Law of Islam*, p. 162.

54. See An-Na'im, "The Islamic Law of Apostasy and Its Modern Applicability," pp. 212–13.

55. See Nu'man A. al-Smarai'i, *Ahkam al-Murtadd fi al-Shari'a al-Islamiya* (Beirut: Dar al-Arabiya lil Tiba'at wa al-Nashr wa al-Tawzi, 1968), pp. 116–17.

56. Al-Mubarak, *Nizam al-Islam fi al-Hukm wa al-Dawla* (Beirut: Dar al-Fikr, 1981), pp. 24–28, 100, 117.

57. As explained by Khadduri in *War and Peace in the Law of Islam*, p. 150, "all the commentators [on the Qur'an] agree that a believer who turns back from his [Islamic] religion *(irtadda)*, openly or *secretly*, must be killed if he persists in disbelief" (emphasis added).

58. Shaikh Abdur Rahman, *Punishment of Apostasy in Islam* (Lahore: Institute of Islamic Culture, 1972).

59. For example, an apostate's marriage is nullified and his civil capacity to deal with his property is restricted. Shafi'i, *Kitab al-Umm*, 5:57 and 6:160–61. See Rudopph Peters and Gert J. J. De Vries, "Apostasy in Islam," *Die Welt des Islams* 17 (1976–77): 7–9; and An-Na'im, "The Islamic Law of Apostasy and Its Modern Applicability," p. 212.

60. For an authoritative statement of these other consequences in the Hanafi school see Majid Khadduri, trans., *The Islamic Law of Nations: Shaybani's Siyar* (Baltimore: Johns Hopkins Press, 1966), pp. 195–209.

61. These restrictions are commonly known as *al-hijab*, the requirement that women stay at home or cover their whole body when they have to leave the home under specific circumstances. This notion is based on such verses of the Qur'an as 24:31, 33:33, 33:53, and 33:59 and related Sunna. Once again, we are concerned with the position under Shari'a as it exists today. The possibility of reinterpreting these sources so as to abolish *al-hijab* is being advocated here, but that should not be confused with the currently established interpretation of these verses and Sunna.

62. Rahim, *Principles of Muhammadan Jurisprudence*, p. 389.

63. Khadduri, *War and Peace in the Law of Islam*, pp. 163–69.

64. Ibid., p. 176; *The Encyclopedia of Islam, New Edition*, 2:227.

65. See both sources cited in the preceding note. For example, Abu Yusuf in *Kitab al-Kharaj*, pp. 128–30, accepted Magians as *ahl al-Kitab* on the assumption that they had a heavenly revealed scripture.

66. Qur'an, 9:29. See Shafi'i, *Kitab al-Umm*, 4:172ff.; and Khadduri, *War and Peace in the Law of Islam*, pp. 177, 195–99.

67. There was no mention of it, for example, in the Prophet's early compacts with the Jews of Medina. Moreover, it was not mentioned in the Qur'an until the ninth year of Hijra. See Aun Al-Sharif, *Dublumaciyat Muhammad* (Khartoum: Khartoum University Press, n.d.), pp. 109–10.

68. The relationship between *jizya* and other taxes, such as *khiraj*, has not always been clear. See Khadduri, *War and Peace in the Law of Islam*, pp. 187–92.

69. See, for example, Muhammad Hamidullah, *Muslim Conduct of State*, 5th ed. (Lahore: Sh. M. Ashraf, 1966), pp. 244–45.

70. T. W. Arnold, in *The Preaching of Islam* (Lahore: Shirkat-i-Qualam, 1956), pp. 62–63, cited a number of examples of Christian groups who were exempt from payment of *jizya* in exchange for serving in Muslim armies. This was obviously an exception to the general rule of Shari'a; otherwise it would not have been worth noting.

71. Verse 9:29 of the Qur'an expressly states that *dhimmis* must pay *jizya "an yadin wahum saqirun,"* that is, in submission and humiliation. See al-Tabari, *Jami al-Bayan*, 10:109; Al-Tusi, *Tafsir al-Tibyan*, 5:237–38; and al-Qasmiy, *Tafsir al-Qasmiy*, 8:3108.

72. As will be explained in Chapter 6, this is clear from the way in which *jizya* has been offered as an alternative to having to fight the Muslims. Thus it has been noted that people in Syria, Mesopotamia, and Persia have sometimes embraced Islam to escape payment of *jizya*. See P. Hitti, *History of the Arabs*, 4th ed., rev. (London: Macmillan, 1949), p. 145.

73. S. D. Goitein, "Minority Selfrule and Government Control in Islam," *Studia Islamica* 31 (1970): 101-16.

74. Khadduri, *War and Peace in the Law of Islam*, p. 198. As noted in *The Encyclopedia of Islam*, 2:228-29, this doctrinal view was not maintained in practice because the administrative and bureaucratic abilities of *dhimmis* were often needed by Muslim rulers. This may demonstrate that Muslim rulers did not comply with Shari'a in this regard but does not change the fact that Shari'a did not permit the participation of *dhimmis* in the government of Muslims.

75. These seem to be the common features of most of the earliest compacts of *dhimma*. For English translations of examples of these compacts see Khadduri, *War and Peace in the Law of Islam*, pp. 184-85, 214.

Some compacts, however, were exceptionally humiliating and oppressive to certain *dhimmi* communities. See, for example, the so-called Covenant of Umar, attributed to the second caliph. For an English translation of the text of this compact see A. S. Tritton, *The Caliphs and Their Non-Muslim Subjects* (Oxford: Oxford University Press, 1930), pp. 6-8.

76. Shafi'i, *Kitab al-Umm*, 6:105-6.

77. Ibn Rushd, *Bidayat al-Mujtahid* (Cairo: Dar al-Fikr al-Arabi, n.d.), 2:330.

78. This is based on verse 2:282 of the Qur'an.

79. See Schacht, *Introduction to Islamic Law*, pp. 161-66; and John L. Esposito, *Women in Muslim Family Law* (Syracuse: Syracuse University Press, 1982), pp. 20, 29-35.

80. Qur'an, 4:34; Al-Tabari, *Jami al-Bayan*, 5:57-70. Shafi'i, in *Kitab al-Umm*, 5:193-94, discusses this verse in light of a report that the Prophet said: "The best among you will not beat their wives." He concluded that beating one's wife is permissible but discouraged.

81. Shafi'i, *Kitab al-Umm*, 5:6-9, 44, 50.

82. Verses 4:11 and 176 of the Qur'an. See Schacht, *Introduction to Islamic Law*, pp. 169-74, for a brief explanation of the complex rules of inheritance under Shari'a.

83. McIlwain, *Constitutionalism Ancient and Modern*, p. 93.

84. Ibid., pp. 141-44.

85. Nwabueze, *Constitutionalism in the Emergent States*, pp. 14-15.

86. Coulson, "The State and the Individual in Islamic Law," pp. 55-56.

87. There is always, of course, the possibility of violent revolution, which many would argue is justifiable in Islam. But this drastic option should be seen as signifying the failure of constitutionalism rather than an aspect thereof.

88. See Mehdi, "Constitutionalism Western and Middle Eastern," p. 143; and Ishaque, "Al-Ahkam Al-Sultaniya," for English translations of some of these authorities.

89. Khadduri, "The Juridical Theory of the Islamic State" pp. 184-85; Gibb, "Constitutional Organization," p. 12; and Mehdi, "Constitutionalism Western and Middle Eastern," pp. 143-44.

Faruki in *The Evolution of Islamic Constitutional Theory and Practice*, pp. 44-46, 48, 58, reviewed all the major historical Muslim authors on this subject and found that none of them explained how the caliph or imam may be deposed in a peaceful and orderly manner.

　　90. Arnold, *The Caliphate,* pp. 48–50; Gibb, "Constitutional Organization," pp. 14–16.

　　91. Al-Nabhani, *Al-Dawla al-Islamiya,* p. 41.

　　92. As indicated earlier, the masculine pronoun is being used advisedly here because Shari'a required the ruler to be male. For modern and future applicability of Islamic public law, there should be no such requirement.

　　93. Muhammad Asad, *Principles of State and Government in Islam* (Berkeley and Los Angeles: University of California Press, 1961), pp. 14–24. The first pages of the book are devoted to arguments against secularism and a plea for an Islamic state.

　　94. Ibid., pp. 22–29.

　　95. Ibid., pp. 39–40.

　　96. Ibid., pp. 42, 45.

　　97. Ibid., pp. 65–67.

　　98. Ibid., chaps. 3, 4, and 5, respectively.

　　99. Al-Azhar, *Majma al-Buhuth al-Islamiyya, Idarat al-Secrtariya al-Faniya* (Cairo: Council for Islamic Research, Technical Secretariat, October 15, 1978). The copy used in the present discussion is in Arabic. In the following survey, I shall paraphrase the Arabic text and link it to the relevant points made in this chapter.

　　100. Mahmoud Mohamed Taha, *Usus Dastur al-Sudan* (Omdurman, Sudan: Matabi Sudan Ayco, 1955), pp. 11–12.

　　101. Taha, *Second Message of Islam,* p. 65.

　　102. See, for example, Frank Michelman, "In Pursuit of Constitutional Welfare Rights: One View of Rawls' Theory of Justice," *University of Pennsylvania Law Review* 121 (1973): 962; and "Welfare Rights in a Constitutional Democracy," *Washington University Law Quarterly* (1979): 659.

5. CRIMINAL JUSTICE

　　1. It is not assumed here that governments, whether of Muslim or non-Muslim countries, do in fact observe the letter and spirit of their constitutions. What is taken to be significant in constitutional provisions is that they represent the standards the particular state sets for itself and by which it expects to be judged. Since a government seeks domestic and international legitimacy through the constitutional standards it sets for itself, it is only fair and appropriate to hold it bound by those standards.

　　2. G.A. Res. 217A (III), U.N. Doc. A/810, at 71 (1948).

　　3. The Civil and Political Rights Covenant was adopted on December 16, 1966, and entered into force on March 23, 1976 (G.A. Res. 2200 [XXI], 21 U.N. GAOR, Supp. [No. 16] 52, U.N. Doc. A/6316 [1966]).

　　4. All Muslim countries that were members of the United Nations in 1948, except Saudi Arabia, supported the Universal Declaration. Saudi Arabia, together with the Soviet bloc and South Africa, abstained, enabling adoption of the declaration without dissenting vote. Moreover, the declaration was cited in a variety of subsequent United Nations documents which were endorsed by almost all Muslim countries that have become independent since the adoption of the declaration. For example, the International Convention on

the Elimination of All Forms of Racial Discrimination, which cites and relies on the Universal Declaration of Human Rights, was ratified by no less than twenty-five Muslim countries. This convention was adopted on December 21, 1965, and entered into force on January 4, 1969 (660 U.N.T.S. 195).

5. At least thirteen Muslim countries are party to this treaty.

6. The significance of religious faith will become clear in the subsequent discussion.

7. It is true that the Saudi Nationality Regulation of 1374 Hijri (1954) does not explicitly link citizenship to religious status, but the restriction of Saudi nationality to Muslims is clearly required by the Hanbali school of Islamic jurisprudence, which constitutes the official legal system of Saudi Arabia.

8. This general proposition and its specific aspects mentioned below are provided for in Articles 10 and 11 of the Universal Declaration of Human Rights and Article 14 of the Civil and Political Rights Covenant.

9. Safeguards for the pretrial stage are required by Articles 9 and 12 of the Universal Declaration and Articles 9 and 10 of the Civil and Political Rights Covenant.

10. This principle is provided for in Article 11(2) of the Universal Declaration and Article 15(1) of the Civil and Political Rights Covenant.

11. See, for example, Article 5 of the Universal Declaration and Article 7 of the Civil and Political Rights Covenant.

12. Use of the masculine pronoun here and in other parts of this chapter with reference to the ruler and his officials is deliberate because both the ruler and his high-ranking officials have to be men under Shari'a.

13. See, for example, G. Baer, "The Transition from Traditional to Western Criminal Law in Turkey and Egypt," *Studia Islamica* 45 (1977): 139.

14. Ann Mayer, Review of M. Cherif Bassiouni, ed., *The Islamic Criminal Justice System, American Journal of Comparative Law* 31 (1983): 363–64.

15. For which verse 5:38 of the Qur'an prescribes the punishment of amputation of the hand.

16. Verse 5:33 of the Qur'an provides a number of possible punishments for this offense: death, crucifixion, cross-amputation of one hand and the opposite foot, or banishment from the land. The implications of the broad difference in the ways the nature and scope of this offense may be conceived will be discussed below.

17. Verse 24:2 of the Qur'an sets one hundred lashes for this offense. As will be noted later, however, Sunna makes the punishment stoning to death if the offender is a married person.

18. Verse 24:4 of the Qur'an prescribes eighty lashes for this offense.

19. The Qur'an disapproves of intoxication and prohibits drinking wine without providing for a specific punishment for either type of conduct. The Prophet is reported to have said, however, that it is *haram*, a religious sin, to take any substance in however small an amount, if taking that substance in large amounts would cause intoxication. Sunna is also reported to have prescribed forty lashes as punishment for *sukr*.

20. Again, although the Qur'an disapproved of *ridda*, it did not provide for its punishment in this life. Sunna is cited as authority for prescribing the death penalty for *ridda*.

21. Safia M. Safwat, "Offenses and Penalties in Islamic Law," *Islamic Quarterly* 26 (1982): 169–71.

22. The verse of the Qur'an usually cited for this *hadd* is 49:9, which may be translated as follows:"If two parties of believers [Muslims] fall to fighting, then make peace between them. But if one of them transgresses beyond bounds against the other, then you all shall fight against the one that transgresses until it complies with the command of God. Once it complies, then make peace between them with justice and be fair [just]; for God loves those who are fair [just]." The Arabic verb translated here as *transgresses* is *baghat*. The noun *baghy*, the name of the alleged *hadd al-baghy*, is derived from the same root.

23. It is reported that the Prophet said that one who drinks wine should be whipped, without specifying the number of lashes, but he himself had such an offender whipped forty lashes. See Safwat, "Offenses and Penalties in Islamic Law," p. 160.

The question is controversial because, according to other reports, the Prophet never specified the number of lashes. Moreover, there are reports that he did not impose any punishment in some cases which were reported to him. If this is true, the offense cannot be *hadd* since the distinguishing feature of *hudud* is that the ruler has no choice but to impose the punishment once the offense is reported to him.

24. See Al-Shawkani, *Nayl al-Awtar* (Cairo: Maktabat al-Qahirah, 1357 Hijri), 7:138–43; and *Encyclopedia of Islamic Jurisprudence*, vol. 1 (Kuwait: Ministry of Awqaf, 1969).

25. Abd al-Qaldir Auda, *Al-Tashri al-Jana'iy al-Islamiy* (Beirut: Dar al-Kitab al-Arabi, 1960), paragraph 580.

26. See Rahman, *Punishment of Apostasy in Islam*, pp. 54–55.

27. M. A. Nasif, *Al-Taj al-Jami lil-Usul*, 4th ed. (Cairo: Dar Ihya' al-Kutub al-Arabiyah, n.d.), 3:18; Hamidullah, *Muslim Conduct of State*, pp. 172ff.

28. This position has been taken, for example, by Muhammad Abduh and Muhammad Ridda in *Tafsir al-Manar*, 5:327; Rahman, *Punishment of Apostasy in Islam*, chap. 2; and El-Awa, *Punishment in Islamic Law*, chap. 2.

29. El-Awa, *Punishment in Islamic Law*, pp. 15–17, prefers to argue that although the punishment of stoning for fornication by a married person is based on Sunna, it was a particular type of *Sunna* which was directly expressing revelation *(wahy)*. Although he cited a number of primary sources in support of this view, one can see difficulties with distinguishing between Sunna texts as to whether or not they express revelation. The religious authority of all Sunna is that it emanates from the Prophet, who was the recipient of revelation, and as such it is assumed to be divinely guided. Moreover, there is no clear criteria by which the two types of Sunna can be distinguished in practice.

30. See, for example, El-Awa, *Punishment in Islamic Law*, p. 7; and Safwat, "Offenses and Penalties in Islamic Law," p. 163.

31. As reported by Ibn Taymiyya in *The Public and Private Law of Islam*, pp. 88–98, early Muslim jurists have differed on most aspects of this *hadd*.

32. An essential element of *sariqa*, as defined by the founding jurists, is the secret taking of property. Since the taking of property in robbery is not secretive, the offense would not qualify as *sariqa*.

33. All wrongful taking of property raises liability for exact restitution or sufficient compensation under Shari'a.

34. Many verses of the Qur'an emphasize this point, but the clearest example may be 33:36, which may be translated as follows: "Once a matter has been decided by God and His Apostle [the Prophet], no believer, man or woman, has a choice about their decision. Anyone who disobeys God and His Apostle is clearly on a wrong path."

An equally clear imperative to submit to the Prophet's rulings or decisions can be found in verse 4:65 of the Qur'an.

35. David F. Forte, in "Islamic Law and the Crime of Theft: An Introduction," *Cleveland State Law Review* 34 (1985–86): 51–53, seems to be seeking cultural sources for imposing the punishment of amputation for the *hadd* of *sariqa.* On page 51 he states: "The source from which Mohammed derived the idea of amputation for theft is unclear." After dismissing what he describes as weak and vague references to the punishment of theft in pre-Islamic Arabia, he concludes that "there is little cultural indication as to what may have influenced Mohammed to impose such a penalty."

36. Taha, *Second Message of Islam,* pp. 74–75.

37. Ibid., p. 74.

38. Auda, *Al-Tashri al-Jana'iy al-Islamiy,* paragraph 508.

39. According to well-established Sunna, reported in all major treatises, *hudud* should be avoided in practice by construing any *shubha,* doubt, to the benefit of the accused. In contrast, however, there is equally well-established Sunna to the effect that once all the conditions and requirements of a particular *hadd* are satisfied, the punishment must be imposed. These Sunna may be reconciled by seeing the second type of text as prohibiting favoritism in applying *hudud.* Much leeway is left by the first-mentioned Sunna in setting the conditions and requirements of applying *hudud.* Once that is exhausted, however, the second-mentioned Sunna requires that the punishment must be imposed. See Rahim, *Principles of Muhammadan Jurisprudence,* pp. 361–62.

40. In Jewish law, which is believed by Jews to be divine, jurists were able to restrict the practical application of the specified capital punishment for some fifty offenses through extremely strict rules of evidence and procedure. On this see *Encyclopedia Judaica* (Jerusalem: Keter Publishing House, 1971), under "Capital Punishment," 5:142–47, and under "Evidence," 6:991–93.

41. For a concise statement of these rules showing the strong historical influence see J. N. D. Anderson, "Homicide in Islamic Law," *Bulletin of the School of Oriental and African Studies* 13 (1951): 811.

42. Ibn Rush, *Bidayat Al-Mujtahid,* 2:447; and Auda, *Al-Tashri al-Jana'iy al-Islamiy,* paragraphs 155 and 214.

43. See, for example, the Qur'an, verses 4:11 and 2:282.

44. Auda, *Al-Tashri al-Jana'iy al-Islamiy,* paragraphs 144 and 215. Shafi'i, for example, maintains that a believer may never be killed for killing an unbeliever and that *diya* for killing a *dhimmi* is one-third of *diya* for killing a Muslim. See Shafi'i, *Kitab al-Umm,* 7:290–91. See also Anderson, "Homicide in Islamic Law," pp. 815–16, for a summary of the relevant rules.

45. Coulson, *History of Islamic Law,* p. 18.

46. Mahmoud Shaltut, *Al-Islam Aqida wa Shari'a* (Cairo: Dar al-Qalam, 1966), p. 314. Although neither Qur'an nor Sunna expressly sanctions the power of *ta'zir* in the sense developed by the jurists, the power was seen to arise by implication because the Qur'an sometimes authorized punishment without fixing it, as in verses 4:15–16. The need to penalize conduct other than *hudud* and *jinayat* is not disputed here. The question is how to structure and regulate this power.

47. Coulson, "The State and the Individual in Islamic Law," pp. 53–55.

48. Safwat, "Offenses and Penalties in Islamic Law," p. 175.

49. Coulson, "The State and the Individual in Islamic Law," p. 56.

50. For a brief summary of the principle of the rule of law, as drawn from a wide international range of legal systems and traditions, see International Commission of Jurists,

The Rule of Law and Human Rights: Principles and Definitions (Geneva: International Commission of Jurists, 1966).

51. Auda, *Al-Tashri al-Jana'iy al-Islamiy*, paragraphs 93–109.

52. The injunction to rule in accordance with justice and fairness is one of the predominant themes of the Qur'an. The word *adl*, justice, and its derivatives are mentioned no less than ten times in relation to adjudication and administration of justice. The most directly relevant verses include 5:8, 4:58, and 16:90.

53. For example, sophisticated and detailed principles of criminal responsibility on homicide were developed by the founding jurists. See Anderson, "Homicide in Islamic Law," pp. 818ff.

54. The question of joint liability, for example, is discussed in relation to homicide, whether a group of people who participate in the murder of a single person can all be killed in *qisas* (exact retaliation). For discussion of the views of leading jurists on this question see Shaltut, *Al-Islam Aqida wa Shari'a*, p. 393. No general principles for joint liability were developed to apply to all categories of offenses or to criminal responsibility in general. The same is true about other issues such as the requirement of intention *(qasd or amd)* and the defense of insanity *(junun)*.

55. For the example of the joint responsibility for homicide see Anderson, "Homicide in Islamic Law," p. 817.

56. In accordance with his general claim that Shari'a is ready for immediate application, Auda argues in *Al-Tashri al-Jana'iy al-Islamiy*, paragraphs 247ff., that all the general principles of criminal responsibility are settled in Shari'a. But he quotes only examples from specific offenses and cites too much controversy on many issues for his claim to be accepted as valid.

57. Ibid., paragraphs 440, 535, 571, 618, and 637.

58. Some jurists recommended the use of torture for the purpose of extracting confessions from individuals of reputedly bad character. See Coulson, "The State and the Individual in Islamic Law," p. 52.

In paragraphs 427 to 433, Auda, *Al-Tashri al-Jana'iy al-Islamiy*, surveyed the differences and agreements among the early jurists on the definition of coercion as grounds for excluding confessions. Since these jurists' views were not directly derived from Qur'an or Sunna, they may now be revised without much difficulty.

59. Awad M. Awad, "The Rights of the Accused under Islamic Criminal Procedure," in M. Cherif Bassiouni, ed., *The Islamic Criminal Justice System* (London: Oceana Publications, 1982), p. 91.

60. Mayer, Review of Bassiouni, ed., *The Islamic Criminal Justice System*, p. 363.

61. For recent examples of the huge amount of literature discussing these two issues and their continuous adjustment and change within and outside the common law tradition, see Suzanne B. McNicol, *A Non-Crucial Privilege against Self-Incrimination* (Canberra, Australia: Monash University, Faculty of Law, 1984); William T. Pizzi, "The Privilege against Self-Incrimination in a Rescue Situation," *Journal of Criminal Law and Criminology* 76 (1985): 567; Donald V. MacDougall, "The Exclusionary Rule and Its Alternatives: Remedies for Constitutional Violations in Canada and the United States," *Journal of Criminal Law and Criminology* 76 (1985): 608; and Walter Pakter, " Exclusionary Rules in France, Germany and Italy," *Hastings International and Comparative Law Review* 9 (1985): 1–57.

62. This was because Britain had dominated Egypt, its partner in the Anglo-Egyptian Condominium, which ruled the Sudan between 1989 and 1956. See generally Zaki Mustafa, *The Common Law in the Sudan* (Oxford: Clarendon Press, 1971).

63. M. I. Khalil, "The Legal System of the Sudan," *International and Comparative Law Quarterly* 20 (1971): 626–27.

64. Egon Guttmann, "Reception of the Common Law in the Sudan," *International and Comparative Law Quarterly* 6 (1956): 402.

65. Khalil, "The Legal System of the Sudan," p. 627.

66. M. A. Abu Rannat, "The Relationship between Islamic and Customary Law in the Sudan," *Journal of African Law* (1960): 9.

67. The Mahdist revolution started in central Sudan around 1881 and spread to the west and east of the country before it captured the capital, Khartoum, and controlled the majority of the territory now known as the Sudan in early 1885.

68. Guttmann, "The Reception of the Common Law in the Sudan," pp. 403–5, 409.

69. Khalil, "The Legal System of the Sudan," pp. 639–41; and Cliff F. Thompson, "The Sources of Law in the New Nations of Africa: A Case Study from the Republic of the Sudan," *Wisconsin Law Review* (1966): 1149–50.

70. These powers were initially granted under the Village Courts Ordinance of 1925 and the Powers of Sheiks Ordinance of 1928 and further regularized in the Chiefs' Courts Ordinance of 1931 and the Native Courts Ordinance of 1932.

71. An-Na'im, "The Elusive Islamic Constitution," p. 329.

72. Following the coup d'état of May 25, 1969, an attempt was made in 1971 to replace English common law with Egyptian-European codes, but this effort was soon aborted. By 1974, the previous legal system was fully reinstated. See Zaki Mustafa, "Opting Out of the Common Law: Recent Developments in the Legal System of the Sudan," *Journal of African Law* (1973): 133.

73. In that year, former President Numayry concluded a pact of national reconciliation with his political opponents which brought Islamic elements into his administration and initiated a policy of gradual Islamization. A committee was appointed to revise Sudanese laws to bring them into conformity with Shari'a. Although the draft bills produced by that committee were not enacted into law at the time, it is clear that those drafts and the background studies produced by the committee influenced the introduction of Shari'a in 1983.

74. For detailed accounts and assessments of the changes see C. N. Gordon, "Islamic Legal Revolution: The Case of Sudan," *International Lawyer* 19 (1985): 793.

For analysis of political factors at play in the adoption and implementation of the 1983 Laws see, for example, Esposito, "Sudan's Islamic Experiment," p. 181; and Duran, "The Centrifugal Forces of Religion in Sudanese Politics," p. 572.

75. The Road Traffic Act was revised to incorporate Shari'a rules of *jinayat* for homicide and bodily injury caused in road accidents.

76. Sections 18 and 308, respectively.

77. Some changes in the powers of public prosecutors were introduced by the 1983 code, but these were a natural continuation of a policy to institute the system of public prosecution which started since the 1974 revision and reenactment of the code. See A. A. El Naiem, "The Many Hats of the Sudanese Magistrate: Role Conflict in Sudan Criminal Procedure," *Journal of African Law* 22 (1978): 50. This policy and the changes it mandated in the 1983 Code of Criminal Procedure were not related to the newly adopted policy of Islamization.

78. Sections 78–81, 82–92, and 93, respectively, of the 1983 Penal Code.

79. Ibid., sections 55–63.

80. Ibid., sections 53 and 51, respectively.

81. More than 200 of the 350 sections of the Penal Code specifying punishments for specific offenses use the phrase "shall be punished with whipping, fine and imprisonment" or the phrase "shall be punished with whipping and fine or imprisonment," without specifying the maximum number of lashes or the maximum length of the term of imprisonment.

82. Ibid., sections 334, 336, 337, 338, and 339.

83. Ibid., sections 318, which penalizes a person who maintains premises for the commission of illicit sexual acts, and 457, which penalizes a person who maintains or participates in the maintenance of a network of organized crime. The same *hadd* punishment is applied to a number of offenses involving breaking and entering into premises even when no property is taken and no violence is actually used. See ibid., sections 393, 394, 395, and 396. Although the offenses defined in these sections include breaking and entering with intent to commit a crime or after having prepared to use violence, such intended crime or preparation for use of force need not actually happen for the *hadd* punishment to arise under the 1983 code.

84. As reported in Ibn Taymiyya, *The Public and Private Law of Islam*, pp. 88–89, leading early Muslim jurists such as Ibn Abbas, Abu Hanifa, Shafi'i, and Ibn Hanbal maintained that selection among these apparently alternative punishments should be graded in accordance with the degree of harm inflicted by the aggressor upon his victim. If he killed his victim and plundered his possessions, the guilty person should be killed and crucified, but if he only killed his victim without plundering his property, the guilty person should be killed but not crucified.

Other jurists, however, have stated that all options should be open to the ruler, who may impose any of them in accordance with his view as to which punishment will best serve the public good.

85. Ibid., sections 321, 334, and 434, respectively.

86. Safwat, "Offenses and Penalties in Islamic Law," p. 159.

87. Auda, *Al-Tashri al-Jana'iy al-Islamiy*, paragraph 245.

88. The death sentence was executed in that case following confirmation by the president of the republic, Numayry, who also invoked arguments peculiar to *ridda* in his confirmation speech. An-Na'im, "The Islamic Law of Apostasy and Its Modern Applicability," pp. 208–10.

In a constitutional suit brought by the daughter of *Ustadh* Mahmoud after the overthrow of former President Numayry, the Supreme Court held that the 1985 trial and execution of *Ustadh* Mahmoud were null and void for a variety of procedural defects. But the court had nothing to say on the constitutionality of punishing *ridda* as such, nor did it rule specifically on the constitutionality of section 458(3).

89. The same general condition set by section 81 of the 1983 Evidence Act can be used to object to the competence of a non-Muslim expert witness under section 66(2) of the act since such an objection is valid under Shari'a.

90. See Esposito, "Sudan's Islamic Experiment," pp. 198–99.

91. This information is based on my own personal observations while being detained without trial, for political reasons, in the same Khartoum Central Prison from which those unfortunate offenders were released and returned to suffer the penalty of amputation of their hands and feet for *hudud* offenses.

92. Thousands of Muslim offenders were sentenced to whipping for drinking alcohol throughout the Sudan, including women who made their living for many years by selling intoxicating beverages.

Although comprehensive official statistics and scientific studies are lacking, these facts were widely reported in the local and international media and have been cited by other authors who wrote on the subject. See, for example, Ann Mosely Lesch, "The Fall of Numeiri," in *Universities Field Staff International Reports* (1985/No. 9. Africa [AML-2-'85]), pp. 9–10.

A report prepared by the International Commission of Jurists stated: "According to the figures received by the mission from the government, 106 amputations including 17 cross-limb [one hand and the opposite foot] amputations were carried out during the period 19 August 1983 to 27 March 1985. Amnesty International has reported that thousands of men and women were flogged, often severely" (International Commission of Jurists, *The Return of Democracy in Sudan* [Geneva: International Commission of Jurists, 1986], pp. 72–73).

93. Ann Mosely Lesch, "Rebellion in the Southern Sudan," in *Universities Field Staff International Reports* (1985/No. 9. Africa [AML-2-'85]), p. 12.

94. For the full text of this statement see "Christians Protest Imposition of Islamic Law," *Origins* (Washington, D.C.: Documentary Service, National Catholic News Service, September 6, 1984), pp. 180–81.

The Sudanese Catholic church had voiced its opposition as early as September 23, 1983. See *Mashrek International*, February 1985, pp. 28–30.

95. See generally, Mohamed Omer Beshir, *The Southern Sudan: Background to Conflict* (London: C. Hurst, 1968).

96. On this first phase of the civil war in the Sudan and its political resolution see generally, Cecil Eprile, *War and Peace in the Sudan, 1955–1972* (London: David and Charles, 1974); and Mohamed Omer Beshir, *The Southern Sudan: From Conflict to Peace* (New York: Barnes and Noble, 1975).

97. Lesch, "Rebellion in the Southern Sudan," p. 8.

98. The leaders of the three main northern political parties (the Umma, Democratic Unionists, and Islamic National Front) advocated the introduction of substitute Islamic laws to replace those introduced by former President Numayry. Yet the only draft penal code to date turned out to be more objectionable than the Penal Code of 1983.

99. In the Sudan, for example, the Muslim Brothers, currently known as the Islamic National Front, were part of President Numayry's government which enacted and implemented the 1983 laws. The leaders of this group fully endorsed these laws and their implementation from the beginning. See, for example, the interview with Hassan al-Turabi, leader of the Muslim Brothers in the Sudan, with *Arabia* (July 1984): 38–40. Other leaders of the movement expressed similar support and endorsement. See, for example, interview with Ahmed Abdel Rahman Mohammed, a leader of the Muslim Brothers and Numayry's minister of interior, with *New Africa*, June 21, 1984. Even after the overthrow of Numayry, this party, which came third in the general elections of April 1986, continued for some time to support the 1983 laws and opposed their repeal.

Traditional Islamic scholars have also endorsed the 1983 laws as fully consistent with Shari'a. See, for example, the statement of a group that calls itself Jama'at ulama Al-Sudan (Organization of the Religious Scholars of the Sudan) in *Al-syasa* (daily newspaper), July 24, 1987, p. 9.

6. SHARI'A AND INTERNATIONAL LAW

1. Several writers have suggested a reexamination of the scope and basic principles of international law if it is to become truly the public law of humankind. See generally, for example, Philip C. Jessup, *A Modern Law of Nations: An Introduction* (Hamden, Conn.: Archon Books, 1968); C. W. Jenks, *The Common Law of Mankind* (London: Stevens, 1958);

and Quincy Wright, *The Strengthening of International Law* (The Hague: Academy of International Law, 1960).

2. As will be explained later, this conception of international law is a very recent phenomenon. Ancient and premodern international law did not presuppose recognition of the equal sovereignty and peaceful relations among states.

3. O'Connell, *International Law*, 2d ed. (London: Stevens and Sons, 1970) 1:108. Jessup, in *A Modern Law of Nations*, pp. 15–42, shows how the limited examples of recognition of individuals as subjects of international law can be extended further and responds to the usual arguments against his position.

4. H. Lauterpacht, "The Grotian Tradition in International Law," in Richard Falk, Friedrich Kratochwil, and Saul H. Mendlovitz, eds., *International Law: A Contemporary Perspective* (Boulder, Colo.: Westview Press, 1985), pp. 10–36.

5. J. H. W. Verzijl, *International Law in Historical Perspective* (Leiden: A. W. Sijthoff, 1968), 1:436.

6. William E. Hall, *International Law*, 8th ed. (Oxford: Clarendon Press, 1924), p. 48; and R. P. Anand, *Confrontation or Cooperation? International Law and the Developing Countries* (New Delhi: Banyan Publications, 1984), pp. 23–27.

7. Ibrahim Shihata, "Islamic Law and the World Community," *Harvard International Club Journal* 4 (1962): 101. See also the sources cited in note 1 of this chapter.

8. Anand, *Confrontation or Cooperation?* pp. 32–36; Gidon Gottlieb, "Global Bargaining: The Legal and Diplomatic Framework," in Falk et al., eds., *International Law*, pp. 210–35.

9. Myres S. McDougal and Harold C. Lasswell, "The Identification and Appraisal of Diverse Systems of Public Order," in Falk et al., eds., *International Law*, pp. 163–87. Louis Henkin, *How Nations Behave* (New York: Columbia University Press, 1979), chaps. 1–4, discusses various aspects of the relationship between law and international behavior.

10. See generally, R. B. J. Walker, ed., *Culture, Ideology and World Order* (Boulder, Colo.: Westview Press, 1984).

11. Some of these developments will be explained in subsequent sections of this chapter and in the next chapter.

12. The Charter of the United Nations was signed on June 26, 1945, and entered into force on October 24, 1945. The few states which are not members of the United Nations, such as Switzerland, are nevertheless bound by the substance of those principles of customary international law codified by the U.N. Charter.

On the foundations of the charter in preexisting international law see Richard Falk, "The Interplay of Westphalia and Charter Conceptions of International Legal Order," in Falk et al., eds., *International Law*, pp. 116–42.

13. Haykal, *Life of Muhammad*, pp. 115–30; Hamidullah, *Muslim Conduct of State*, pp. 48–61; and Hitti, *History of the Arabs*, pp. 23–29.

14. Haykal, *Life of Muhammad*, pp. 15–16; and Fred M. Donner, *The Early Islamic Conquests* (Princeton: Princeton University Press, 1981), pp. 20ff.

15. Hamidullah, *Muslim Conduct of State*, p. 51; Hitti, *History of the Arabs*, pp. 30–48.

16. Donner, *Early Islamic Conquests*, pp. 37ff.

17. Khadduri and Liebesny, *Law in the Middle East*, pp. 353ff.

18. Hamidullah, *Muslim Conduct of State*, pp. 52ff.

19. Khadduri, *The Islamic Law of Nations*, pp. 3, 10ff. See also Khadduri, *War and Peace in the Law of Islam*, pp. 42–58.

20. See generally, Ingrid Detter De Lupis, *The Law of War* (Cambridge: Cambridge University Press, 1987), chap. 2.

21. Majid Khadduri, "Islam and the Modern Law of Nations," *American Journal of International Law* 50 (1956): 359.

22. Al-Kaya Al-Harasiy, *Ahkam al-Qur'an* (Beirut: Al-Maktaba al-'Ilmiya, 1983), 1:89.

23. See, for example, the Qur'an 2:190, 193, and 244, 4:76, and 9:12, 29, and 123.

24. Other primary sources are in agreement with Ibn Kathir on the sequence of revelations on *jihad/qital*. See, for example, Al-Kaya Al-Harasiy, *Ahkam al-Qur'an*, 1:78–88.

25. The principle and application of abrogation, *naskh*, was explained in Chapter 3 of this book.

26. See Zayd, *Al-Naskh fi al-Qur'an al-Karim*, 1:289–501, 2:503–83; and Hasan, *Early Development of Islamic Jurisprudence*, pp. 67–68.

27. Such as verses 10:99, 16:125, 18:29, 29:46, and 88:21–24 of the Qur'an.

28. Noor Mohammad, "The Doctrine of Jihad: An Introduction," *Journal of Law and Religion* 3 (1985): 385.

29. See, for example, Abu Zahrah, "*Nazariayt al-Harb fi al-Islam*," *Revue Egyptienne du Droit International* 14 (1958): 6; and Mahmud Shaltut, *Al-Islam wa al-Alaqat al-Dawliya* (Cairo: Matba'at al-Azhar, 1951), p. 58. This claim was made by Ibn Taymiyya in the fourteenth century. See Ibn Taymiyya, *Qa'ida fi Qital al-Kuffar*, ed. Al-Fiqqi (Dawha, Qatar: Matabi 'Ali ibn Ali, 1983?), pp. 115–46.

30. For an English translation of an early account of these conquests by a Muslim historian see Philip K. Hitti, *The Origins of the Islamic State*, a translation of *Kitab Futuh al-Buldan*, by al-Baladhuri (New York: AMS Press, 1968).

31. There is little agreement among Western scholars over the role of religious factors in the nature and causes of the early Islamic conquests. For a brief survey of the main Western views on the subject, see Donner, *Early Islamic Conquests*, pp. 3–7. As Donner argues, however (p. 8), any explanation of the phenomenon must take into account the revolutionary impact of Islam on Arab society at the time.

32. Schools of Islamic jurisprudence disagreed on who was qualified to receive an offer of *dhimma*. Shafi'i and Hanbali schools maintain that *dhimma* may be offered only to the Christians, Jews, and Magians as the only People of the Book, and never to polytheists. The Hanafi and Maliki schools allow *dhimma* to be offered to all non-Muslims except the Arab polytheists. See Abu Sulayman, Abdul Hamid, *The Islamic Theory of International Relations* (Herndon, Va.: International Institute of Islamic Thought, 1987), pp. 9–10.

33. For a translation of this Sunna and references to many other records of similar instructions by the Prophet, see Hamidullah, *Muslim Conduct of State*, pp. 305–6. Khadduri, in *The Islamic Law of Nations*, pp. 75–77, gives an English translation of this Sunna as reported in Shaybani's *Siyar*.

34. Hamidullah, *Muslim Conduct of State*, pp. 167–69.

35. Mohammad, "The Doctrine of Jihad," p. 389.

36. Hamidullah, *Muslim Conduct of State*, p. 165; Shihata, "Islamic Law and the World Community," p. 110.

37. See Ibn Kathir, *Mukhtasar Tafsir ibn Kathir*, on the interpretation of this verse.

38. See Khadduri, *War and Peace in the Law of Islam*, pp. 94–137. See also Khadduri's translation of the relevant chapter of Shaybani's *Siyar*, in *The Islamic Law of Nations*, pp. 95–105.

39. Hamidullah, *Muslim Conduct of State*, pp. 190–92.

40. See, for example, Ibn Kathir, *Mukhtasar Tafsir ibn Kathir*, in commentary on verses 2:190–93 of the Qur'an.

41. For translations of these instructions and references to their original sources see Hamidullah, *Muslim Conduct of State*, pp. 305–9.

42. For the formulation of some of the relevant rules by Shaybani, see Khadduri, *Islamic Law of Nations*, pp. 106–29. The rules on the spoils of war under various schools of Islamic jurisprudence are summarized in Khadduri, *War and Peace in the Law of Islam*, pp. 118–32.

43. See, for example, verses 48:19–20, 8:41 and 69. The fact that these verses are from the Medina revelation supports the proposition that the use of force against non-Muslims relates to the subsequent stage of Medina and not the earlier stage of Mecca.

Shari'a rules on enemy property are explained in Khadduri and Liebesny, *Law in the Middle East*, pp. 356–58; and Hamidullah, *Muslim Conduct of State*, pp. 237–52.

44. Khadduri, *War and Peace in the Law of Islam*; Khadduri and Liebesny, *Law in the Middle East*, chap. 15; Khadduri, "Islam and the Modern Law of Nations," pp. 358–60; Shihata, "Islamic Law and the World Community," p. 107; and Hans Kruse, "The Islamic Doctrine of International Treaties," *Islamic Quarterly* 1 (1954): 152.

45. Khadduri and Liebesny, *Law in the Middle East*, pp. 354, 358. The significance of the term of ten years is that it was the period of truce between the Prophet and the polytheists of Mecca in what is known as *sulh al-hudybiya* of 628 A.D. For translations of the text of that treaty see Khadduri, *War and Peace in the Law of Islam*, p. 89; or Hamidullah, *Muslim Conduct of State*, pp. 274–75.

46. Khadduri, *War and Peace in the Law of Islam*, pp. 56–57; and *The Islamic Law of Nations*, p. 15.

47. Khadduri, *War and Peace in the Law of Islam*, pp. 59, 64.

48. Hamidullah, *Muslim Conduct of State*, pp. 171–88. Reference has already been made to the notions of *ridda* and *baghy*, apostasy and rebellion, in the domestic context, in Chapters 4 and 5.

49. Khadduri, *The Islamic Law of Nations*, pp. 39–40.

50. See Khadduri, *War and Peace in the Law of Islam*, pp. 76–80, on Shari'a on the use of force against apostates, rebels, and renegades.

51. This point was partly appreciated by al-Mawardi, who said that these classes come under international law only when they are of sufficient power or have acquired territory and rule over it. See Hamidullah, *Muslim Conduct of State*, p. 170.

52. Majid Khadduri, "International Law, Islamic," in R. Bernhard, ed., *Encyclopedia of Public International Law*, Installment 1 (Amsterdam: North-Holland, 1981), pp. 231–32.

53. Khadduri, "Islam and the Modern Law of Nations," p. 358.

54. Mohammad, "The Doctrine of Jihad," p. 393.

55. Since this section was written, Iran and Iraq have accepted a cease-fire arranged by the United Nations and undertaken protracted peace negotiations. While hoping that a lasting peace will be achieved between the two countries, I still feel that the war can be used to illustrate the ambiguity and untenability of Shari'a principles on the use of force.

56. See generally, for example, Shirin Tahir Kheli and Shaheen Ayubi, eds., *The Iran-Iraq War: New Weapons, Old Conflicts* (New York: Praeger, 1983); J. M. Abdulghani, *Iraq and Iran: The Years of Crisis* (Baltimore: Johns Hopkins University Press, 1984); and R. K. Ramazani, *Revolutionary Iran: Challenge and Response in the Middle East* (Baltimore: Johns Hopkins University Press, 1988), pp. 57-85.

57. Richard W. Bulliet, "Time, Perceptions, and Conflict Resolution," in Tahir Kheli and Ayubi, eds., *Iran-Iraq War*, p. 65.

58. Piscatori, *Islam in a World of Nation-States*, chap. 2.

59. Ibid., chap. 3.

60. As will be suggested in the next chapter, international law may establish principles and mechanisms whereby states may be held accountable for violating the human rights of their own citizens. Such action by the international community should be distinguished from the unilateral and officious intervention found objectionable in the present discussion.

61. It has thus been said that to understand terrorism "one must seek to understand what is happening to whom, where, how, why and with what outcomes and effects" (Jordan Paust, " Definitional Focus," in Yonah Alexander and Seymour Maxwell Finger, eds., *Terrorism: Interdisciplinary Perspectives* [New York: John Jay Press, 1977], p. 19).

62. Differences in the purposes of the definition may explain the lack of consensus. On this lack see Norman W. Provizer, "Defining Terrorism," in Martin Slann and Bernard Schechterman, eds., *Multidimensional Terrorism* (Boulder, Colo.: Lynne Pienner Publishers, 1987), p. 4.

63. In an analysis of 109 definitions of terrorism, the element of violence/force was mentioned in 83.5 percent of the definitions, followed by political intent in 65 percent, emphasis on fear/terror in 51 percent, psychological effects and anticipated reactions in 47 percent and 41.5 percent, respectively (Alex Schmid, *Political Terrorism* [New Brunswick, N.J.: Transaction Books, 1983], pp. 76-77).

Although the clandestine nature of the violence is mentioned in only 9 percent of the definitions analyzed in that study, I think it is important for our legal purposes here. Clandestine use of political violence signifies the lack of fair warning and a desire to avoid compliance with prevailing norms of war.

64. As translated in Hamidullah, *Muslim Conduct of State*, p. 168.

65. Hamidullah, *Muslim Conduct of State*, pp. 267-77, 142-53; Khadduri and Liebesny, *Law in the Middle East*, pp. 367-71; and Kruse, "Islamic Doctrine of International Treaties," pp. 154-55.

66. See Christopher Joyner, "Reflections on the Lawfulness of Invasion," *American Journal of International Law* 78 (1984): 131. Cf. J. N. Moore, "Grenada and the International Double Standard," ibid., p. 145.

67. 1984 *ICJ*, p. 169 (Provisional Measures); 1984 *ICJ*, p. 392 (Jurisdiction). For a summary of the issues and findings of the International Court of Justice in this case see Henkin et al., *International Law*, pp. 633-45.

7. SHARI'A AND BASIC HUMAN RIGHTS

1. See generally, *United Nations Action in the Field of Human Rights*, U.N. Doc. ST/HR/2/Rev. 1, U.N. sales no. E.79.XIV.6 (1980); and B. G. Ramcharan, ed., *Human Rights Thirty Years after the Universal Declaration of Human Rights* (The Hague: Martinus Nijhoff, 1979).

2. These are the European Convention for the Protection of Human Rights and Fundamental Freedoms of 1950, the American Convention on Human Rights of 1969, and the African Charter on Human and Peoples' Rights of 1981.

3. See, for example, Jack Donnelly, "Human Rights and Human Dignity: An Analytic Critique of Non-Western Conceptions of Human Rights," *American Political Science Review* 76 (June 1982): 303; and Rhoda Howard and Jack Donnelly, "Human Dignity, Human Rights and Political Regimes," *American Political Science Review* 80 (September 1986): 801.

For a survey of the main problems and theories in justification and support of universal standards of human rights, see Jerome J. Shestack, "The Jurisprudence of Human Rights," in Theodore Meron, *Human Rights in International Law: Legal and Policy Issues* (Oxford: Clarendon Press, 1985), p. 69.

4. Warwick McKean, *Equality and Discrimination under International Law* (Oxford: Clarendon Press, 1983), pp. 280-81.

5. Official spokesmen of the Islamic Republic of Iran have voiced their belief that they are bound by Islamic law and not international human rights standards. See a collection of these statements in Edward Mortimer, "Islam and Human Rights," *Index on Censorship* 12, no. 5 (1983): 5-6.

6. The same would be true of other differences such as race or ethnicity, language, and so on. But because Shari'a does not sanction discrimination on any other grounds except gender and religion, this chapter will focus on these two grounds of discrimination.

7. In the context of the modern nation-state, this tendency is reflected in general intolerance of minorities, whether religious or otherwise. Thus it has been said that "the ideals of national unity manifested by a central concentration of power; by a common language, culture and religion; and by economic and geographical limits, all so fundamental to the self-identification of the new states, tended also to express themselves in intolerant and repressive attitudes toward those who were perceived or perceived themselves as 'others.'" (Partick Thornberry, "Is There a Phoenix in the Ashes? International Law and Minority Rights," *Texas International Law Journal* 15 [Summer 1980]: 421).

8. Although this is the unavoidable conclusion of the briefest survey of the relevant principles and rules of Shari'a, it is rarely admitted by contemporary Muslim writers on the subject.

One of the rare exceptions in modern Muslim writings is Sultanhussein Tabandeh, *A Muslim Commentary on the Universal Declaration of Human Rights* (London: F. T. Goulding and Co., 1970), pp. 17-20 and passim, where the author states clearly and defends the exclusion of women and non-Muslims from the full range of human rights under Shari'a.

9. For example, the theories surveyed by Shestack, "Jurisprudence of Human Rights," pp. 85ff., appear to be primarily based on the Western tradition. In fact, the available literature on the philosophical notions of "rights" and "universal human rights," reviewed in ibid., pp. 70-85, is not very useful for our purposes because it is primarily based on Western cultural tradition.

10. Oscar Schachter, in his editorial comment "Human Dignity as a Normative Concept," *American Journal of International Law* 77 (1983): 853, has suggested that it may be philosophically significant to derive human rights from the inherent dignity of human beings. But as Schachter himself has shown the term *human dignity* has its own definitional problems.

11. Here I am adopting the analysis of *Ustadh* Mahmoud Mohamed Taha, *Second Message of Islam*, pp. 80ff.

12. Myres S. McDougal, Harold D. Lasswell, and Lung-chu Chen, *Human Rights and World Public Order* (New Haven: Yale University Press, 1980), pp. 473–508; and V. Nanda and C. Bassiouni, "Slavery and the Slave Trade: Steps towards Eradication," *Santa Clara Law Review* 12 (1972): 424.

Article 8 of the Supplementary Convention on the Abolition of Slavery, the Slave Trade, and Institutions and Practices Similar to Slavery of 1956 requires states party to the convention to communicate to the secretary general of the United Nations copies of any laws, regulations, and administrative measures enacted or put into effect to implement the provisions of this convention. This documentation is to be used by the Economic and Social Council of the United Nations as a basis for further Recommendations on this subject.

13. McKean, *Equality and Discrimination under International Law*, pp. 116–21.

14. Henkin et al., *International Law*, p. 982.

15. The main current slavery convention was signed on September 25, 1926, and entered into force on March 9, 1927 (60 L.N.T.S. 253). More recent international treaties on the subject include the Supplementary Convention on the Abolition of Slavery, the Slave Trade and Institutions and Practices Similar to Slavery, which was signed on September 7, 1956, and entered into force on April 30, 1957 (18 T.I.A.S. No. 6418, 266 U.N.T.S. 3).

16. See, for example, Article 5 of the African Charter on Human and Peoples' Rights and Article 8 of the International Covenant on Civil and Political Rights. This last article is exempt by Article 4 of the convention from derogation, that is, no state party to the convention may ever derogate from its obligation to prohibit slavery and the slave trade and servitude under any circumstances. Moreover, Articles 6 and 7 of the International Covenant on Economic, Social and Cultural Rights, providing for the right to work, render slavery obsolete.

17. Arcot Krishnaswami, *Study of Discrimination in the Matter of Religious Rights and Practices* (New York: United Nations, 1960), pp. 11–12; and Francisco Capotorti, *Study of the Rights of Persons Belonging to Ethnic, Religious and Linguistic Minorities* (New York: United Nations, 1979), pp. 1–3.

18. This was true among states professing different sects within the same religion as well as among those adhering to different religions. Thus various European peace treaties since the seventeenth century have provided for the protection of Protestants within Catholic territory and vice versa. See Thornberry, "Is There a Phoenix in the Ashes?" p. 426 and accompanying notes.

19. See, for example, Articles 1.3 and 55(c) of the U.N. Charter, Article 2 of the African Charter, and Article 2 of the Civil and Political Rights Covenant.

For a comprehensive survey and analysis of current treaty-based guarantees against such discrimination since the end of World War II see Capotorti, *Study of the Rights of Persons Belonging to Ethnic, Religious and Linguistic Minorities*, pp. 26–41.

20. The principle of nondiscrimination provided for in the articles cited in the previous note apply equally to discrimination on grounds of gender. Moreover, several specialized conventions specifically apply to the rights of women, such as the Convention on the Political Rights of Women of 1953 (193 U.N.T.S. 135). The most comprehensive of this class of international treaties is the Convention on the Elimination of All Forms of Discrimination against Women of 1979.

21. Vernon Van Dyke, *Human Rights, Ethnicity and Discrimination* (Westport, Conn.: Greenwood Press, 1985), p. 194.

22. This differential treatment, known as affirmative action or positive discrimination, has its own problems in practice. See, for example, Marc Galanter, *Competing Equali-*

ties (Berkeley and Los Angeles: University of California Press, 1984), for an explanation of these problems as they have arisen through the recent application of this principle in the Indian context.

23. Henkin et al., *International Law*, p. 999.

24. The vast majority of Islamic states are party to treaties prohibiting slavery. A similar treaty obligation exists with respect to prohibition of discrimination on grounds of gender and religion for those party to the International Covenant on Civil and Political Rights of 1976.

Despite its high moral and political authority, the 1948 Universal Declaration of Human Rights is not a legally binding treaty, although some of the human rights it guarantees, including freedom from discrimination on grounds of religion, may have become part of customary international law.

25. Cf. Henkin et al., *International Law*, p. 998: "While gender-based discrimination is still practiced in many states in varying degrees, freedom from gender discrimination as state policy, in many matters, may already have become a principle of customary international law."

26. See generally, Richard Falk, *Human Rights and State Sovereignty* (New York: Holmes and Meier, 1982).

27. G.A. Res. 2625 (XXXV 1970). For the full text of this declaration see Louis Henkin, Richard C. Pugh, Oscar Schachter, and Hans Smit, *Basic Documents Supplement to International Law: Cases and Materials*, 2d ed. (St. Paul: West Publishing, 1987), pp. 75-83.

As can be expected, the legal nature of this declaration has been debated from the beginning. But as noted by Robert Rosenstock, in "The Declaration of Principles of International Law Concerning Friendly Relations: A Survey," *American Journal of International Law* (October 1971): 715, "the principles [of the Declaration] involved, however, are acknowledged by all [states] to be principles of the [U.N.] Charter. By accepting the respective texts [of the Declaration], states have acknowledged that the principles represent their interpretations of the obligations of the Charter [in accordance with Article 31.3 of the Vienna Convention on the Law of Treaties]."

28. Henkin et al., *Basic Documents Supplement to International Law*, p. 81.

29. C. W. Jenks, *The World Beyond the Charter in Historical Perspective* (London: George Allen & Unwin, 1969), pp. 177-78.

30. See generally, Pomerance, *Self-Determination in Law and Practice*, which includes an extensive bibliography on the subject.

See also Hector Gros Espiell, *The Right to Self-Determination: Implementation of United Nations Resolutions* (New York: United Nations, 1980); and Aureliu Cristescu, *The Right to Self-Determination: Historical and Current Development on the Basis of the United Nations Instruments* (New York: United Nations, 1981).

31. Jessup, *Modern Law of Nations*, pp. 40-42.

32. Richard Falk, *Legal Order in a Violent World* (Princeton: Princeton University Press, 1968), p. 339; emphasis added.

33. This charge was leveled against India's intervention in East Pakistan, now Bangladesh, in 1971. On the legality and limitations of the principle of humanitarian intervention see material quoted in Henkin et al., *International Law*, pp. 695-702; and Richard Lillich, *Humanitarian Intervention and the United Nations* (Charlottesville: University Press of Virginia, 1983). See generally, Fernando R. Teson, *Humanitarian Intervention: An Inquiry into Law and Morality* (Dobbs Ferry, N.Y.: Transnational Publishers, 1988).

34. As was explained in Chapter 4, the status of *dhimma* under Shari'a guaranteed non-Muslims security of person and property and a degree of communal autonomy. Shari'a also recognized for women an independent legal personality, including the full capacity to hold and dispose of property in their own right and certain minimum rights in family law and inheritance. See generally, Jane I. Smith, "Islam," in Arvind Sharama, ed., *Women in World Religions* (Albany: State University of New York Press, 1987), p. 235.

35. Majid Khadduri, "Human Rights in Islam," *Annals of the American Academy of Political and Social Science* 243 (1946): 79.

36. In a recent substantially revised version of this paper Khadduri omitted the above-quoted statement. Though emphasizing the need for reform and compliance with current international standards of human rights, Khadduri's revised version does not dispute the accuracy of the statement from his 1946 paper. See Majid Khadduri, *The Islamic Conception of Justice* (Baltimore: Johns Hopkins University Press, 1984), p. 233.

37. See, for example, Ali Abdel Wahid Wafi, "Human Rights in Islam," *Islamic Quarterly* 11 (1967): 64; Khalid M. Ishaque, "Human Rights in Islamic Law," *International Commission of Jurists Review* 12 (1974): 51; and Isma'il al-Faruqi, "Islam and Human Rights," *Islamic Quarterly* 27 (1983): 12.

38. Riffat Hassan, "On Human Rights and the Qur'anic Perspectives," *Journal of Ecumenical Studies* 19 (1982): 51.

39. Tabandeh, *Muslim Commentary on the Universal Declaration of Human Rights*, pp. 18–20 and 35–45. Reference to these and other points made in this book was made in Chapter 4 above.

40. Rahman, *Islam*, p. 38; and Khadduri, *War and Peace in the Law of Islam*, p. 130.
For a comprehensive treatment of slavery in Shari'a and in history see R. Brunschwig, "'Abd," in *Encyclopedia of Islam*, new ed., 1:24–40. See also Reuben Levy, *The Social Structure of Islam* (Cambridge: Cambridge University Press, 1957), pp. 73–85.

41. Modernist arguments that slavery should have been abolished by Shari'a will be considered below.

42. I am not concerned here with secret slavery and semislavery, which exist in many parts of the world.

43. Tabandeh, *Muslim Commentary on the Universal Declaration of Human Rights*, p. 27.

44. For reports of Sunna and other early traditions showing the free practice of slavery during the Prophet's time see Khadduri, *Islamic Law of Nations*, pp. 80ff.

45. This, of course, does not cover the purchase of slaves, which is treated by Shari'a jurists as part of the law of sale. See Brunschwig, "'Abd."

46. Khadduri and Liebesny, *Law in the Middle East*, pp. 355–56. For a documented account of these options and differences of opinion among the jurists in matters of detail see Khadduri, *War and Peace in the Law of Islam*, pp. 126–30.

47. For example, verse 4:36 of the Qur'an instructs Muslims to "do good" and to treat their parents, relatives, orphans, slaves, and others well.

48. Khadduri, *War and Peace in the Law of Islam*, pp. 131–32.

49. Hassan, "Human Rights and the Qur'anic Perspectives," p. 59.

50. In his explanation of this verse, Ibn Kathir does not mention any implication of prohibition of the enslavement option. Rather, he quotes Shafi'i's statement of the four options open to the ruler over captives of war: execution, enslavement, or release with or without ransom.

51. Slavery was abolished in Bahrain in 1937, Kuwait in 1947, and Quatar in 1952. See C. W. W. Greenidge, "Slavery in the Middle East," *Middle Eastern Affairs* (December 1956): 439.

52. Levy, *Social Structure of Islam*, pp. 91–134 and *passim*, for comparisons between various aspects of the status of women before and during the early Islamic period.

53. On the relative improvements in the status of women introduced by Shari'a see Sayed Ameer Ali, *The Spirit of Islam* (London: Christophers, 1922), pp. 222–57; Fazlur Rahman, "Status of Women in the Qur'an," in Guity Nashat, ed., *Women and Revolution in Iran* (Boulder, Colo.: Westview Press, 1983), p. 37; and Coulson, *History of Islamic Law*, pp. 14–15.

54. On the acquisition of the status of *aman* and its consequences see Hamidullah, *Muslim Conduct of State*, pp. 201–2; Khadduri and Liebesny, *Law in the Middle East*, pp. 361–62; and Shihata, "Islamic Law and the World Community," pp. 108–9.

55. Although this is the position of all major schools of Islamic jurisprudence, it is not based on direct Qur'anic prohibition of such marriages. Rather, it is based on the derivative argument that since verse 4:34 of the Qur'an entitles the husband to exercise authority over his wife while stating, as in verse 4:141, that a non-Muslim may never exercise authority over a Muslim, it follows that a man from the People of the Book, such as a Christian or Jew, may never marry a Muslim woman.

This reasoning will be repudiated at the end of this chapter through the application of the evolutionary principle of construction of Islamic sources.

56. This was the construction given by the founding jurists to verses 2:21, 5:5, and 9:10 of the Qur'an.

57. Schacht, *Introduction to Islamic Law*, p. 170.

58. On the contrast between Shari'a view of the status and rights of women and that envisaged by Article 16 of the Universal Declaration of Human Rights see Tabandeh, *Muslim Commentary on the Universal Declaration of Human Rights*, pp. 35–67.

59. Verse 4:2 of the Qur'an. See Coulson, *History of Islamic Law*, pp. 18–19.

60. This is the construction given by the founding jurists to verses 2:226–32 of the Qur'an. Look under *talaq* in H. A. R. Gibb and J. H. Kramers, eds., *Shorter Encyclopedia of Islam* (Leiden: E. J. Brill, 1953), pp. 564–67.

61. Verses 4:11 and 4:176 of the Qur'an.

62. Reports by nongovernmental organizations, such as Amnesty International and the Arab Human Rights Organization, and other monitoring documentation, such as Human Rights Internet Reporter, may be the best available sources of documentation for human rights violations. But because most Muslim countries are governed by authoritarian regimes, information about human rights violations is difficult to obtain.

63. For an effort to do so see James Dudley, "Human Rights Practices in the Arab States: The Modern Impact of Shari'a Values," *Georgia Journal of International and Comparative Law* 12 (1982): 55.

64. Shari'a is the family law for Muslims in Egypt. See Maitre A. El-Kharboutly and Aziza Hussein, "Law and the Status of Women in the Arab Republic of Egypt," *Columbia Human Rights Law Review* 8 (1976): 35.

SELECTED BIBLIOGRAPHY

SOURCES IN ARABIC

Abd al-Raziq, Ali. *Al-Islam wa Usul al-Hukm.* Beirut: Dar Maktabat al-Haya, 1966.

Abduh, Mohamed, and Mohamed Ridda. *Tafsir al-Manar.* Cairo: Dar al-Manar, 1947–48/1367 Hijri.

Abu Yusuf. *Kitab al-Kharaj.* Cairo: Al-Matba'ah al-Salafiyah, 1962–63/1302 Hijri.

Abu Zahrah. "Nazaria't al-Harb fi al-Islam." In *Revue Egyptinne du Droi International.* 14 (1958): 1–27.

Al-Azhar. *Mashru al-Dastur al-Islamiy.* Cairo: Council for Islamic Research, Technical Secretariat, October 15, 1978.

Al-Jassas, Abu Bakr al-Kazi. *Ahkam al-Qur'an.* Istanbul: Dar al-Khilafah al-Aliyah, 1916/1325 Hijri.

Al-Kaya al-Harasy. *Ahkam al-Qur'an.* Beirut: Al-Maktaba al-Ilmiya, 1983.

Al-Mubarak. *Nizam al-Islam fi al-Hukm wa al-Dawla.* Beirut: Dar al-Fikr, 1981.

Al-Muti'i, Muhammad B. *Haqiqat al-Islam wa Usul al-Hukm.* Cairo: Maktabat al-Nahda al-Haditha, 1344 Hijri.

Al-Nabhani, Taj al-Din. *Al-Dawla al-Islamiya.* Damascus: Al-Manar Press, 1952.

Al-Qasmiy. *Tafsir al-Qasmiy.* Cairo: Eisa al-Bai al-Halabi, 1957.

Al-Qurtubi, Abdulla Muhammad. *Al-Jami li Ahkam al-Qur'an.* Beirut: Dar al-Kitab al-Arabi, n.d.

Al-Shawkani. *Nayl Al-Awtar.* Cairo: Makabat al-Qahirah, 1357 Hijri.

Al-Sharif, Aun. *Dublumaciyat Muhammad* (Khartoum: Khartoum University Press, n.d.).

Al-Smarai'i, Nu'man A. *Ahkam al-Murtadd fi al-Shari'a al-Islamiyya.* Beirut: Dar al-Arabiyya lil Tiba'at wa al-Nashr wa al-Tawzi, 1968.

Al-Tabari. *Jami al-Bayan an Ta'wiyl ayy al-Qur'an*. 2d ed. Cairo: Mustafa al-Babi, 1954.

Al-Tusi. *Tafsir al-Tibyan*. Al-Najaf: Maktabat al-Amin, n.d.

Auda, Abd al-Qadir. *Al-Islam wa Awda'una al-Siyasiya*. Beirut: Mu'assasat al-Risalah, 1980?

———. *Al-Tashri al-Jan'iy al-Islamiy*. Beirut: Dar al-Kitab al-Arabi, 1960.

Bultajiy, Muhammad. *Manhaj Umar ibn al-Khatab fi al-Tashri*. Cairo: Dar al-Fikr al-Arabi, 1970.

Ibn Abd al-Barr. *Jami Bayan al-'Ilm wa Fadlihi wa ma Yanbaghi fi Riwayatihi wa Hamlih*. 2d ed. Vol. 2. Al-Madinah al-Munawarah: Al-Maktabah al-Salafiyah, 1968.

Ibn Hazm. *Al-Ihkam fi Usul al-Ahkam*. Vol. 6. Cairo: Matba'at al-Asimah, 1968.

Ibn Kathir, Muhammad Ali al-Saboni, ed. *Mukhtasar Tafsir ibn Kathir*. Beirut: Dar al-Qur'an al-Karim, 1393 Hijri.

Ibn Qutaybah. *Al-Imama wa al-Siyasa*. Cairo: Mustafa al-Babi, 1957.

Ibn Rushd. *Bidayat Al-Mujtahid*. Cairo: Dar al-Fikr al-Arabi, n.d.

Ibn Sa'ad, Muhammad. *Al-Tabaqat al-Kubra*. Vol. 5. Medina: Al-Jami'ah Al-Islamiyah, 1983.

Ibn Taymiyya, *Qa'ida fi Qital al-Kuffar*. Dawha, Qatar: Matabi'Ali ibn Ali, 1983?

Imarah, Muhammad. *Al-Islam wa al-Sultah al-Diniyah*. Cairo: Dar al-Thaqafah al-Jadidah, 1979.

Kalfallah, Muhammad Ahmed. *Al-Qur'an wa al-Dawla*. 2d ed. Beirut: Al-Mu'asasa al-Arabiya lil Dirasat wa al-Nashr, 1981.

Khalid, Khalid M. *Min Huna Nabda*. Cairo, Mu'assat al-Kharji, 1950.

Khan, Sayyid Ahmad. *Tafsir al-Qur'an*. Lahore, n.d.

Khomeini. *Al-Hukuma al-Islamiya*. Beirut: Dar al-Quds, n.d.

Mutwali, Abdel Hamid. *Mabadi Nizam al-Hukm fi al-Islam*. Cairo: Dar al-Ma'arif, 1977.

Nasif, M. A. *Al-Taj al-Jami lil-Usulll*. 4th ed. Cairo: Dar Ihya' al-Kutub al-Arabiyah, n.d.

Shafi'i, Abu Abdallah Muhammad Ibn Idris al-. *al-Umm*. 8 vols. Cairo: Maktabat al-Kuliyat al-Azhariyah, 1961.

Shaltut, Mahmud. *Al-Islam Aqida wa Shari'a*, Cairo: Dar al-Qalam, 1966.

———. *Al-Islam wa al-alaqat al-Dawliya*. Cairo: Matba'at al-Azhar, 1951.

Shaybani, Muhammad ibn al-Hasan. *Al-Siyar al-Kabir*. Cairo: Matba'at Jami'at al-Qahirah, 1958.

Taha, Mahmoud Mohamed. *Usus Dastur al-Sudan*. Omdurman: Matabi' Sudan Ayco, 1968.

Turabi, Hasan al-. In Rashid al-Ghnnushy and Hassan al-Turabi, *Al-Haraka al-Islamiyya wa al-Tahdith*, pp. 45–76. Beirut: Dar al-Jiyl, 1980.

Zayd, Mustafa. *Al-Naskh fi al-Qur'an al-Karim*. 2 vols. Cairo: Dar al-Fikr al-Abarie, 1963.

SOURCES IN ENGLISH

Books

Abdel Malek, Anouar, ed. *Contemporary Arab Political Thought*. Translated by Michael Pallis. London: Zed Press, 1983.

Abdur Rahim. *The Principles of Muhammadan Jurisprudence According to the Hanafi, Maliki, Shafii and Hanbali Schools*. Westport, Conn.: Hyperion Press, 1981.

Abu Sulayman, Abdul Hamid. *The Islamic Theory of International Relations: New Directions for Islamic Theory and Thought*. Herndon, Va.: International Institute of Islamic Thought, 1987.

Adams, C. C. *Islam and Modernism in Egypt*. New York: Russell & Russell, 1968.

Ahmed, Ishtiaq. *The Concept of an Islamic State: An Analysis of the Ideological Controversy in Pakistan*. New York: St. Martin's Press, 1987.

Al-Azami, Muhammad. *On Schacht's Origins of Muhammadan Jurisprudence*. New York: Wiley, 1985.

Alexander, Yonah, and Seymour M. Finger, eds. *Terrorism: Interdisciplinary Perspectives*. New York: John Jay Press, 1977.

Ali, Abdullah Yusuf. *The Holy Qur-an, Text, Translation and Commentary*. Lahore: Shaikh Muhammad Ashraf, 1938.

Ali, Sayed Ameer. *The Spirit of Islam*. London: Christophers, 1922.

Amnesty International Newsletter. Vol. 16, no. 11, November 1986.

Anand, R. P. *Confrontation or Cooperation? International Law and the Developing Countries*. New Delhi: Banyan Publications, 1984.

Anderson, James Norman D. *Law Reform in the Muslim World*. London: University of London, Athlone Press, 1976.

Arjomand, Said Amir. *The Shadow of God and the Hidden Imam: Religion, Political Order, and Societal Change in Shi'ite Iran from the Beginning to 1890*. Chicago: University of Chicago Press, 1984.

Arnold, T. W. *The Caliphate*. New York: Barnes and Noble, 1966.

———. *The Preaching of Islam*. Lahore: Shirkat-i-Qualam, 1956.

Asad, Muhammad. *The Principles of State and Government in Islam*. Berkeley and Los Angeles: University of California Press, 1961.

Barr, James. *Fundamentalism*. 2d ed. London: SCM Press, 1982.

Bassiouni, Cherif M., ed. *The Islamic Criminal Justice System*. London: Oceana Publications, 1982.

Beer, Lawrence W., ed. *Constitutionalism in Asia*. Berkeley and Los Angeles: University of California Press, 1979.

Beshir, Mohamed Omer. *The Southern Sudan: Background to Conflict*. London: C. Hurst, 1968.

―――. *The Southern Sudan: From Conflict to Peace*. New York: Barnes and Noble, 1975.

Black, Henry C. *Black's Law Dictionary*. 5th ed. St. Paul: West Publishing, 1979.

Blaustein, Albert P., and Gisbert H. Flanz, eds. *Constitutions of the Countries of the World*. Dobbs Ferry, N.Y.: Oceana Publications, 1980.

Burton, John. *The Collection of the Qur'an*. Cambridge: Cambridge University Press, 1977.

Capotorti, Francesco. *Study of the Rights of Persons Belonging to Ethnic Religious and Linguistic Minorities*. New York: United Nations, 1979.

Coulson, Noel. *A History of Islamic Law*. Edinburgh: Edinburgh University Press, 1964.

Cristescu, Aurelin. *The Right to Self-Determination: Historical and Current Development on the Basis of the United Nations Instruments*. New York: United Nations, 1981.

Curtis, Michael, ed. *Religion and Politics in the Middle East*. Boulder, Colo.: Westview Press, 1981.

De Lupis, Ingrid D. *The Law of War*. Cambridge: Cambridge University Press, 1987.

Dennett, Daniel C. *Conversion and the Poll Tax in Early Islam*. Cambridge, Mass.: Harvard University Press, 1950.

Donner, Fred M. *The Early Islamic Conquests*. Princeton: Princeton University Press, 1981.

Donohue, John J. and John L. Esposito, eds. *Islam in Transition: Muslim Perspectives*, New York: Oxford University Press, 1982.

El-Awa, Mohamed S. *On the Political System of the Islamic State*. Indianapolis: American Trust Publications, 1980.

―――. *Punishment in Islamic Law*. Indianapolis: American Trust Publications, 1982.

Encyclopedia of Islamic Jurisprudence. Vol. 1. Kuwait: Ministry of Awqaf, 1969.

Eprile, Cecil. *War and Peace in the Sudan, 1955–1972*. London: David and Charles, 1974.

Espiell, Hector Gros. *The Right to Self-Determination: Implementation of United Nations Resolutions*. New York: United Nations, 1980.

Esposito, John L. *Islam and Politics*. 2d ed., rev. Syracuse: Syracuse University Press, 1987.

―――. *Women in Muslim Family Law*. Syracuse: Syracuse University Press, 1982.

―――, ed. *Islam and Development: Religion and Sociopolitical Change*. Syracuse: Syracuse University Press, 1980.

―――, ed. *Islam in Asia: Religion, Politics, and Society*. New York: Oxford University Press, 1987.

―――, ed. *Voices of Resurgent Islam*. New York: Oxford University Press, 1983.

Falk, Richard. *Legal Order in a Violent World*. Princeton: Princeton University Press, 1968.

Falk, Richard, Friedrich Kratochwil, and Saul H. Mendlovitz, eds. *International Law: A Contemporary Perspective*. Boulder, Colo.: Westview Press, 1985.

Farrukh, Omar A. *Ibn Taimiyya on Public and Private Law in Islam or Public Policy in Islamic Jurisprudence*. Beirut: Khayats, 1966.

Faruki, Kemal A. *The Evolution of Islamic Constitutional Theory and Practice from 610 to 1926*. Karachi, Decca: National Publishing House, 1971.

―――. *Islamic Jurisprudence*. Karachi: Pakistan Publishing House, 1962. Rev. ed. 1975.

Fyzee, A. A. A. *Outlines of Muhammadan Law*. 3d ed. Oxford: Oxford University Press, 1964.

Galanter, Marc. *Competing Equalities*. Berkeley and Los Angeles: University of California Press, 1984.

Geller, Ernest. *Muslim Society*. Cambridge: Cambridge University Press, 1981.

Gibb, H. A. R. *The Arab Conquests in Central Asia*. London: Royal Asiatic Society, 1923.

―――. *Modern Trends in Islam*. Chicago: University of Chicago Press, 1947.

―――. *Mohammadanism*. New York: Oxford University Books, 1949.

―――. *Studies on the Civilization of Islam*. Edited by Standford J. Shaw and William R. Polk. Princeton: Princeton University Press, 1982.

Gibb, H. A. R., and J. H. Kramers. *Shorter Encyclopaedia of Islam*. Leiden: E. J. Brill, 1953.

Goldziher, Ignaz. *Introduction to Islamic Theology and Law*. Translated by Andras Hamori and Ruth Hamori. Princeton: Princeton University Press, 1981.

Haim, Sylvia G. *Arab Nationalism: An Anthology*. Berkeley and Los Angeles: University of California Press, 1964.

Hall, William Edward. *International Law*. Oxford: Clarendon Press, 1924. 8th ed.

Hamidullah, Muhammad. *Muslim Conduct of State*. 5th ed. Lahore: Sh. M. Ashraf, 1966.

Hannum, Hurst, ed. *Guide to International Human Rights Practice*. Philadelphia: University of Pennsylvania Press, 1984.

Hasan, Ahmad. *The Early Development of Islamic Jurisprudence*. Islamabad: Islamic Research Institute, 1970.

Haykal, Muhammad Husayn. *The Life of Muhammad*. Translated by Isma'l al-Faruqi. Indianapolis: American Trust Publications, 1976.

Henkin, Louis. *How Nations Behave*. New York: Columbia University Press, 1979.

Henkin, Louis, Richard Pugh, Oscar Schachter, and Hans Smit. *Basic Documents Supplement to International Law: Cases Materials*. 2d ed. St. Paul: West Publishing, 1987.

————. *International Law: Cases and Materials*. 2d ed. St. Paul: West Publishing, 1987.

Hitti, P. *History of the Arabs*. 4th ed., rev. London: Macmillan, 1949.

Hitti, Philip K. *The Origins of the Islamic State*. Translation of *Kitab Futuh al-Buldan*, by al-Baladhuri. New York: AMS Press, 1968.

Hodgson, Marshall G. S. *The Venture of Islam*. Vol. 1. Chicago: University of Chicago Press, 1974.

Holt, P. M., Ann K. S. Lambton, and Bernard Lewis, eds. *The Cambridge History of Islam*. Cambridge: Cambridge University Press, 1970.

Hourani, Albert. *Arabic Thought in the Liberal Age, 1798–1939*. Cambridge: Cambridge University Press, 1983.

Howard, Rhoda. *Human Rights in Commonwealth Africa*. Totowa, N.J.: Rowan and Littlefield, 1986.

Hussain, Asaf. *Islamic Iran: Revolution and Counter-Revolution*. London: Frances Pinter Publishers, 1985.

Ibn Hisham. *The Life of Muhammad*. Translated by Alfred Guillaume. Oxford: Oxford University Press, 1958.

International Commission of Jurists. *The Return of Democracy in Sudan*. Geneva: International Commission of Jurists, 1986.

————. *The Rule of Law and Human Rights: Principles and Definitions*. Geneva: International Commission of Jurists, 1966.

Irfani, Suroosh. *Revolutionary Islam in Iran: Popular Liberation or Religious Dictatorship?* London: Zed Books, 1983.

Jenks, C. W. *The Common Law of Mankind*. London: Stevens, 1958.

————. *The World Beyond the Charter in Historical Perspective*. London: George Allen & Unwin, 1969.

Jessup, Philip C. *A Modern Law of Nations: An Introduction*. Hamden, Conn.: Archon Books, 1968.

Keddie, Nikki R., and Eric Hooglund, eds. *The Iranian Revolution and the Islamic Republic*. 2d ed., rev. Syracuse: Syracuse University Press, 1986.

Kerr, Malcolm H. *Islamic Reform: The Political and Legal Theories of Muhammad Abduh and Rashid Rida.* Berkeley and Los Angeles: University of California Press, 1966.

Khadduri, Majid. *The Islamic Conception of Justice.* Baltimore: Johns Hopkins University Press, 1984.

————. *Political Trends in the Arab World.* Baltimore: Johns Hopkins Press, 1970.

————. *War and Peace in the Law of Islam.* Baltimore: Johns Hopkins Press, 1955.

————, trans. *Islamic Jurisprudence, Shafi'i's Risala.* Baltimore: Johns Hopkins Press, 1961.

————. *The Islamic Law of Nations: Shaybani's Siyar.* Baltimore: Johns Hopkins Press, 1966.

Khadduri, Majid, and Herbert Liebesny. *Law in the Middle East.* Washington, D.C.: Middle East Institute, 1955.

Khomeini. *Islam and Revolution.* Translated by Hamid Algar. London: KPI, 1985.

Krishnaswami, Arcot. *Study of Discrimination in the Matter of Religious Rights and Practices.* New York: United Nations, 1960.

Lambton, Ann K. S. *State and Government in Medieval Islam.* Oxford: Oxford University Press, 1981.

Laupidus, Ira M., *Contemporary Islamic Movements in Historical Perspective.* Berkeley: Institute of International Studies, University of California, 1983.

Levy, Reuben. *The Social Structure of Islam.* Cambridge: Cambridge University Press, 1957.

Liebesny, Herbert. *The Law of the Near and Middle East.* Albany: State University of New York Press, 1975.

MacDonald, Duncan B. *Development of Muslim Theology, Jurisprudence and Constitutional Theory.* Lahore: Premier Book House, 1972.

Mahmassani, Subhi. *Falsafat Al-Tashri Fi Al-Islam* (The Philosophy of Legislation in Islam). Translated by Farah Ziadah. Leiden: E. J. Brill, 1961.

Marsden, George. *Fundamentalism and American Culture.* Oxford: Oxford University Press, 1982.

Martin, Douglas. *The Persecution of the Baha'is of Iran, 1844–1984.* Ottawa: Association of Baha'i Studies, 1984.

McDougal, Myres S., Harold D. Lasswell, and Lung-chu Chen. *Human Rights and World Public Order.* New Haven: Yale University Press, 1980.

McIlwain, C. H. *Constitutionalism Ancient and Modern.* Ithaca: Cornell University Press, 1947.

McKean, Warwick. *Equality and Discrimination under International Law.* Oxford: Clarendon Press, 1983.

McNicol, Suzanne B. *A Non-Crucial Privilege against Self-Incrimination.* Canberra, Australia: Monash University, Faculty of Law, 1984.

Mehdi, Mohammad. "Constitutionalism Western and Middle Eastern." Manuscript. San Francisco, 1960.

Mernissi, Fatima. *Beyond the Veil*. Bloomington: Indiana University Press, 1987.

Meron, Theodore, ed. *Human Rights in International Law: Legal and Policy Issues*. Oxford: Clarendon Press, 1985.

Mustafa, Zaki. *The Common Law in the Sudan*. Oxford: Clarendon Press, 1971.

Nwabueze, Ben O. *Constitutionalism in the Emergent States*. Rutherford, N.J.: Fairleigh Dickinson University Press, 1973.

O'Connell, Daniel Patrick. *International Law*. 2d ed. London: Stevens and Sons, 1970.

Palley, Claire. *Constitutional Law and Minorities*. Minority Rights Group, Report No. 36. London, 1978.

Pipes, Daniel. *In the Path of God: Islam and Political Power*. New York: Basic Books, 1983.

Piscatori, James P. *Islam in a World of Nation-States*. Cambridge: Cambridge University Press, 1986.

Pomerance, Michla. *Self-Determination in Law and Practice*. The Hague: Martinus Nijhoff, 1982.

Powers, David S. *Studies in Qur'an and Hadith: The Formation of the Islamic Law of Inheritance*. Berkeley and Los Angeles: University of California Press, 1986.

Rahman, Fazlur. *Islam*. Chicago: University of Chicago Press, 1979.

―――. *Islam and Modernity: Transformation of an Intellectual Tradition*. Chicago: University of Chicago Press, 1982.

―――. *Islamic Methodology in History*. Karachi: Central Institute of Islamic Research, 1965.

Rahman, Shaikh Abdur. *Punishment of Apostasy in Islam*. Lahore: Institute of Islamic Culture, 1972.

Ramazani, R. K. *Revolutionary Iran: Challenge and Response in the Middle East*. Baltimore: Johns Hopkins University Press, 1988.

Ramcharan, B. G., ed. *Human Rights Thirty Years after the Universal Declaration of Human Rights*. The Hague: Martinus Nijhoff, 1979.

Robson, James, ed. and trans. *An Introduction to the Science of Tradition by al-Hakim an-Naysaburi*. London: Royal Asiatic Society of Great Britain and Ireland, 1953.

Rosenthal, Erwin I. J. *Islam in the Modern National State*. Cambridge: Cambridge University Press, 1965.

―――. *Political Thought in Medieval Islam*. Cambridge: Cambridge University Press, 1958.

Schacht, Joseph. *An Introduction to Islamic Law*. Oxford: Clarendon Press, 1964.

————. *The Origins of Muhmmadan Jurisprudence*. Oxford: Oxford University Press, 1959.

Schmid, Alex. *Political Terrorism*. New Brunswick, N.J.: Transaction Books, 1983.

Seligman, Edwin R. A., ed. *Encyclopaedia of the Social Sciences*. Vol. 3.

Selvidge, Marla J., ed. *Fundamentalism Today: What Makes It So Attractive?* Elgin, Ill.: Brethren Press, 1984.

Sharama, Arvind, ed. *Women in World Religions*. Albany: State University of New York Press, 1987.

Smith, W. C. *Islam in Modern History*. Princeton: Princeton University Press, 1957.

Tabandeh, Sultanhussein. *A Muslim Commentary on the Universal Declaration of Human Rights*. London: F. T. Goulding and Co., 1970.

Taha, Mahmoud Mohamed. *The Second Message of Islam*. Translated by Abdullahi A. An-Na'im. Syracuse: Syracuse University Press, 1987.

Thompson, Kenneth W. *The Moral Imperatives of Human Rights: A World Survey*. Washington, D.C.: University Press of America, 1980.

Tritton, A. S. *The Caliphs and Their Non-Muslim Subjects*. Oxford: Oxford University Press, 1930.

UNESCO. *Human Rights Teaching*. Vol. 4. Paris: UNESCO, 1985.

United Nations. *United Nations Action in the Field of Human Rights*. New York: United Nations, 1980.

Van Dyke, Vernon. *Human Rights, Ethnicity and Discrimination*. Westport, Conn.: Greenwood Press, 1985.

Verzijl, J. H. W. *Human Rights in Historical Perspective*. Leiden: A. W. Sijthoff, 1968.

Voll, John O. *Islam: Continuity and Change in the Modern World*. Boulder, Colo.: Westview Press, 1982.

Von Grunebaum, G. E. *Islam: Essays in the Nature and Growth of a Cultural Tradition*. London: Routledge & Kegan Paul, 1955.

Walker, R. B. J., ed. *Culture, Ideology and World Order*. Boulder, Colo.: Westview Press, 1984.

Watt, Montgomery. *Islamic Philosophy and Theology*. Edinburgh: Edinburgh University Press, 1962.

————. *Muhammad at Mecca*. Oxford: Oxford University Press, 1953.

————. *Muhammad at Medina*. Oxford: Oxford University Press, 1958.

Wheare, K. C. *Modern Constitutions*. London: Oxford University Press, 1966.

Williams, David R. *World Religions and the Hope for Peace*. Boston: Beacon Press, 1951.

Wright, Quincy. *The Strengthening of International Law*. Leiden: The Hague, Academy of International Law, 1960.

Articles and Chapters

Abu Rannat, S. M. A. "The Relationship between Islamic and Customary Law in the Sudan." *Journal of African Law* 4, no. 1 (1960): 9–16.

Ahmad, Khursid. "The Nature of the Islamic Resurgence." In John L. Esposito, ed. *Voices of Resurgent Islam*, pp. 218–29. New York: Oxford University Press, 1983.

Akhavi, Shahrough. "Ideology and Praxis of Shi'ism in the Iranian Revolution." *Comparative Studies in Society and History* 25 (April 1983): 195–221.

———. "Iran: Implementation of an Islamic State." In John L. Esposito, ed. *Islam in Asia: Religion, Politics, and Society*, pp. 27–52. New York: Oxford University Press, 1987.

Al-Ashmawy, Said. "Islamic Government." *Middle East Review* (Spring 1986): 7–13.

Al-Faruqi, Isma'il. "Towards a Methodology of Qur'anic Exegesis." *Islamic Studies* 1 (1962): 35–52.

———. "Islam and Human Rights." *Islamic Quarterly* 27, no. 1 (1983): 12–30.

Amedroz, H. F. "The Hisba Jurisdiction in the Akham Sultaniyya of Mawardi." *Journal of the Royal Asiatic Society* (1916): 287–314.

An-Na'im, Abdullahi. "The Elusive Islamic Constitution: The Sudanese Experience." *Orient* 26 (1985): 329–40.

———. "The Islamic Law of Apostasy and Its Modern Applicability: A Case from the Sudan." *Religion* 16 (1986): 197–224.

———. "The Many Hats of the Sudanese Magistrate: Role Conflict in Sudan Criminal Procedure." *Journal of African Law* 22 (1978): 50–62.

———. "Religious Minorities under Islamic Law and the Limits of Cultural Relativism." *Human Rights Quarterly* 1 (1987): 1–18.

Anderson, J. N. D. "Homicide in Islamic Law." *Bulletin of the School of Oriental and African Studies* 13 (1951): 811–28.

Awad, Awad M. "The Rights of the Accused under Islamic Criminal Procedure." In Cherif M. Bassiouni, ed., *The Islamic Criminal Justice System*, pp. 91–107. London: Oceana Publications, 1982.

Baer, Gabriel. "The Transition from Traditional to Western Criminal Law in Turkey and Egypt." *Studia Islamica* 45 (1977): 139–58.

Bonderman, David. "Modernization and Changing Perceptions of Islamic Law." *Harvard Law Review* 81 (April 1968): 1169–93.

Brunschvig, R. "'Abd." In *Encyclopaedia of Islam*, new ed., 1:24–40. Leiden: E. J. Brill, 1960.

Bulliet, Richard W. "Time, Perceptions, and Conflict Resolution." In Shirin Tahir Kheli and Shaheen Ayubi, eds., *The Iran-Iraq War: New Weapons, Old Conflicts*, pp. 65–81. New York: Praeger, 1983.

"Christians Protest Imposition of Islamic Law." In *Origins*, pp. 180–81. Washington, D.C.: Documentary Service, National Catholic News Service, September 6, 1984.

Coker, Francis W. "Sovereignty." In Edwin R. A. Seligman, ed., *Encyclopaedia of the Social Sciences*, 14:265–68. New York: Macmillan, 1930.

Coulson, N. J. "The State and the Individual in Islamic Law." *International and Comparative Law Quarterly* 6 (1957): 49–60.

Crick, Bernard. "Sovereignty." In David L. Sills, ed., *International Encyclopedia of the Social Sciences*, pp. 77–81. New York: Macmillan, 1968.

Dekmejian, R. Hrair. "The Anatomy of Islamic Revival: Legitimacy Crisis, Ethnic Conflict, and the Search for Islamic Alternatives." In Michael Curtis, ed., *Religion and Politics in the Middle East*, pp. 31–42. Boulder, Colo.: Westview Press, 1981.

Donnelly, Jack. "Cultural Relativism and Universal Human Rights." *Human Rights Quarterly* 6, no. 4 (1984): 400–419.

———. "Human Rights and Human Dignity: An Analytic Critique of Non-Western Conceptions of Human Rights." *American Political Science Review* 76, no. 2 (June 1982): 303–16.

Donohue, John J. "Islam and the Search for Identity in the Arab World." In John L. Esposito, ed., *Voices of Resurgent Islam*, pp. 48–61. New York: Oxford University Press, 1983.

Dudley, James. "Human Rights Practices in the Arab States: The Modern Impact of Shari'a Values." *Georgia Journal of International and Comparative Law* 12 (1982): 55–93.

Duran, Khalid. "The Centrifugal Forces of Religion in Sudanese Politics." *Orient* 26 (1985): 572–600.

Eliash, Joseph. "The Ithna 'ashari Shi'i Juristic Theory of Political and Legal Authority." *Studia Islamica* 29 (1969): 17–30.

El-Kharboutly, Maitre, and Aziza Hussein. "Law and the Status of Women in the Arab Republic of Egypt." *Columbia Human Rights Law Review* 8 (1976): 35–50.

Encyclopedia Judaica. "Capital Punishment." 5:142–47. Jerusalem: Keter Publishing House, 1971.

Esposito, John L. "Muslim Family Law Reform: Towards an Islamic Methodology." *Islamic Studies* 15 (Spring 1976): 19–51.

———. "Perspectives on Islamic Law Reform: The Case of Pakistan." *New York University Journal of International Law and Politics* 13 (Fall 1980): 217–45.

———. "Sudan's Islamic Experiment." *Muslim World* 76 (1986): 181–202.

Forrest, G. A. "Constitution and Constitutional Law." In *Encyclopaedia Britannica*, 6:398. Chicago: Encyclopaedia Britannica, 1967.

Forte, David F. "Islamic Law and the Crime of Theft: An Introduction." *Cleveland State Law Review* 34, no. 1 (1985–86): 47–67.

Fyzee, A. A. A. "Shi'i Legal Theories." In Majid Khadduri and Herbert Liebesny, eds., *Law in the Middle East*, pp. 113–31. Washington, D.C.: Middle East Institute, 1955.

Gibb, H. A. R. "Constitutional Organization." In Majid Khadduri and Herbert Liebesny, *Law in the Middle East*, pp. 3–27. Washington, D.C.: Middle East Institute, 1955.

Goitein, S. D. "Minority Self-rule and Government Control in Islam." *Studia Islamica* 31 (1970): 101–16.

Goldziher, Ignaz. *Muhammedanische Studien.* Translated and quoted in Herbert Liebesny, *The Law of the Near and Middle East*, pp. 13–14. Albany: State University of New York Press, 1975.

Gordon, Carey N. "Islamic Legal Revolution: The Case of Sudan." *International Lawyer* 19 (1985): 793–815.

Gottlieb, Gidon. "Global Bargaining: The Legal and Diplomatic Framework." In Richard Falk, Friedrich Kratochwil, and Saul H. Mendlovitz, eds., *International Law: A Contemporary Perspective*, 210–35. Boulder, Colo.: Westview Press, 1985.

Greenidge, C. W. W. "Slavery in the Middle East." *Middle Eastern Affairs* (December 1956): 435–40.

Guttman, Egon. "Reception of the Common Law in the Sudan." *International and Comparative Law Quarterly* 6 (1957): 401–17.

Hallaq, Wael B. "Was the Gate of Ijtihad Closed?" *International Journal of Middle East Studies* 16 (1984): 3–41.

Hasan, Ahmad. "The Classical Definition of 'Ijma': The Nature of Consensus." *Islamic Studies* 14 (1975): 261–70.

Hassan, Riffat. "On Human Rights and the Qur'anic Perspectives." *Journal of Ecumenical Studies* 19 (1982): 51–65.

Hill, Enid. "Comparative and Historical Study of Modern Middle Eastern Law." *American Journal of Comparative Law* 26 (1978): 279–304.

Howard, Rhoda, and Jack Donnelly. "Human Dignity, Human Rights and Political Regimes." *American Political Science Review* 80 (September 1986): 801–17.

Hudson, Michael C., "Islam and Political Development." In John L. Esposito, ed., *Islam and Development*, pp. 1–24. Syracuse: Syracuse University Press, 1980.

Humphrey, J. H. "The Universal Declaration of Human Rights: Its History, Impact and Juridical Character." in B. G. Ramcharan, ed., *Human Rights Thirty Years after the Universal Declaration of Human Rights.* The Hague: Martinus Nijhoff, 1979.

Ishaque, Khalid M. "Al-Ahkam Al-Sultaniya: Laws of Government in Islam." *Islamic Studies* 4 (1965): 275–314.

———. "Human Rights in Islamic Law." *International Commission of Jurists Review* 12 (1974): 30–39.

Khadduri, Majid. "Human Rights in Islam." *The Annals of the American Academy of Political and Social Science* 243 (1946): 77–81.

———. "International Law, Islamic." In R. Bernhard, ed., *Encyclopedia of Public International Law.* Installment 1, pp. 227–33. Amsterdam: North-Holland, 1981.

———. "Islam and the Modern Law of Nations." *American Journal of International Law* 50 (1956): 358–72.

———. "The Juridical Theory of the Islamic State." *Muslim World* 41 (1951): 181–85.

———. "Nature and Sources of Islamic Law." *George Washington Law Review* 22 (1953): 3–23.

———. "The Nature of the Islamic State." *Islamic Culture* 21 (1947): 327–31.

Khalil, M. I. "The Legal System of the Sudan." *International and Comparative Law Quarterly* 20 (1971): 624–44.

Krausz, Ernest. "Religion and Secularization: A Matter of Definitions." *Social Compass* 18 (1971–72): 203–12.

Kruse, Hans. "The Islamic Doctrine of International Treaties." *Islamic Quarterly* 1 (1954): 152–57.

Lauterpacht, H. "The Grotian Tradition in International Law." in Richard Falk, Friedrich Kratochwil, and Saul H. Mendlovitz, eds., *International Law: A Contemporary Perspective*, pp. 10–36. Boulder, Colo.: Westview Press, 1985.

Layish, Aharon. "The Contribution of the Modernists to the Secularization of Islamic Law." *Middle Eastern Studies* 14 (October 1978): 263–77.

Lesch, Ann Mosely. "The Fall of Numeiri." *Universities Field Staff International Reports*, pp. 1–14. No. 9 Africa [AML-2-1985], 1985.

———. "Rebellion in the Southern Sudan." *Universities Field Staff International Reports*, pp. 1–18. No. 8 Africa [AML-1-1985], 1985.

Lewis, Bernard. "The Return of Islam." In Michael Curtis, ed., *Religion and Politics in the Middle East*, pp. 9–29. Boulder, Colo.: Westview Press, 1981.

Liebesny, Herbert. "Comparative Legal History: Its Role in the Analysis of Islamic and Modern Near Eastern Legal Institutions." *American Journal of Comparative Law* 20 (Winter 1972): 38–52.

———. "Impact of Western Law in the Countries of the Near East." *George Washington Law Review* 22 (1953): 127–41.

MacDougall, Donald V. "The Exclusionary Rule and Its Alternatives: Remedies for Constitutional Violations in Canada and the United States." *Journal of Criminal Law and Criminology* 76, no. 3 (1985): 608–65.

Makdisi, George. "The Juridical Theology of Shafi'i: Origins and Significance of *Usul Al-Fiqh*." *Istudia Islamica* 59 (1984): 5–47.

Margoliouth, D. S. "Omar's Instructions to the Kadi." *Journal of the Royal Asiatic Society* (April 1910): 307–26.

Mashrek International. February 1985.

Mayer, Ann. Review of M. Cherif Bassiouni, ed., *The Islamic Criminal Justice System. American Journal of Comparative Law* 31 (1983): 361–68.

McDougal, Myres S., and Harold C. Lusswell. "The Identification and Appraisal of Diverse Systems of Public Order." In Richard Falk, Friedrich Kratochwil, and Saul H. Mendlovitz, eds., *International Law: A Contemporary Perspective*, pp. 163–87. Boulder: Colo.: Westview Press, 1985.

Mohammad, Noor. "The Doctrine of Jihad: An Introduction." *Journal of Law and Religion* 3 (1985): 381–97.

"Montreal Statement of the Assembly for Human Rights." *Journal of the International Commission of Jurists* 9 (1968): 94–112.

Mortimer, Edward. "Islam and Human Rights." *Index on Censorship* 12, no. 5 (1983): 5–7.

Mustafa, Zaki. "Opting Out of the Common Law: Recent Developments in the Legal System of the Sudan." *Journal of African Law* 17, no. 2 (1973): 133–48.

Nanda, Ved P., and M. C. Bassiouni, "Slavery and Slave Trade: Steps toward Eradication." *Santa Clara Lawyer* 12 (1972): 424–42.

New Africa. June 21, 1984. Interview with Ahmed Abdel Rahman Mohammed.

Pakter, Walter. "Exclusionary Rules in France, Germany and Italy." *Hastings International and Comparative Law Review* 9 (1985): 1–57.

Paret, R. "Istihsan and Istislah." In *Encyclopedia of Islam* 4:255–59. Leiden: E. J. Brill, 1978.

Peters, Rudopph, and Gert J. J. DeVries. "Apostasy in Islam." *Die Welt des Islams* 17 (1976–77): 1–25.

Pizzi, William T. "The Privilege against Self-Incrimination in a Rescue Situation." *Journal of Criminal Law and Criminology* 76, no. 3, (1985): 567–607.

Rahman, Fazlur. "Concepts of *Sunnah*, *Ijtihad* and *Ijma'* in the Early Period." *Islamic Studies* 1 (1962): 237–51.

———. "Islamic Modernism: Its Scope, Methods and Alternatives." *International Journal of Middle East Studies* 1 (1970): 317–33.

———. "A Recent Controversy over the Interpretation of *Shura*." *History of Religion* (1981): 291–301.

———. "Status of Women in the Qur'an." In Guity Nashat, ed., *Women and Revolution in Iran*, pp. 37–54. Boulder, Colo.: Westview Press, 1983.

———. "Towards Reformulating the Methodology of Islamic Law." *New York University Journal of International Law and Politics* (Fall 1979): 219–24.

Rosenstock, Robert. "The Declaration of Principles of International Law Concerning Friendly Relations: A Survey." *American Journal of International Law* 65 no. 5 (October 1971). 713–735.

Safwat, Safia M. "Offenses and Penalties in Islamic Law." *Islamic Quarterly* 26 (1982): 149–81.

Schacht, Joseph. "Islamic Law in Contemporary States." *American Journal of Comparative Law* 8 (1959): 133–47.

Schachter, Oscar. "Human Dignity as a Normative Concept." *American Journal of International Law* 77, no. 4 (1983): 848–54.

Seaman, Bryant W. "Islamic Law and Modern Government: Saudi Arabia Supplements the *Shari'a* to Regulate Development." *Columbia Journal of Transnational Law* 18, no. 3 (1980): 413–81.

Semaan, K. I. "Al-Nasikh wa Al-Mansukh: Abrogation and Its Application in Islam." *Islamic Quarterly* 5 (April–July 1959): 11–29.

Shamma, Samir. "Law and Lawyers in Saudi Arabia." *International and Comparative Law Quarterly* 14 (1965): 1034–39.

Shestack, Jerome J. "The Jurisprudence of Human Rights." In Theodore Meron, ed., *Human Rights in International Law: Legal and Policy Issues*, pp. 69–113. Oxford: Clarendon Press, 1985.

Shihata, Ibrahim. "Islamic Law and the World Community." *Harvard International Club Journal* 4 (1962): 101–13.

Spiro, Herbert J. "The True Constitution." in C. Peter Magrath, ed., *Constitutionalism and Politics: Conflict and Consensus*, pp. 4–12. Glencoe, Ill.: Scott, Foresman, 1968.

Thompson, Cliff F. "The Sources of Law in the New Nations of Africa: A Case Study from the Republic of the Sudan." *Wisconsin Law Review* 4 (1966): 1146–87.

Thornberry, Patrick. "Is There a Phoenix in the Ashes? International Law and Minority Rights." *Texas International Law Journal* 15 (Summer 1980): 421–58.

Tisdall, W. St. Clair. "Shi'ah Additions to the Koran." *Moslem World* 3, no. 3 (1913): 227–41.

UNESCO, ed. "Human Rights, Comments and Interpretations." A Symposium edited by UNESCO. London: 1949. Reprinted in *Human Rights Teaching*, vol. 4. Paris: UNESCO, 1985).

Vesey-Fitzgerald, S. G. "Nature and Sources of the Shari'a." In Majid Khadduri and Herbert Liebesny, eds., *Law in the Middle East*, pp. 85–112. Washington, D.C.: Middle East Institute, 1955.

Voll, John O. "Renewal and Reform in Islamic History: *Tajdid* and *Islah*." In John L. Esposito, ed., *Voices of Resurgent Islam*, pp. 32–47. New York: Oxford University Press, 1983.

Wafi, Ali Abdel Wahid. "Human Rights in Islam." *Islamic Quarterly* 11 (1967): 64–75.

INDEX